William Kirkpatrick of Málaga

Doré, Gustave, Catedral y Puerto, Málaga.

# WILLIAM KIRKPATRICK
# OF MÁLAGA
## 1764 – 1837
### CONSUL, NÉGOCIANT AND ENTREPRENEUR, AND GRANDFATHER OF THE EMPRESS EUGÉNIE, CONSORT TO NAPOLEON III, EMPEROR OF FRANCE.

*Colin Carlin*

The Grimsay Press

The Grimsay Press
An imprint of Zeticula
57, St Vincent Crescent
Glasgow
G3 8NQ
Scotland
http://www.thegrimsaypress.co.uk


First published 2011
Copyright © Colin Carlin, 2011.

Front Cover: David Roberts, *View of Málaga*, 1837-8.

ISBN 978-1-84530-071-5
Excerpts from *Aspects of the French Revolution* by Alfred Cobban, published by Jonathan Cape Limited, are used by permission of the Random House Group Limited.

Excerpts from *Ebb and Flow*, by Richard Herr, Chapter 7, *In Spain a History*, edited by Raymond Carr, are used by permission of Oxford University Press.

Excerpts from *Fernando Sor, Composer and Guitarist*, are used by permission of Dr. Brian Jeffery, Tecla Editions.

Excepts from Dr Jan Parmentier's study *Het Gezicht van de Oostendse Handelarr* - are used with the permission of The Archivist, Oostende Historische Publicaties.

Every effort has been made to contact all the illustration copyright holders. The author and the publishers will make good, in future editions, any errors or omissions brought to their attention.

# Dedication

This study is dedicated to Don Luis Kirkpatrick O'Donnell, Baron of Closeburn, born in Madrid on the 19 August 1910, Patriarca de la familia Kirkpatrick.

"History, if it is to be something more than pure chronology, has also to be something more than straight political history. It has to be the history of human activity in a specific form, such as religion or law or politics or production"

*Professor Alfred Cobban*

# Contents

Family trees:

# Acknowledgements

I am especially grateful to Mike Truman of the Open University and María Jesús Torres Giménez of Málaga who made this project possible by opening so many doors in Málaga. I am indebted to them and to their friends who have had to listen to the story of Ella Rosa far too many times.

The support and encouragement of Professor Amparo Quiles Fax and Professor López de Coca Castañar of the University of Málaga, has been invaluable and led to many new discoveries.

Don Enrique Kirkpatrick Mendaro, Marqués de Placetas, a direct descendent of William and Fanny Kirkpatrick, has given me a wealth of detail on his family and valuable insights into the lives of his ancestors. I am immensely appreciative of his contribution.

Carlos Trías Vejarano of Trías, Kirkpatrick & De Grivegnée of Marbella was very welcoming and introduced me to his cousin don Enrique. He has provided a great deal of information and valuable advice.

I am truly grateful to Catherine Kirkpatrick for her generous contribution of time and skill to the production of this book, and to Christopher and Liz Carlin of Seattle, WA for their assiduous searching for Ella Rosa in archives across the United States.

I would also like to give special thanks to Esther Cruces Blanco, the Director, and her staff at the Archivo Histórica Provincial de Málaga and to Sr. José Manuel Calderón of the d'Alba Archives at the Liria Palace in Madrid.

María Pepa Lara García and her colleagues at the Málaga Municipal Library have responded to my ill-put queries with tolerance and forbearance and have been most liberal with their help and support. Similarly Alberto Palomo Cruz and Susana Rodríguez de Tembleque of the Málaga Cathedral Archives, have been enduringly patient and helpful, as was Dr Trinidad Farcie Merron at the Archivo Díaz de Escovar at the Museo Unicaja de Artes Populares.

Francisco Marmolejo Cantos, Director del Archivo Histórico de la Fundación García Agüera of Coín, and Michelle Consuela Heidi, Carmen Nueda and Vanessa Cary of Bath, have all worked hard at transcribing and translating old Spanish documents.

Thanks also go to Cathy Gibb, Archives Assistant, Dumfries Archive Centre, for help with Kirkpatrick records.

There are many others, in libraries around the world, who have helped my research including the staff of the Library at the Centro Cultural Provincial in Málaga and the National Archives in Washington D.C. and the British National Archives at Kew.

Special credit must go to Marie Weinel of the Bath Central Library for her diligent searching of library shelves on my behalf.

All errors, misunderstandings, mistakes and omissions are entirely due to my own shortcomings.

# A Guide to the Kirkpatrick Family and their Relations.

*The traditional Spanish method of giving double surnames has been used for clarity. Generally one of the father's surnames is followed by one of the mother's surnames.*

**William Kirkpatrick y Wilson of Málaga** and his wife Françoise or **Fanny de Grivegnée y Gallegos**.

**John Kirkpatrick y Wilson of Ostende**, his older brother.

**Thomas Kirkpatrick y Wilson of Hamburg and Málag**a, his younger brother.

**William Kirkpatrick y Gillespie of Conheath** and Mary Wilson of Kelton, their parents,

**Robert Kirkpatrick of Glenkiln**, their grandfather, who was beheaded by the Jacobites in 1745.

**James Kirkpatrick of Cullompton**, William's great uncle, and the father of **Robert** and **John/Juan Kirkpatrick** and **Abraham** and **James**. The first three brothers were merchants in Málaga and London. Their sisters Ana and Elizabeth were also in Málaga. Elizabeth married Mr Escott. James was a lawyer in Bristol.

Their great grandfather was **Thomas Kirkpatrick of Knock** who was probably descended from Alexander Kirkpatrick, Lord of Kirkmichael and through him to the Kirkpatricks of Closeburn.

**Baron Henri de Grivegnée** was William's father-in-law and father of William's wife Françoise or Fanny, as she was known in the family.

**Antonia Gallegos** was the mother of Fanny de Grivegnée y Gallegos and also Manuel, and José Gallegos. An uncle, Francisco Gallegos, was a senior priest at Málaga Cathedral.

William and Françoise's children were **María Manuela**, **Henrietta** and **Carlota**. A son, Guillermo and a first-born daughter Antonia Maria Ann are said to have died young.

María Manuela married **Cipriano Palafox y Portocarrero**, the Count de Teba and later Count de Montijo. Their daughters were **Paca** who became the Duchess d'Alba and **Eugénie** who married Louis Napoleon III, Emperor President of France and the nephew of the Emperor Napoleon I. Eugénie and Louis Napoleon had one son who died tragically in 1879 in a mishandled skirmish in the Zulu Wars in South Africa.

More detail is shown on the genealogical diagrams after Appendix Ten.

Málaga Dockside in the first decades of the Nineteenth Century

# Illustrations

# Foreword

This biography has its origins in an old family tale of Spanish Princesses and dashing gunrunners. I grew up in a remote part of what was then Northern Rhodesia, in the heart of Central Africa. The small colonial settlement of Abercorn was an African haven of perfect climate, mountain air, fresh streams and clear, safe lakes.

In this idyllic spot, I first heard of our romantic tradition of a Carlin family connection to the brilliant Eugénie, Countess de Teba, often known as the Countess de Montijo. This link was said to come through our great grandmother who had married a Rhett Butler figure from *Gone With the Wind*, that tale of the American "Old South". Maybe it was not quite like that; but an Empress, Charleston and the Carolinas and Virginia, and a Commodore and blockade running and fast frigates, all featured strongly in the family consciousness and drew me to the story of the Empress Eugénie and the Kirkpatricks of Málaga.

Some years later, when I was 19, I was in Johannesburg, in South Africa, having lunch with my 90-year old grandfather, George Carlin, at his "Club". This turned out to be the dining room of a well-known department store, and his table was in the front row, just below the stage, where models paraded the latest Paris fashions. I know that my grandfather tried to tell me what he knew of this story, and I know that much of his tale was wiped from my teenage memory by the sight of those wonderful lithe girls.

After many years of searching, I have been able to reconstruct most of the history of George's father, Captain James Carlin, the gunrunner. The story he tried to tell me about Ella Rosa, his exotic mother, is still a mystery.

I have recovered much of our family romance of the Sea Captain from the letters, stories and the writings of my family in England and Scotland, and California, Washington State, and Florida in the USA, and in South Africa, and records from around the world.

The gunrunning proved to be a fraction of Captain Carlin's activities between 1861 and 1880. He disappeared from view for ten years between 1881 and 1891, when he emerged, washed up on the Bowery waterfront in New York, in need of help from his friends in the city. He may have lost his ship in a disaster off Western Greenland or perhaps some other calamity. He died in that city in 1921. My attempts to fill in the gaps in his life led to a re-examination of his wife's story, and a hunt for information and corroboration. This study of William Kirkpatrick is the outcome of my search to prove or disprove my grandfather's story of Ella Rosa.

The 1860 Texas Census shows my great Grandmother, Ella Rosa Carlin, as born in Louisiana in 1841. Be that as it may, we know she was married in Charleston, South Carolina, on the 5th of May (an iconic date for Bonapartists) in the year 1857, to Captain James Carlin, an Englishman working with the United States Coastal Survey Department. At the outbreak of the American Civil War, and the imposition of a United States Naval blockade on the Southern Confederate States, he became a famous Commander of the swift, pale grey, Clyde-built steamers which he designed specially to run over the coastal shallows, and through the blockading fleet of the United States Navy, into the ports of the Confederacy.

He was Superintending Captain for the South Carolina Importing and Exporting Company, a large shareholder in the company, and the Commodore of our tale. He imported munitions and supplies for the Confederate Army and exported cotton to Europe. After numerous adventures, including two short spells as a civilian prisoner of war, he and his family left for Liverpool at the end of 1863. Following more adventures he reappears in the records, running artillery, supplies, uniforms and men onto the coast of Cuba, in support of Céspedes's attempt to overthrow the Peninsular government in Havana, the first Cuban Ten Year War of Liberation.

So what of Ella Rosa? Her legend was that she was a niece or a cousin of Eugénie de Montijo; accounts vary. She claimed on her "deathbed" – she later recovered – that her "aunt" Eugénie was the source of the secret funds she used to educate her family (three of her sons went to university in Germany) and to live in some style near Nairn, in Scotland, and later to preserve a modest middle class home in Victorian London. She used Montijo and de Montijo as her maiden name on the birth certificates of many of her 15 children including her oldest son; her most successful daughter Louise Harriet, used de Montijo as a middle name.

Was she a fantasist, or did she invent this extravagant romance to explain exotic Spanish American origins in the Old South? Perhaps it was an elaborate cover story to preserve whatever funds her usually absent husband had managed to save from the wreck of the Confederacy,

The Empress Eugénie,
Franz Xaver Winterhalter, Chateau de Compiegne, Olse, France

and later from lawyers, creditors and government agents? But there was much talk of Spanish blood, the real thing, and supposedly characteristic Spanish features. Her daughters were all educated women for the period, and clearly believed the tale. One was certainly a romantic. She was a scriptwriter with some early films to her credit. Another was the proprietor of a well-known Harley Street convalescence home, and famously hard-headed, and realistic. There seems to be no association with any of the Montijo families in America who are probably named after the town near Badajoz in the Spanish province of Extremadura.

My grandfather wrote that Ella Rosa's father was a wealthy planter in Virginia who lost all his money in Confederate bonds. There were plenty of ruined planters in the Southern States after Sherman's march to the sea and Union expropriations. But our family in the United States say that Ella Rosa's mother died in childbirth, and that the child was raised in a Convent. Family in Johannesburg say that the nuns tried to take her money. This implies she may have been an orphaned Ward of Court with her own capital. After many years searching, we have found no trace of her origins in the United States. She married as Ella Rosa Jenkins, but stated on several occasions that her surname was previously de Montijo, and once that it was Richardson. Was she a runaway bride hiding her identity?

Could there be a link to Eugénie through the Lesseps family of New Orleans who were real but remote Montijo cousins? These Lesseps were married into a Richardson family in Louisiana. Family members in Jupiter, Florida connect Ella Rosa to New Orleans.

A centenarian Carlin, a 102 year old U.S. Navy Captain, remembers his grandmother's conversation about Ella Rosa, and how the old aunts would "shush" when a child approached or appeared interested. Other relations make the same comment about old aunts gossiping about Ella Rosa.

The 1860 Census records of New Braunfels, Texas, show her with her husband and first child, and an Edward Jenkins, who may be a step or half-brother. They also show her as born in Louisiana, where her husband is said to have had a sugar plantation after the Civil War. Ella Rosa died in Chelsea in London in 1914.

How can these stories be reconciled? Are there stray daughters or nieces from the wider Kirkpatrick, de Grivegnée, Gallegos, Cabarrús or even Portocarrero y Palafox y Guzman families, who could be the mother who died in childbirth, leaving an orphan in the care of Nuns in far away America?

While I have found no direct evidence to support this proposition there are a range of tantalising possibilities. The report that Ella Rosa kept her origins secret until her "deathbed" suggests that either it really was an important element in her life which had to be kept hidden, or that it was made up to cover some other hidden source of funds which could not be revealed to the family. Her husband had earned big money as a blockade-runner and may have secreted some of it away, but a relationship to the fabled Empress seems a very elaborate story to fabricate when a simpler, more credible explanation would be more believable.

A very straightforward solution could lie with the idea of a "lost" daughter. Eugénie's grandfather William Kirkpatrick y Wilson had three daughters who survived to adulthood and one other who may have died young and seems to be lost to the family. There were numerous foreign specialists in Málaga in the 18$^{th}$ and early 19$^{th}$ Centuries. Cotton, and sugar growing and processing, and mining were all big business for the Kirkpatricks, the de Grivegnées and the de Lesseps in Málaga. It is reasonable to suppose that some of their success was owed to American expertise brought in from the Southern States, perhaps with the help of the Lesseps and Richardson "cousins" in New Orleans. We can easily imagine a young Andalusian beauty being whisked back to America by just such a young American returning home after a contract in Spain. Her family may have viewed this as an unsuitable match, or perhaps religious differences played a part; all Ella Rosa's children grew up Protestant Anglicans. Her family may have disapproved of such a bridegroom, and written her out of the record, and indeed there are hints that this may have happened.

William Kirkpatrick y Wilson delayed the hand-over of his U.S. Consular post for a few days in order to complete the arrangements for the estate for Nathaniel Richardson, an American who had committed suicide in Málaga in 1818. A Mademoiselle E. Richardson was on the roll of the Ursuline Convent in New Orleans in about the right period. William Kirkpatrick and his wife Fanny are sometimes recorded with two extra children who "died young". One of these was their son Guillermo. Another was a their first born, a daughter baptised Antonia Maria Ann. Was the Elisabeth, who was with the family in London in 1812, the young woman who died far away in America? At the time Ella was sometimes used as diminutive of Elizabeth.

Ella Rosa Carlin, Charleston, South Carolina.

But there are other possibilities too. If we take Ella Rosa's deathbed admission that Eugénie was her aunt, then we have to look at the way in which that could have happened. Leaving aside other definitions and translations of "aunt", Ella Rosa's clear implication is that her mother was either the unrecorded daughter of Eugénie's sister Paca, later the Duchess d'Alba, or of some other sister who has disappeared, or was hidden from view.

Extraordinary as this may seem, it is not completely beyond the circumstantial and contemporary evidence. Eugénie and her older sister Paca went on a riding excursion through the wilds of Granada in 1839 with both Paca's future husband, the Duke d'Alba and the young Marquis d'Alcanizes, later Duke de Sesto, who was wildly in love with Paca. Eugénie meanwhile was "in love" with d'Alba, and later with d'Alcanizes. They were un-chaperoned and accompanied only by servants. There are reports that suggest that Eugénie may have had a romantic adventure during this excursion. Prosper Mérimée wrote to their mother, María Manuela, showing alarm at certain events around this period, and Paca's grand wedding to d'Alba was delayed for a year or more on the excuse that dresses had be obtained from Paris.

There are two families in England who have curious stories of descent from a secret child of Eugénie or Paca who could date from this incident.[1] Their mother, that redoubtable and brilliant lady, María Manuela Kirkpatrick y Grivegnée, acted in an extraordinary and perhaps reckless way by allowing her teenage daughters to go away into the wilds of *la Mancha* for some weeks with their two beaux.

She may have hoped to cement the d'Alba tie and the Duke of Sesto was also a grand match for a girl from a merchant's family in Málaga. If Ella Rosa was the daughter of the rather saintly Paca, later Duchess d'Alba, then her mother would indeed almost qualify for being called a "Spanish Princess"; the description given to Ella Rosa's mother by the Carlins in Johannesburg. Perhaps they merely picked up on Hillaire Belloc's scurrilous doggerel about Napoleon III and his Spanish Princess bride?

There remains another possibility which would not have passed the notice of any passing aunt. María Manuela was by no means an innocent. She was widely rumoured to have taken George Villiers, later Lord Clarendon and British Foreign Secretary, as a lover and there were stories of others. Napoleon III was concerned at the behaviour of his mother-in-law, and paid her handsomely to leave Paris. The Spanish Ambassador in Brussels complained to the Count de Montijo about the activities of his somewhat estranged wife.

Cipriano Portocarrero y Palafox, the Count in question, replied in pained tones, that she was beyond his control. These rumours may have just been the result of her boasts about her lovers, in the sense of those who flirted with her in her salon, and not any physical way. But that is not what contemporary observers thought. A half-sister is possible from such more or less casual relationships. Eugénie, when Empress of France, is recorded as sending secret funds to poor Spanish refugees in America via Dr. Evans, her Philadelphia-born dentist.

"Eugenia drew this scene in Romanillos in which it is seen the Duchess of Alba next to Pepe Alcañices and Eugenia reclining on the ground".

Perhaps there was another Kirkpatrick daughter of an earlier generation who was spirited off to distant relations in America or married off to a passing foreigner? Was this the "despised daughter who married beneath her position" mentioned by my cousin Ethel Jones, in her letter recalling her mother's memories of family conversation in San Francisco many years before? But Cipriano had Montijo sisters too. Maybe one of them had a daughter who became a Spanish exile in the States during the disturbances of the Carlist Wars in Spain. Such a descent would make a perfectly reasonable explanation for Ella Rosa's use of Montijo.

The Countess of Montijo-Teba with her daughters.
Bibliothèque Nationale, Paris

William Kirkpatrick's wife, Françoise de Grivegnée y Gallegos, had an uncle in Richmond, Virginia. José or Joseph Gallegos was very prosperous and left his nieces in Málaga a useful bequest on his death in 1817. Perhaps he left a legacy to a niece or daughter who became Ella Rosa's mother in 1840, thus fitting the Virginia link mentioned by my grandfather? Perhaps there is a Cuban connection through the later Kirkpatricks who settled there or from Alexander Kirkpatrick of Wilmington N.C.?

Whatever these old aunts' tales may really mean and however romantic the story, they have led me to a detailed exploration of the Kirkpatrick family in Málaga, and they have given me a wonderful glimpse of the 18th and early 19th century life of a very international mercantile family.

*Colin Carlin*
*Bath*
*2010*

# Introduction

The continuing fame of the Kirkpatrick family of Málaga derives in large part from their granddaughter Eugénie, Countess de Teba and Consort to Napoleon III, and as such Empress of France during the glorious years of the Second Empire. Eugénie has also been kept in the public eye by the celebrity of her great niece, Cayetana — María del Rosario Cayetana Alfonsa Victoria Eugenia Francisca Fitz-James Stuart y de Silva, the 83 year old Duchess d'Alba — who is still a centrepiece for society magazines in Spain. Eugénie was a dynamic role model and trendsetter for women around the world, and her rise and fall was widely reported in both the political news, and the gossip and social columns, from New Zealand and San Francisco to the capitals of Europe and the smallest town which boasted a weekly newspaper. Even today in villages in Spain, old ladies will grin with delight when asked about "Eugenia". Her sister Paca was only slightly less famous in her day in her role as an earlier Duchess d'Alba, but her fame faded after her early death.

Eugénie married Louis Napoleon, the elected Emperor President of France on the 25 January 1853. While she may not have been the first non-royal foreign-born woman to sit on the throne of France, she was probably the last.

The Louis Napoleon who became the third Bonaparte Emperor of the French was officially the son of Louis Bonaparte and Hortense de Beauharnais. This Louis was the favourite brother of the first Emperor Napoleon Bonaparte who appointed him King of Holland. Hortense was the daughter of Josephine, Napoleon Bonaparte's wife by her first marriage, and thus Napoleon's stepdaughter.

But rumours, and a study of the movements of all parties concerned, suggest that Napoleon III might really have been the son of the great Emperor. The issue of the dates is complicated by the undisputed fact the child was born one month premature. Both Napoleon and Louis Bonaparte were in Paris at the relevant time. Hortense and Louis Bonaparte were notoriously incompatible and Louis was consumed with jealousies and asked for a divorce shortly after the birth of her son.

Whatever the truth, their son Louis Napoleon ruthlessly exploited his family name to gain election as President of France, and then as Emperor. He was an able man, far sighted, with an enquiring, modern cast of mind, but he would never have achieved these heights without the loyal support of the Bonaparte diehards, and his own overwhelming personal ambition.

Napoleon III.

Much of the France that we see today, the great boulevards of Paris, the grand provincial cities, the banks and agricultural credit unions and much more, are his handy work. He spent some time in the United States and England and had observed how a modern state should function and was determined to reform France.

The Montijo daughters had been infused with the ideals of Napoleon I. Their father, the dashing colonel Cipriano Portocarrero, who had fought for Napoleon in the defence of Paris, had filled the head of his daughter, the young Eugénie, with tales of the Emperor's glory and military successes. While England, and the countries he occupied, may have a different view of the tyrant who dominated Europe for almost two decades, Napoleon revolutionised law and government in France and much of the rest of Europe too. He cast away the remnants of the *ancien regime*, transforming the ideals of the French revolution into a republican form of democracy, even if the great Bonaparte was not himself a subscriber.

The young Louis Napoleon, Bonapartists' heir and torchbearer, had been Eugénie's childhood hero. But her fascination with Napoleon's legend, and the imminent prospect of the throne of France, did not prevent her making one more attempt to marry Pepe Alcañices, Duke de Sesto, her teenage beau, and the man she really loved, before accepting Napoleon III's insistent offer of marriage.

But Eugénie is distinctive for another important reason. Ever discreet, she was very much a power behind the throne. Napoleon III suffered from severe kidney stones and was often in such pain that he was unable to attend to the governance of the country. Eugénie deputized for him at meetings of the French Cabinet as his Regent in 1859, 1865, and 1870 and thus became the first non-royal woman to hold direct sway over the fate of a major European power. She tended to take a conservative stance which countered her husband's more liberal tendencies.

During the Imperial couple's first State visit to England, Eugénie formed a close friendship with Queen Victoria which was to last the rest of their lives. Victoria was a shrewd judge of character and appreciated many of the Spanish countess's qualities.

So we can ask the question; how was it that the granddaughter of a Scottish merchant rose to become the Empress Consort and Regent of France and personal friend of the Queen of Great Britain and the British Empire, then at its mightiest? Her story has been told often enough, but much of what follows, the story of her Málaga family and their origins and connections has not been examined in detail. The role of William Kirkpatrick y Wilson in setting the foundations for María Manuela's successful progression through the Royal courts of Europe, and the glittering arrival of her daughter, Eugénie, on the European scene, has been down played or ignored.

The Kirkpatricks were in Andalusia in the 1730s. They may have settled in Spain before that date and they have been in the country ever since. This study concentrates on the life of William Kirkpatrick and his immediate family. The fame of his offspring, and the glamour of their association with the Second Empire, means that his origins in Scotland have been extensively researched and recorded. Passing travellers in Spain made a point of noting their contacts with the family, and writing about them in their travelogues, and recalling long distant meetings when Eugénie's celebrity became international news.

It is possible to make an in depth study of the family Kirkpatrick y Grivegnée of Málaga, because of the universal interest in their extraordinary progeny which has developed over the last 150 years. First their eldest daughter, the brilliant and flamboyant María Manuela, and then her daughter, Eugénie and their association with the glory and tragedy of Napoleon III and his Second Empire. The numerous biographies of Eugénie and Napoleon III, Prosper Mérimée's letters to María Manuela, and a host of more casual references to William Kirkpatrick, all provide material to illustrate the life of a merchant family in Málaga during, the 100 or more years between 1730, when Juan Kirkpatrick appears in official documents, and the death of William in 1837.

The more contemporary references give a reasonably unbiased view of their social origins, their continuing relationship with Great Britain, their life in Málaga and their international trade contacts in Europe and the United States. We also get a glimpse of the work of a Foreign Consul in troubled times. While Kirkpatrick's true allegiances and views remain obscure, they can be guessed at from his associates and his reaction to events.

We have only a few dozen business and consular letters in his own hand, to help us judge his personality. But his colleague, the American Consul in Alicante, made some critical comments to James Monroe about what he regarded as Kirkpatrick's excessive French sympathies. For Americans, his association with the famous Commodore Bainbridge of the United States Navy is especially striking. Informal letters, written by his friend, the British Consul, suggest a man of wry Scots humour and a keen sense for business. His character and his attitude to events are reflected by the lives and reactions of his business partners and friends and the men his daughters married. His lengthy association with Henri de Grivegnée, his friendship with Cipriano, Count de Teba, and with William Laird, the British Consul, and the social position and extensive business interests of the Cabarrús family are evidence of his political views and allegiances.

The Kirkpatricks of Málaga came from a large and complex Scottish family with many diverse strands. Over the generations they became associated with other equally extended families, the Cabarrús, Grivegnées, Gallegos and Quiltys, and also the Powers and Neumanns and other Málaga settlers. Some of these relationships have to be explored in detail to achieve an understanding of their associations and methods of business.

The American academics Jesus Cruz and David Ringrose, have studied the rise of the Spanish capitalist class and shown how the aristocracy co-opted members of the merchant and middle class to manage their finances and expand the economy. Jesus Cruz has used the example of the Cabarrús family and the San Carlos Bank to show this process at work in Madrid. He has detailed "the systematic use of family network building, consanguineal marriage and recruitment of clients by a large number of Madrid families". His study of the rise of the Cabarrús family prompted him to call for more research on the foreign sugar barons of 19th Century Andalusia. Ringrose has made a detailed study of the Spanish economy and trade in the 18th and 19th Century. But he also makes a point that is significant in relation to the origins of the Kirkpatrick family's links to Spain. While there were similar patterns in Scotland, the Kirkpatricks closely followed the Spanish pattern in the recruitment of partners in their business. Ringrose[2] explains the Spanish system of *mancebos* or apprenticeships. Young men with potential were recruited from the family home in the provinces to learn the trade and strengthen the families' business concerns. Spouses were also found from similar sources, to be married to promising *mancebos* or to widowed business partners. Recently Manuel Muñoz Martín has written about the promoters of Málaga's economy in the 19th Century and has described in some detail the financial disaster which befell the whole family in the years that followed the French occupation of the City.

These and other Spanish academics have researched the social and economic aspects of the large foreign community in Málaga. Their studies tend to look at the colony as a whole and examine, in a general way, the difficulties that this group of settlers faced in the turmoil of the late 18th and early 19th Centuries. Their demography has been mapped and their society has been described. Their ways of raising capital, their financial arrangements, their social stratification and religion affiliations and degree of literacy have been presented in the context of their relations with local producers and the existing Spanish population. Work has been done on the foreign residents' reactions to the political upheavals of the period, but no one has yet examined in detail, the social origins and development of one of these families from the British Isles.

Blanca Heredia Krauel has studied the many early British visitors to Spain and has described their reactions to the country and its peoples. She has also shown that the adverse comments these visitors often made in their subsequent publications rebounded on their friends and acquaintances back in Spain. María Begoña Villar García has also examined the foreign residents in some detail and put them in their Spanish social context. Their work sets the wider social and academic context for this more personal look at one large and dynamic family.

This study attempts to show that William Kirkpatrick was a prominent member of an extensive inter-related network of trade and influence. He was not a penniless Jacobite refugee as put about for propaganda reasons by both French Republicans and Bourbon Legitimists after the fall of the Second Empire. Nor was he an Irish tradesman making good in Málaga as claimed by some Irish Nationalists, nor was he a naturalised American. He went about the family business with energy and initiative, aided by an important Consular appointment and family, trade and political connections in America and across Europe.

William Kirkpatrick plays a shadowy role in the numerous histories and biographies of the Empress Eugénie and Napoleon III. References to him in secondary sources, especially 20th century biographies of Eugénie, are often factually inaccurate and drawn from similar, late 19th Century works, heavily influenced by the anti-Bonapartists and the Paris Communards, encouraged by the sensationalist press.[3]

Andalusia, with its ancient sites at Granada and Cordoba, and its romantic appeal, was on the itinerary of many Englishmen making the Grand Tour. The English speaking American and British Consuls and their friends and associates were an essential part of the Spanish tour. They dispensed advice, and letters of introduction to city governors, cashed or renewed letters of credit, and provided a safe haven for anxious visitors.

Sir Arthur de Cappell Brooke wrote[4] in 1831.

> "I do not know, indeed that robbery or assassination is more general (in Málaga) than in other parts of Andalusia, but quite frequent enough to make a quiet inoffensive traveller like myself

feel rather uncomfortable when leaving the hospitable roofs of my friends, Mr Kirkpatrick and Mr Mark, (the British Consul) and pursuing my way along the silent Alameda towards my hotel."

These English language sources provide a commentary from afar, another voice. They give a distant perspective on events in Spain. I have used extracts from many foreign authors to reveal details of their history which may not always be familiar to Malagueños.

It is a curiosity that some contemporary French sources tend to credit Kirkpatrick with being very wealthy, "riche à millions"[5], while some English language sources make much of his running a bodega, sometimes mistranslated as "wine bar".[6]

To Spanish eyes the Kirkpatricks, de Grivegnées and their associates were all strong *afrancesados* and their affiliation to the ideals of French Republicanism and Napoleon's early reformist sentiments was to permeate their lives and influence their reactions to events in Spain and beyond.[7] Napoleon's eclipse was also to bring to an end to their prosperous and comfortable lives as settlers in what was in reality a foreign land which came to resent their wealth and their apparent unfaithfulness to their adopted country. But William Kirkpatrick and his foreign associates showed the way for the rapid expansion of Spanish commercial and industrial activities in the years following the end of the Carlist wars.

The reality is that William Kirkpatrick appears as a man of liberal and progressive ideas, and great initiative. He was very prosperous at times, but he suffered a series of losses starting with the effects of the British blockade during the long years of the French Revolutionary and Napoleonic wars. His difficulties continued under Napoleon's Continental System of trade embargos, and extended to the periods of popular unrest which followed the French invasion, the Spanish War of Independence, the occupation of Málaga and their aftermath, and the second French invasion and the disturbances of the 1820s. Following the example of his brother John, William was not beyond a little sanctions busting business on the side.

Napoleon's Berlin Decree of November 1806 stopped Frances's allies, and the countries they occupied, trading with Britain. This was extended by the Milan Decree of 1807, and was countered by the British with an Order in Council which stopped Britain's traditional partners trading with France.

William Kirkpatrick had to play out his public life in tumultuous times. To fully understand his difficulties and his successes we need to look again at these historical events. As the generations pass, this once well-known history has become distant and unfamiliar. Somehow he found a way to survive, many did not. Málaga was in a disastrous state by the time the French left the City in 1812. He emerges as a shrewd man of business, caught out by shifts in the political wind. He seems to have rebuilt his prosperity in later years but not to have regained his former wealth.

"Málaga, Viewed from the Anchorage"

# 1. The Kirkpatricks of Málaga

*The descent and relationships of the earlier Málaga Kirkpatricks have been calculated from their Wills in various Archives, extensive research by Don Enrique Kirkpatrick Mendaro and contemporary biographical and official listings in the journals of the period. They have not been examined in any detail by General Charles Kirkpatrick or by other commentators. There is still some uncertainty about all their exact relationships.*

William of Málaga was born in Scotland on the 24th May 1764, the son of William Kirkpatrick y Gillespie of Conheath and Mary Wilson. His descendent, Enrique Kirkpatrick y Mendaro, the Marqués de Placetas, records that William spent his early years at Caerlaverock, where his parents lived from 1761 after they moved from Garrel. He and his numerous brothers and sisters filled Conheath House in Glencaple, which his father built some years later to accommodate his large family of 19 children. An old friend from childhood days in Dumfries recorded that "Willie Kilpatrick was her playmate and schoolfellow in her early days for they were neighbour lairds' children". She says that he went to "push his fortune in London where he became a merchant. He later proceeded to Spain and settled in Málaga where he married a lady of a grand Spanish family"[8].

His Consular appointment papers state that after a "liberal education" he went to Ostende to join a trading house. William probably made his way to London to the trading firm of his first cousin once removed, Robert Kirkpatrick, and thence to Ostende where his older brother John Kirkpatrick y Wilson was a prosperous merchant. Other family members followed him to Ostende and on to Málaga on the death of their father in 1787. There are records in Ewart Library, Dumfries, showing that his father suffered financial difficulties towards the end of his life and the Conheath Estate and his personal effects were sold to pay his debtors.[9] But his eldest son John had the means to purchase Conheath and preserve it in family ownership for a few more years.

The Scottish poet Robert Burns, despairing of making a living as a tenant farmer, served with the Customs and Excise Department at the port of Dumfries for a salary of £50 a year. William Kirkpatrick y Gillespie of Conheath would have been his colleague and superior; his testament documents show that he was Surveyor of Customs of the

Port of Dumfries at the time of his death on the 2 December 1787. His younger son Thomas, who was born on 25 July 1766 and who later went to Dunkirk, Hamburg and then Málaga, was named as his only executor.

This testament was contested on the 14 November of the same year by Robert Riddick, acting for William Riddick deceased, for an amount of five hundred pounds plus interest. The document mentions the firm of Riddick Kirkpatrick & Ross, of whom William Kirkpatrick y Gillespie senior was a partner, and also mentions the Gatehouse Wine Company. This legal action successfully deposed Thomas Kirkpatrick y Wilson as executor and replaced him with Robert Riddick. From this we can deduce that both these William Kirkpatricks, father and son, were in a similar line of business.

Dutch and Belgian records show that John Kirkpatrick y Wilson, of Ostende, the eldest brother, had extensive trade with Dumfries. John had to return to Dumfries to deal with difficulties over his father's estate and residual creditors. His nephew, the son of his uncle John Kirkpatrick y Gillespie of the Isle of Man, helped him to settle his father's affairs. His uncle even contributed his portion of the inherited family lands, nearly two fifths of Nether Glenkiln, towards this final settlement of William senior's debts.[10]

William Kirkpatrick y Wilson was not the first Scotsman, nor the first member of the family, to make a living in southern Spain. The National Archives in London hold a very early petition from "Malek", Spain, which refers to the period 1325 – 1350. The Archives also hold the Wills of early traders like John Corny, an English Merchant who died in 1622, and a Robert Wilson who died there in about 1691. Robert Bowden and Robert Warner were English merchants in Málaga in 1664.

In 1696 English Consuls, Deputies and others of the Royal English factory in Málaga sent a congratulatory petition to King William II of England. That they named him as William the Second suggests their Scottish bias, as this King William was the Second of that name for the Kingdom of Scotland, but the Third for England. This was a declaration of their loyalty to the new Protestant King, and was probably designed to show that they were not Jacobite sympathisers. Their loyal message may have been somewhat blunted by their error. While no Kirkpatricks, Escotts or Aiskills are listed; thirteen British residents are named, representing a sizeable community before the turn of the 17th Century.[11]

Another early settler from the British Isles was John Galwey from Ireland. He held the office of Síndico Personero, (one who is

Nominated) and was awarded the Grand Cross of Charles III and gained recognition as a Hidalgo on 24 August 1765. He married into the Quilty family who also were early Málaga settlers from Ireland. Galwey stayed on in Spain after inheriting his father's large fortune. One of his sons entered the Army of the Honourable East India Company (HEIC), demonstrating their continued attachment to Britain, other children stayed on in Málaga, and one grandchild married a Cabarrús y Kirkpatrick descendant.[12]

These early "English" merchants profited from special trade arrangements, the "most favoured nation status" concessions the Spanish had surrendered to England, under the Anglo-Spanish treaty of 1667, renewed in 1713, 1715, and 1750. These beneficial trading agreements were likened to "como a Indias de la Europa" by an 18th century Spanish economist.[13]

The Kirkpatricks who settled in Andalusia divide into two confusing collateral lines which descend from Thomas of Knock, of the Kirkmichael branch of the Kirkpatrick family in Dumfries in Scotland. This Thomas had three sons, Robert of Glenkiln, who was executed as a Jacobite in the "forty five"; George, who founded the Irish branch of Coolmine Kirkpatricks but later returned to Glenkiln; and James, who went to England and prospered.

James is mentioned in various Kirkpatrick and Escott Wills, which tie him to the Dumfries family and is named as head of the family. He married Elizabeth Capper of Cullompton, Devon in 1686 and is the father of the early Kirkpatrick settlers in Málaga.

James and Elizabeth had four sons, Robert of Málaga and of Woodford in the county of Essex; Abraham, a merchant in Málaga and later of London; and John, the Juan of Málaga. Their sister Elizabeth married William Escott of Málaga. Abraham was a partner in the Málaga enterprises and is mentioned in documents in the Málaga archives. Another son James was a lawyer. He was a barrister-at-law, and held the judicial post of Master in Extraordinary in Chancery.[14] He was also Town Clerk of the Corporation of Bristol[15] and Recorder of the Corporation of Bridport in Devon, close to the home of the Escott family near Bicknoller in the Quantock Hills.[16] This was probably the James Kirkpatrick who died on 23 May 1787, in the Adelphi, that fine Adam terrace between the Strand and the Embankment in London.

The Jacobite Robert Kirkpatrick of Dumfriesshire also had four sons with similar names to their cousins. The oldest was William of

Conheath, the father of William of Málaga. The next son was Thomas, who married into the Craig family of Tobago in the West Indies. The third son was also a Robert who reportedly stayed in Dumfries, and then a John who settled in the Isle of Man (see Appendix Eight for more on this John).

William of Conheath had a very large family, some of whom will appear in this story as they settled abroad and ended their days near Málaga. His oldest son John was an international merchant and ship owner in Ostende, joining an earlier, but unidentified John Kirkpatrick, who was also a local ship owner, and could have been the Juan of Málaga, of the same date who owned a ship with a Mr. Browne. The next surviving son was William who is the subject of this study and the progenitor of the Spanish Kirkpatricks. His younger son Thomas was a merchant in Dunkirk and in Hanover for some years before moving to Málaga as Hanoverian Consul.

Records in the Municipal Archives in Málaga show that a Juan Kirkpatrick was involved in shipping and trading in the city in 1730. This date may be significant as the Spanish and British Governments had signed the Treaty of Sevilla in 1729, bringing to an end the disturbed period of hostilities which followed the War of Spanish Succession. He was followed by his brothers, Robert and Abraham Kirkpatrick y Capper, and a Mr Escott who married their older sister, Elizabeth Kirkpatrick y Capper. Their son, John Kirkpatrick Escott, also appears in the 18th Century archives, and was active in the affairs of the Málaga Maritime Council, which did so much to modernise the Port and increase trade. William's brother Thomas was also a Consul and négociant. William's nephew Thomas James Kirkpatrick y Stothert and his grand nephew Alexander Thomas Kirkpatrick y Kirkpatrick were Honorary British Consuls some years later. It is a sign of their increasing integration that the Kirkpatricks of the first generation married into the British and foreign community, while their Spanish born children tended to marry into prominent Spanish families.

At a time when marriage alliances sealed business partnerships, and opened doors which were otherwise firmly closed to those of different social rank, religion or nationality, these matters were of the greatest importance and must have occupied the minds of many an anxious mother or maiden aunt. William Kirkpatrick cemented an earlier business alliance between John Kirkpatrick Escott and Robert Kirkpatrick and Henri de Grivegnée by marrying Henri's daughter Françoise.

William and Françoise's daughter, María Manuela, made a spectacular match when she married the Count de Teba, the unlikely heir presumptive of the splendid list of Montijo titles and their very considerable estates.

Her sister Henriette also made a very good catch. She married Domingo Cabarrús, the son of the Spanish King's banker, and in due course, became the Countess de Cabarrús. The Cabarrús were of French origin and first generation nobility who had made their way by their father's ability. The Count de Teba, with other Málaga associates, was a leading shareholder in the Bank San Carlos which had been formed by Francisco, the first count de Cabarrús.[17]

Colonel Cipriano Portocarreo y Palafox, Count de Teba and later of Montijo

Carnival Ball given by the Countess of Montijo on in February 1843, with Paca, Eugenia and their Aunt Carlota Kirkpatrick y Kirkpatrick in fancy dress. From the collection of the Duke of Peñaranda.

The third sister, Catalina Carlotta Kirkpatrick y Grivegnée, married back into the extended Kirkpatrick family, her husband being her cousin, Thomas James Kirkpatrick y Stothert from Ostende. He is described as a British Subject and a member of the Alto Comerció Marítimo de Málaga, and dedicated to commerce. He was the son of Juan Kirkpatrick y Wilson of Ostende and of Dona Juana Stothert of Dumfries. Don Thomas Jaime added some 100,000 Reales de Vellón (rsvs.)[18] deposit to the 31,644 rsvs. that his fiancée had contributed as her dowry.[19]

This marriage re-enforced ties within the family's trading partnership and the dowry formed a substantial portion of the capital of their enterprises. But they were also to cause many difficulties in the years that followed. Such alliances followed the path of many leading foreign merchants in Málaga like the Quiltys, Lorings, Rellies, Gordons, Powers, Terrys and others.

In contrast their Gallegos aunts, the sisters of Francesca Kirkpatrick y Gallegos, married into families of parallel rank, one to the Polish Consul with extensive local connections, and another to a leading foreign merchant family long settled in southern Spain. While the Scotsmen were able to find wives from the local population, it seemed more difficult for their women folk. William had five sisters who survived to adulthood. Harriett followed him to Spain but did not marry even though she converted to Roman Catholicism.

Today it is difficult to appreciate the gulf that existed between prosperous merchants' families and the noble old families of Spain, the grandees, whose aristocratic exclusivity relied on land ownership and purity of blood, *pureza de sangre,* especially an unbroken line of Catholic blood.[20] The Palafox Portocarrero Guzman family, of whom Cipriano, Count de Teba was a descendent, was the grandest of the grand. But he married María Manuela Kirkpatrick at a time when his grandee status was heavily discounted. He had renounced his title, and reverted to plain Colonel Portocarrero when there was reason to think that his older brother, Eugenio, the count of Montijo and renowned lothario, might produce an heir.

But in 1817 Cipriano was also at a financial low. His brother was withholding the rents due to him from the estates at Teba which were rightfully his as second son. But more significantly in this context, his political fortune was also spent. As a Liberal and a notorious supporter of the French, he had forfeited any influence which might have been due his status in the ranks of the foremost nobility. His very presence in Spain was licensed by the King, and was meant to be of short duration.

Cipriano had great difficulty persuading his brother that the match was a suitable one for a grandee of Spain. Eugenio was a conservative and supporter of the nobility who played a very public role in the politics of Court life in Madrid. But María Manuela was described as "riche a millions et belle comme le jour"[21]. She was also highly intelligent and cultured in five languages and had an excellent singing voice and, as we shall see, a very forceful personality. She must have caused William and Fanny many an anxious moment. Enrique Kirkpatrick Mendaro comments that, on reading the biographies of the Empress Eugenia and her mother María Manuela, he sees her as a woman of great temperament and much character, causing numerous rows with her father, who must also had a strong character.

María Manuela's marriage can be seen as a great coup for the daughter of a négociant, but it was also a very timely moment to seize the chance to enter the highest ranks of Spanish society, which she crowned by becoming, for a short time, the chief lady-in-waiting for the Queen at the Court in Madrid.

While William Kirkpatrick's initial reaction is said to be against the match, as Cipriano appeared to be without sufficient funds to maintain an appropriate position in society, he eventually agreed on condition that the dowry his daughter brought to the marriage, regarded in law as her own funds and future security, were held in trust by the Marques de Benalua. William did not want to see the substantial resources he committed to the marriage consumed by his daughter's extravagance or Cipriano's desperate need for money. Hardheaded Scots pragmatism won against his daughter's demands and his ties of friendship to the Count de Teba, and indeed against any thoughts of further social advancement for his family.

Clearly William was a man of resolute character to hold out against the blandishments of so strong a daughter as María Manuela. Her successful bid for upward social progression gave this audacious lady the platform she would later need to launch her daughters in the most exclusive sections of European Society. She achieved this with the most astounding success. But her relations with her father appear to have remained stormy and it was noticeable that although María Manuela rushed from Paris to be beside her dying husband in Madrid, she did not visit her father in his last days in Málaga, not did she observe the customary protocols of mourning.[22]

The Kirkpatricks progression from Western Scotland to the staterooms of the palaces of Europe occurred over at least five generations, and is a tribute to the talents of earlier members of the family who eased the road by gathering wealth and useful contacts along the way.

The discovery of this early group of Kirkpatrick settlers shows that young "Willie" Kirkpatrick was following a well-worn route when he stepped out from the farmlands of Dumfriesshire to join the London road one morning in the early 1780s. He went armed with a good Scottish education, letters of introduction, and recommendations to relations across Europe.

The surviving records suggest that Juan Kirkpatrick y Capper was the first member of the family to settle in Spain. His brother Abraham Kirkpatrick y Capper was described as a merchant in London when he died in 1777. But Abraham Kirkpatrick was closely associated with Francis Aiskill, merchant of Málaga and British Consul, and he had close trade relations with his Kirkpatrick brothers in Málaga. He spent time in Málaga forming Abraham Kirkpatrick et Cíe. which specialised in ship handling and dock works. Abraham's Will of 16 January 1777 left a substantial legacy to his brother, Robert, and his Aiskill grandchildren and shows that he was a resident of Clapham in the County of Surrey.[23] Juan Kirkpatrick's Spanish Will confirms that he is Abraham and Robert's brother, and thus the third son of James Kirkpatrick of Cullompton, in Devonshire.

Documents dated between 1730 and 1732 in the Málaga City Archives show a Juan Kilpatrick [also Kxikpatxick and other various spellings] in the context of an importation of 2903 fanegas of flour where the maximum load for a mule was 2.5 fanegas. This consignment amounted to about a hundred and thirty metric tons, and was distributed as famine relief to the residents of the city. [24]

He owned a ship jointly with Francisco Bowne, which brought this wheat to Málaga at a time of great need. John or Juan Kirkpatrick is not mentioned in Abraham's will so he may have been dead by 1777. Clearly Francis Aiskill introduced Juan Kirkpatrick to the Málaga trade and Robert Kirkpatrick y Capper joined him and took charge of their trading house. By then they were linked by family ties to the Escotts who are also mentioned in Abraham's will. This link to the Escotts and

Aiskills confirms that these early Málaga Kirkpatricks were part of the extended family of Kirkpatrick of Dumfries and connects them to the family in Ostende and later Brussels. Further documents show that Robert Kirkpatrick and Juan Escott were still merchants in the city in the middle of the 18th Century.

James's son, Robert, is shown in family records as unmarried although there are hints that he may have been widowed in Spain. Documents in the Provincial Archives in Málaga dated 1777 state that he was a native of Cullompton in Devonshire. Robert was described in his death notice in *The Gentleman's Magazine* of 1781 as a "very confidential merchant in the Spanish trade". [25] His bequests confirm that this is the same Robert Kirkpatrick y Capper.

He died leaving a large fortune to his scattered grand-nephews and -nieces. These include Charlotte and Francis Aiskill, the children of his younger brother, Abraham Kirkpatrick. His sister Anne married Mr Francis Aiskill, British Consul in Málaga from at least 1763. [26] The son of John Escott and Elizabeth née Kirkpatrick was John Kirkpatrick Escott, who was resident in Málaga for some 30 years prior to 1781. [27] He had business relations with Henri de Grivegnée and left his affairs in Henri's charge when he had to leave Spain.

Francis Aiskill is recorded writing to William Pitt as late as 11 January 1757. [28] Thus he was the British Consul in the city when Juan, Abraham and Robert Kirkpatrick y Capper and Mr Escott were residents. His daughter Charlotte married James Reed Esq., High Sheriff of Essex and Director of the Bank of England. This is the James Reed who had been in business with John Kirkpatrick Escott when he moved back to England. Reed was sponsor of William Kirkpatrick's appointments as US Consul, in 1800 and also a referee to his business probity and a partner with Jeremiah Parkinson in Robert Kirkpatrick's various businesses in London. [29]

Robert of Glenkiln's execution in 1746 scattered his family, and even some of his granddaughters made their way to Spain or married men who spent much of their lives in Málaga. Their relative success, despite such a loss, indicates that the family had resources beyond Scotland. Such external resources may only have been social and business contacts, but the later marriages of grand nieces to a governor of the Bank of England and to a deputy governor of the Tower of London, show they were part of an extensive social group which held positions of some influence in the City of London.

The earlier Spanish agreements with the English had allowed trade to prosper and the commerce of Málaga was stimulated by the defeat of the British in North America and the liberalisation of trade with the newly independent United States. But the long period of war and revolution which followed, and the loss of Spanish trade with the newly independent Spanish colonies in South and Central America, contributed to a period of economic decline. Generations of Kirkpatricks had prospered in the city and had been able to return to comfortable retirement in England, but William ended his days in more modest circumstance at his villa in Adra in the Province of Almería.

# 2. The Scottish Hinterland

*The Kirkpatrick family repeated the same set of Christian names across generations. The Closeburn lines of descent are very complicated and best left to genealogists to unravel from Scottish land records, Patents and other ancient legal documents. Those interested in even more family detail are referred to General Charles Kirkpatrick's book referenced below.*

The origins of this enterprising family lay in the farmlands of Dumfriesshire in the South West of Scotland. Their landholdings were clustered around the ancient Royal Burgh of Dumfries, and along the valley of the river Nith, Nithsdale. They looked out to the Solway Firth, and beyond to the Irish Sea. The villages and hamlets of Closeburn, Kirkpatrick and Conheath are all near by. The English border is 25 miles to the east at Gretna, where the Dumfries road meets the main road to Carlisle, and on to London. It is an area with a troubled history of Jacobite rebellions, and English invasions. The Kirkpatricks survived by adapting to events, and ensuring that a family member somewhere, somehow, ended up on the winning side. They brought to their businesses, their native advantages of Scots shrewdness with money and commerce.

But they were more than provincial gentry. In 1596 King James gave a Protection to the head of the house.

> "grantis and gevis licence to one trusty and familiar servator Thomas Kirkpatrick of Closeburn and to his eldest son to depairt and pas furth of our realme to the parties of France, Flanders and utheris beyond sea, and thair in, for the space of five years meanwhile their lands, stedings, possessions, offices, tenants, servants, to remain in our special protection, to be unharmit, untroublit unmolested or unquieted in any sorte be any person or personis for quhat somever cause". [30]

General Charles Kirkpatrick comments that: "perhaps Sir Thomas took a wise precaution in arranging a long holiday with the safety of his property thus assured". But the Kirkpatrick's internationalist outlook may have stemmed from this trip to France and Flanders which was then ruled by Spain, and would have included Ostende.

The young Willie Kirkpatrick y Wilson, who became United States Consul in Málaga, was the second surviving son of William Kirkpatrick y Gillespie of Conheath (1737 – 1787), in Nithsdale. Bernard Burke of

Burke's Peerages, writing in 1855 states, that these Kirkpatricks "held the position of provincial gentry connected by intermarriages to some of the leading local families".[31] His mother was Mary, the daughter of John Wilson of Kelton of Kirkcudbright, some miles further the west.

William of Málaga was thus the grandson of the Robert Kirkpatrick y Gillespie of Glenkiln who supported the "Bonnie Prince", Charles Edward Stuart, in the '45, the Jacobite Rebellion, and was beheaded on the scaffold in 1746 as a consequence. This connection is probably the source of the romantic notion that William was a Jacobite fleeing to Spain for political reasons. But this view confuses William's motives with those of earlier generations who dispersed around the world following the failed First Jacobite Rebellion of 1715, the "Fifteen" as it was known to differentiate this earlier rebellion from the more famous "Forty-five". Following the path of many in his family before him, he left his homeland to make his way in the world, not to escape the English troopers. He achieved fortune, and a remarkable place in history through the fame of his granddaughter Eugénie, Countess de Teba.

This relationship to Robert of Glenkiln and thus to Thomas Kirkpatrick of Knock of the Kirkmichael line, gave the Conheath Kirkpatricks an important connection to the greater honours, and social standing of the Closeburn Kirkpatricks and their historic lineage and large landholdings.

These ancient Kirkpatricks had ties to various Kings of Scotland and Robert the Bruce and Lord Darnley, husband of Mary Queen of Scots, and the Hamiltons, the premier Dukes of Scotland. In the mid 15th Century, the family divided into the Closeburn and Kirkmichael septs, or clan divisions, which continued to intermarry in succeeding generations.

After the death of the last lord of Kirkmichael 1689, his estate was divided between his two sons, George Kirkpatrick of Knock and Robert Kirkpatrick of Glenkiln, from whom William of Conheath was descended. George joined the English Army and served in Ireland where his son Alexander settled and was successful becoming High Sheriff of Dublin, and later of the surrounding County. James Kirkpatrick of Cullompton seems to have made his own way in the world. His marriage to Elizabeth Capper may have carried advantages of property or estates.

Sir Thomas Kirkpatrick, the head of the main Closeburn line, was granted a baronetcy of Nova Scotia by Charles II in 1685 "for unswerving fidelity" and a substantial donation to the plantation of that remote colony.[32]

As a result of the Jacobite rebellions and other misfortunes the Closeburn Kirkpatricks lost much of their remaining lands which had amounted to some 14,000 acres. Their castle had been much reduced and the family built a substantial manor house nearby. A careless servant burnt it down in 1748 and they moved back to the renovated castle tower. The estate was sold in 1778 for the very substantial sum of £50,000 and the family dispersed. In 1889, Closeburn Castle was described as "less like a palatial residence than a small gaol that had seen better days".[33] Closeburn Hall was further reduced by the British Army during the Second World War. Closeburn is a few miles north of Dumfries on what is now the A76. Now renovated, Closeburn Castle is owned by Don Luis Kirkpatrick, the direct descendent of Thomas Kirkpatrick Stothert and Carlotta Kirkpatrick y Grivegnée, and through them to the Kirkpatricks of Conheath and beyond to the original owners of Closeburn Castle.

But this extensive and scattered family held together through numerous generations, made successful marriages and retained their position in Scottish and English society without large land holdings.

Cousins married cousins and the family was linked by these relationships and by patronage within the family. Evidence of its social position is found in the government posts held by senior members, their Consular appointments and their distinguished Military service.

Both the sons and daughters contracted advantageous marriages. The oldest sons of the Closeburn line enjoyed the status of Scottish laird or landowner and served in the Army, Navy and Judiciary, often achieving high rank. The younger sons and those of the cadet lines made their way in commerce as international merchants as was usual in Scottish families of this kind. The Kirkpatricks, and related families like the Aiskills, Escotts, and Parkinsons, used marriage alliances and family relationships to maintain networks of more or less interconnected trading partnerships. These stretched from London to the Low Countries, Hamburg and Paris, and to Adra and Málaga in Spain, and to the Caribbean and the United States.

The Tower of Closeburn Castle rebuilt with stone from the Old Hall

Closeburn Hall in the 19th Century

# 3. The Hidalgo, and the Lineage of the Kirkpatricks of Conheath

The twenty-four year old William Kirkpatrick y Wilson arrived in Málaga in 1788 as a young man of good family, but with no established position other than as a foreign merchant. His relations had been away from the city for some years, and his task was to reorganise the House of Kirkpatrick and re-vitalize their trade. To do this he had to establish his status within Málaga society and integrate himself into Spanish ways.

As part of this process he set about the complicated procedure of obtaining Hidalgo status in 1795. If William Kirkpatrick can be accused of inflating his family pedigree, it was for the tax exceptions and other privileges and advantages associated with this rank. It was not to prove that his daughter was noble enough to marry his old friend Colonel Portocarrero in 1817, as suggested by later detractors. Hidalgo translates in English as "noble", but in this context it holds a literal sense closer to the older English class of "Gentleman".

The title of Hidalgo was granted to wide categories of individual. There were those who earned the right for meritorious service or valour. A more common qualification was by descent from those who were or had been nobles or by property rights. Owning the main family house was also a qualification, as was land holding by purchase. Even those who could prove that they were descended from a sequence of seven legitimate sons would be eligible.

It was not a class of nobility, but the status carried numerous privileges. Their houses, horses and arms could not be confiscated for debts, nor could they be jailed for economic reasons or put to torture. Hidalgos were exempted from Council service and enjoyed separate prisons. They were also permitted to resolve certain disputes by duels and they were not to be condemned to death by insulting means, nor placed on "bonfires and carving up with the sword" or by bleeding or exile supposing that their lives had been spared. They were exempted from a fifth of the levies of provincial militias if they could show their certificates of hidalguía.[34]

In those uncertain and brutal times theses were obviously privileges worth achieving and William went to considerable lengths to obtain this quality.

He was proposed by a number of local commercial figures including William Laird, whom was later to become British Consul in the city and a very long-term friend. He also had to obtain from Dumfries records of his family's descent and certified copies of baptismal records going back at least three generations. These had to be signed by both the Church Minister and a number of local worthies in Dumfries and Edinburgh.

James Cummyn, the Lyon Kings of Arms in Edinburgh, confirmed that John Kirkpatrick y Wilson's Patent was in accordance with the Genealogies of the Families of Scotland. It was even necessary for William, Baron Grenville of Wotton, one of His Majesty's Lords of the Illustrious Privy Council, and principal Secretary of State for Foreign Affairs, or his clerk to certify and confirm that The Lyon King of Arms was the man he said he was.

The documents were again certified or notarised in London by James Sutherland, and confirmed by the British Consul in Málaga, William Douglas Brodie. Even the British Embassy in Madrid was involved. Finally all the documents had to be translated, and the translator, D. Lorenzo Wasberg had to have his qualifications certified. It is significant that "Sir" (Caballero) James Kirkpatrick of Cullompton is named as the head of the family.[35]

On the 23 of February of 1797, the Royal Chancellery sitting in Granada confirmed his qualification. This patent was not only a validation of religious and social status in the homeland. It was also a question of blood; noble, or at least respectable and honourable, bloodlines had to be evidenced and certified.

From today's perception of pre 20th Century Spanish Catholicism, and the horrors of the Inquisition, it is striking that religious denomination seemed to play a minor role in the qualification process. While it was important that the baptisms of his forebears were recorded, this was to be to prove their legitimacy, respectability and Christian heritage, rather than their actual religious creed. The fact that these were Christian baptisms in the Church of Scotland was sufficient. It was understood and accepted that they were not Roman Catholic rites.

This emphasis on blood rather than religion would have originated from the time of the Reconquista, when the Moors were expelled from Spain and it became vital to prove Christian bloodlines to the exclusion of the Moor's Islamic belief or Sephardic Jewish faith. Protestantism was not part of the equation. Baptism in a Christian church was enough, and numerous merchants seemed to do perfectly well in Málaga without the need to convert to the Roman doctrine.

While it may have been true that Protestant families were excluded from the best Andalusian society, and Spanish marriage alliances were out of the question for this group, there was a comfortable level of society where foreigners could prosper without conversion.

William's family lineage was closely examined again in 1817 at the time of his daughter's marriage to Colonel Cipriano Palafox y Portocarrero (1784 – 1839). The Colonel was by birth a grandee of Spain, and first in line to inherit the great honours and estates of his brother Eugenio, 7th Count de Montijo.[36] The King's permission had to be sought and the alliance licensed by the Court officials in Madrid.

William's claim to membership of Scottish landed gentry was hardly exaggerated. These Kirkpatricks of Dumfriesshire were local notables and landowners from ancient times. The estate of Conheath had been part of the possessions of the Closeburn Kirkpatricks but had passed out of the family.[37] It was later re-purchased by William Kirkpatrick's father. Old maps show Conheath as a separate house with a row of associated cottages. Today Conheath is just to the east of the B725, four miles south of Dumfries in Nithsdale, on the road to Caerlaverock Castle in a parish of the same name.

But William's ancestry once again came in for much sarcastic comment, from those who opposed or scorned his granddaughter Eugénie's far loftier alliance with Louis Napoleon in 1853. Propagandists against the new Napoleon's Second Empire, and Republicans in general, raised doubts about the genealogy Kirkpatrick had produced for the Spanish Monarch in 1817. They scorned Napoleon's marriage to a Spanish countess when more suitable brides had been on offer from the royal houses of Europe.

William Kirkpatrick y Wilson did not commission the Kirkpatrick patent he used for his application. He contacted his kinsman, the Scottish antiquarian, Charles Kirkpatrick Sharpe, and obtained a copy of the 1791 Patent his older brother, John Kirkpatrick y Wilson of Ostende, had commissioned from the Lyon King of Arms at the Edinburgh College of Heralds. This was based on a family history which a local antiquarian, Dr Clapperton, had drawn up for their father William of Conheath in 1784 in support of various issues with land titles.[38]

Although, there are doubts about which documents were shown to King Ferdinand VII in 1817, he doubtless saw the 1791 Patent, as a fine illuminated copy survives in pristine freshness in the Municipal Archives in Málaga. But the King was probably shown Clapperton's pedigree as well, for he famously commented, "Let the good man (The Count de Teba) marry the daughter of Fingal". Clapperton had previously written a history of the Closeburn line from earliest times to 1811 that included references to a connection with Robert the Bruce. Perhaps the King was making a deeply ironic statement, as Fingal was more a figure of Irish legend, than of Scottish genealogy.

The validity of the original pedigree was compromised in the eyes of the Edinburgh College of Arms by subsequent additions by Richard Godman Kirkpatrick which were not properly endorsed by the Herald. But it was essentially the document drawn up by Dr Clapperton for William's father some thirty-three years before.[39]

Conheath House as it is today

William Escott Kirkpatrick, in a letter of 18 January 1853 written from Brussels, states that the Edinburgh Herald Offices' Patent of Arms of 16 May 1791, was granted to his father, John Kirkpatrick of "Cullock", that being the name of his wife's property in Kirkcudbright. This John is William's older brother who settled in Ostende. The Patent must have been approved by Sir Thomas Kirkpatrick, the 5th Baronet of Closeburn, and was granted on the contemporary evidence of the local antiquarian Dr Clapperton, who produced a complete pedigree dating from earliest times, for William Kirkpatrick of Conheath in 1784.

John Kirkpatrick required the Patent for reasons connected with his own succession. When his father died he had to return to Dumfries to settle his Father's complicated estate. As part of the process John needed to prove his own connection to Conheath. Thus the reasons for seeking the Patent were completely separate and long predate the events around María Manuela's marriage in 1817.[40]

Occasionally William Kirkpatrick is called a "Baron" but there is no evidence of his ever being raised to this position, and it probably reflects a misinterpretation of his supposed Scottish "rank" as the son of a Laird, and his relationship to the main Closeburn line. Closeburn was described as a Barony and certain lands comprising the Conheath estates may also have been described as Baronies. Certainly his father William of Conheath was described as a "Baron" but this was because he owned the Barony of Conheath. But these land holding did not necessarily award the owner any right to be called Baron in the European sense of the word. In any case, these lands would have become the property of the oldest son, John Kirkpatrick y Wilson, if they had not been forfeited to his father's debtors.

There may still be some uncertainly as to quite where the cadet Conheath line parted from the older and better connected Closeburn line. The Edinburgh Herald's Office shows a date in the mid 15th Century. But connected they were, as is shown by ties of marriage and business across the succeeding generations. The link is also established by a land grant made in 1774 by the 4th Baronet, Sir James Kirkpatrick, to William of Conheath. This was a valuable life tenure on certain lands in the Closeburn barony. It is a significant document as it proves that the two branches of the family were in close contact, and the Closeburn line was prepared to support the Conheath family when they needed help. The link between the two branches was re-enforced in later generations by the marriages of cousins.

# 4. Family and Extended Connections

We can imagine the young Willie Kirkpatrick landing in Málaga in 1788. His first call must have to been to the house of Henri de Grivegnée who had been acting as the Kirkpatrick's agent during their enforced absence. The young Scotsman would have received a warm welcome in a household full of daughters who needed husbands. The arrival of the twenty-four year old merchant, perhaps tall and fair, would surely have caused great excitement. A romantic and probably speculative view describes him thus:

> "Tall and sinewy, ruddy skinned and fair haired, he was the fortunate possessor not only of the physical traits of his race, but of the sagacity that enables them to see and grasp the chances of success."[41]

There was much family and commercial business to catch up on, and reminiscences of the time when his cousins, Robert and Juan and John Escott, were in the city. The two families worked together, but to what extent this was an informal arrangement of shared consignments and cargoes and business projects or a formal partnership is unclear although they usually traded under a joint name. William would have enjoyed the help and encouragement and business connections of the more experienced Henri. He may have lived with them and worked from their offices in his first year or so in the city before setting up in the Plazuela de los Moros, then moving to the calle Santo Domingo[42]. An attachment to the eldest daughter Fanny would have been a natural result and a very satisfactory arrangement for both parties and their extended business.

The assimilation of the numerous foreign merchants and artisans into Spanish society was an important component in the success of many of these enterprises. This is shown by the Flemish Grivegnée family, who originated as merchants in Liege in what is now Belgium, and their association through marriage with the local Gallegos family from Alhaurin el Grande inland between Málaga and Marbella. Their lives, travels and travails illustrate their internationalist approach, and the extent to which Paris was the centre of their cultural universe.

Henri de Grivegnée became a highly successful négociant who had effectively integrated into governance of the commerce of the city. He was well placed to ride the storms ahead, although he was totally ruined in 1814 from too close an association with the French occupation forces. He married Doña Antonia de Gallegos in 1766 when she was just 15. She was born in 1751, and died during the troubled period following the financial disaster. She was from an established local family who appear frequently in the City records and the records of Churriana in the country to the west of the Málaga. This marriage alliance may have provided capital and land for Henri and his sugar and cotton projects in Churriana, and a comfortable country house for the Kirkpatricks a few years later. He was associated with the Company of de Housse, Nenot y Francisco de Selick, Caballero in 1795.[43] His brother Guillermo Grivegnée was active as a pioneer industrialist in Marbella.

The political stance of this group of prosperous merchants and their Enlightment views are revealed by their membership of *La Sociedad Económica de Amigos del País de Málaga*. This was an extensive 18th and 19th Century network of forward thinkers in both Spain and her colonies. Vitalized by the Bourbon rule of Charles III, men and sometimes women came together to hold discussions and publish papers on topical and reformist issues. Some articles were highly technical agricultural discussions others were literary or cultural. They were aware that Spain lagged behind many other European countries and they were determined to bring the ideas of the new European Enlightenment into the governance of the country.

Many clubs faded away over time, but the Málaga Society remained active during the later years of the 19th century. In 1790 it included both Don Enrique Grivigny (sic) del comerció alto maritime, and Conciliarlo, and don Juan Rein, and don Diago Power del comerció alto maritime, also Thomas Cwilti (should read Quilty), and Gallegos, Muller, Murphy, and others, many of whom were foreigners. Foreign consuls also attended meetings but were not named. William Kirkpatrick had links to all these and it can be taken that he was sympathetic to their cause. The Count de Montijo, perhaps in his role as Duke of Granada, was listed as a correspondent.[44]

The Gallegos also had an international outlook. Doña Antonia's brother, José Gallegos, set up as a merchant in Richmond, Virginia, in the United States, and prospered greatly. On his death in 1818 he left a large sum to his family in Spain. He was the very wealthy founder of the Gallego Flour Mills (whose burnt-out building is the centrepiece of an iconic photograph of the sacking of Richmond on 2 April 1865 before the advance of the Union Army). Gallego developed extensive connexions and maintained his links with his brother in law, Henri de Grivegnée, and his sisters and brothers in Spain. His business partner and joint heir was Peter Chevallie, the son of the French Consul of the American revolutionary period, John Augustus Chevallie, originally from La Rochelle, who had used his own money to fit out a ship with military supplies for the American Revolutionary forces.

Ruins of the Gallego Flour Mills, Richmond, Virginia, 1865

*Oxford Notes and Queries* (a curious sort of 19th Century academic "blog") refers to the marriage of a "granddaughter of Baron Grivegnée of Málaga with Napoleon III, some account of his family. The marriages of four daughters are disclosed, but not their Christian names. One married Neumann, Consul for Poland, another Lesseps; another Michael N. Power of Málaga; another William Kirkpatrick".[45]

The de Grivegnée daughters made noteworthy marriages, which reveal patterns of relationships in the local society of the period. Francisca (or Fanny) Maria de Grivegnée y Gallegos was born in 1769 and married William Kirkpatrick in 1791[46], some three years after his arrival in Málaga. Francisca died tragically in Málaga on the 3 or 4 of February 1822 from the fatal effects of arsenic, taken by mistake for a dose of cream of tartar.[47] The note on her tomb on the Family Pantheon in the Cemetery at Churriana states that she died as a result of a seizure induced by ingesting a dose of arsenic taken by mistake when confused with a food sauce.[48] Arsenic was regularly used as an insecticide in this period.

Their next daughter was Catherine who married Mathieu de Lesseps in Málaga Cathedral on 21 May 1801. She died in Paris on 27 January 1853, three days before her niece Eugénie's wedding to Napoleon III on the 30th. She was the mother of Ferdinand de Lesseps of Suez Canal fame. The Lesseps were a French family which claimed Scottish origins but had been settled in Biarritz many years. They had close cousins in Louisiana who maintained their French connections and were well known plantation owners near New Orleans. Their strong Bonapartiste political allegiance and their difficulties after the fall of Napoleon Bonaparte are illustrated by a brief review of her life, which also reveals the family's international outlook.

Catherine accompanied Mathieu on his Consular postings to Alexandria, and then to Pisa where she remained when her husband was appointed Imperial Commissioner to the Ionian Islands. She is described at this time as an "attractive grass widow". "Her salon was the social centre of Tuscany."[49] The political situation in Corfu, then controlled by unpopular French forces, was too volatile for the security of the family of a French "governor". After Napoleon's disaster in Russia and the collapse of French power, Mathieu refused to surrender to the British fleet then besieging Corfu until he received instructions from Paris. He stayed on with the starving French garrison and even paid their wages from his own funds. Eventually Mathieu had his orders, but the Emperor was in captivity in Elba, and the orders came from Louis XVIII. The Imperial Commissioner had been dismissed and was not to be reimbursed for his expenditures on behalf of the French garrison. He made his way back to his house near Versailles deeply out of pocket and with no prospect of employment.

Francisca de Grivegnée y Gallegos
(Miniature Portrait from Don Enrique Kirkpatrick Mendaro)

"Catherine brought further bad news when she arrived with the children from Pisa. Her own people had been ruined by the Emperor's eclipse, so the family's position was now serious."[50]

By her own people Catherine must have meant her Grivegnée and Kirkpatrick relations in Málaga, who had been ruined by French expropriations and the consequent debts.

The escape of Napoleon and his triumphant return to Paris for the glorious "100 days" brought some respite. Mathieu was remembered and his loyalty to the Empire was rewarded. He was raised to the rank of Count of the Empire and nominated Prefect of the Department of Cantal. But this episode was soon over; Mathieu again lost his post when Louis XVIII was restored after Waterloo, and Mathieu and later Catherine made their way back to Paris. An incident during this confused period gives a rare snapshot of Catherine's character and again illustrates the family's commitment to the Napoleonic cause.

When Mathieu lost the Prefecture of Cantal he had to leave the Prefect's residence but Ferdinand was ill with a high fever and it was thought unwise to move him. Thus Catherine stayed on in part of the residence.

> "She in turn offered to lend him – the new Prefect, Baron Locard – her carriage, only to discover that it had been used to bring back to Aurillac under arrest no less a personage than Marshall Ney, who had been hiding with a relative of hers. Years later Ferdinand recalled: "I shall never forget the indignation of my mother when she learned to what use my father's carriage had been put. With her Spanish fire she poured the most violent reproaches upon Baron Locard and she was never able to forgive his part in the proceeding." [51]

They left for Paris where they still had a house near Versailles. Just as they reached the end of their financial resources Mathieu was restored to favour, and in November 1818 he was offered the post of French Consul General in Philadelphia. Catherine remained in Paris to oversee the education of their sons. The de Lesseps became famous, some would have said infamous, over the dealings of their son Ferdinand. He achieved the heights of success using his force of character and high-level connections to push through the Suez Canal, a triumph that was celebrated in Egypt in the presence of his cousin the Empress Eugénie. But his efforts in Panama met with disaster and he was accused of mismanagement of the scheme and its finances.

These relationships and their more extended connections are established by an extensive subscription list for the *Miscellaneous Works of David Humphreys late Minister Plenipotentiary from the United States of America to the Court of Madrid,*[52]. It also demonstrates their wider intellectual interests and their awareness of developments in science and technology. A Henry Neumann, Esq., merchant of Málaga, was a subscriber as was Nickolas Plinck the father of "Senora Doña Juana Plinck of Nagel, relict of Thomas Kirkpatrick Esq. for many years Hanoverian Consul of Málaga".[53] Doña Juana was a niece of M. Rein[54] of the house of Rein and Domecq, wine exporters, who was a Merchant and President of the Consulate Court of Málaga. When James Busby was on his vine-collecting tour of Spain he called Reins' the "First Mercantile House in Málaga", meaning the leading one.

The next de Grivegnée y Gallegos daughter, Maria Juana, married Michael Narciso Power, a merchant whose family was long established in

Andalusia and Gibraltar. A James Power, a merchant of Málaga, is also on the list. He would have been associated with William Power and Co. of Cadiz and was probably the son of Michael Power of Málaga, who married Juana de Grivegnée. Michael Power was an Irish wine merchant, whose granddaughter Emily Jane Power married Benjamin Carver of the firm of Carver Brothers Ltd., long established cotton merchants of Gibraltar.[55] The records reveal numerous other combines between the foreign merchant of Málaga and Gibraltar often forged by joint business interests. While these were concentrated on wines and sherry, cotton and sugar, the American trade also played a large part. Other subscribers were George Trenholm of Charleston, Sir Henri Grivegnée and Henry Grivegnée junior, both of Málaga, and, of course, William Kirkpatrick, who took two copies.

This list links a wide range of Kirkpatrick associates and shows a possible connection to George Trenholm, the uncle of George Alfred Trenholm, a leading businessman of Charleston, South Carolina. He was instrumental in forming the South Carolina Importing and Exporting Company that ran the blockade of Charleston in the early 1860s. Whether the two are linked by more that the subscriptions is unknown, but there are hints of other Kirkpatrick connections with the Trenholm family of Charleston S.C.[56]

Their fourth daughter, Maria Josefa de Grevignée y Gallegos married Henri Neumann, a native of Hamburg and Polish Consul in the city. Their children married into extended Málaga families, developing connections with the Reissig* and the Huelín y Silver families who trace their origins to an Englishman from Southampton, William Huelín Silver, who settled in Málaga in the 18th Century, marrying Josefa Mandly de Rueda in 1777. Their son, Matías Huelín Silver-Mandly de Rueda, married Enriqueta Neumann y Grivegnée settling in Granada. He was to play a major role in the administration of William's estate and the arrangements for his lead mines. The Huelín Madley Reissig family became early industrialists and iron smelters in Málaga.[57]

* Founded by Zacarías Gaspar Reissig y Künike-Osstin, native of Hamburg and Danish Consul. (Muñoz Martin, page 187-188, has extensive notes on these connections.)

Portrait of Ferdinand de Lesseps (1805-1894).

# 5. William and Fanny

From this distance in time we cannot tell how William and Fanny de Grivegnée managed the marriage they contracted on 2 of November 1791, in the Church of the Parish of San Juan Dios on the west side of the city. There were long separations, but these were of necessity. Fanny was in Paris for some years staying with her sister Catherine and educating their daughters. William appears to have visited them and may have been with them in England and introduced them to his London relations and John Kirkpatrick Escott. But there are signs the marriage worked well. The daughters were well regarded for their social brilliance and appearances. Invitations to their musical events were highly prized. William seems to have been greatly affected by Fanny's tragic death. He moved to Motril at about that time and is spoken of as "pauvre Guillerimo" in later letters, but whether in sympathy at his loss or because of his business difficulties is unknown. He suffered ill health to end the end of his life, which must have prompted his return to Málaga in the months before his death.

William Kirkpatrick and Fanny produced five children, four daughters, and a son who died early.[58] Málaga Cathedral records show that their first daughter was Antonia Maria Ann baptised on 8 September 1792. María Manuela Elisabeth[59] who was born in Málaga in 1793 was also known in the family as Mariquita, an Andalusian diminutive of Maria. Then followed Henriquita, born in 1795 and Carlotta Catalina born on 18 January 1796. Their only son Guillermo Enrique Joaquin Thomas was born on 11 March 1797, but died young.

William and Fanny Kirkpatrick were living in Santo Domingo in 1795 but the church records for this parish were destroyed during the shelling and bombing of the Civil War era. Baptismal records for the Parish of San Juan, held in the library of Málaga Cathedral for 1790 to June 1825, show a series of Kirkpatrick y Grivegnée baptisms. The critical volume for 1794 – 1795 is missing. This would have shown the baptism of María Manuela. This is typical of the curious gaps we have found in a wide range of official records concerning María Manuela, Countess de Montijo. Numerous members of the Gallegos family are recorded in Churriana Parish. These records are in the archives of Málaga Cathedral.

In the financial accounts for Fanny's expenses in London in 1814 that Juan de Lesseps sent to William Kirkpatrick in 1836, five girls are listed: Marie Quita (María Manuela), Henriette, Carlotta and Elisabeth and Mathilde.[60] The last two were Fanny's nieces. Only Juan de Lessep's letter names Elisabeth and Mathilde as part of the family circle at this time.

Mathilde Maria Rafael Neuman was baptised at the Sagrario Chapel of Málaga Cathedral in 1801, the daughter of don Enrique Neuman and Donna Mañuela (Maria Josefa) de Grivegnée y Gallegos and thus Fanny de Grivegnée's niece. A son, Guillermo Neumann is shown in other records[61]. Elisabeth must have been another Gallegos or Power niece or a perhaps there is some confusion over the name of first daughter who died young.

Juan de Lesseps accounts for the nieces in the same way as the three known sisters and includes them in the same bills for board and minor purchases. The parents of Elisabeth and Mathilde had not paid their bills either. Don Enrique Neuman is shown as a native of Hamburg and the Polish Consul in Málaga, and the Powers were prominent wine merchants..

A Scottish source records that:

> "a scion of the family of Sir James Kirkpatrick settled in Málaga early in the present century as agent to a Scottish wine merchant, and was very useful to the commissariat department of the British Army in the Peninsular War. He had three daughters whose brilliant complexion and fair hair, as well as handsome fortunes, were the admiration of the Spanish Dons. One daughter married a wine grower in Andalusia and the third, an official employed in the commissariat of the British Army." [62]

This and similar other statements confirm that Thomas James Kirkpatrick was with Wellington's forces. The available evidence does not support this suggestion that William was helpful to the British Army. He was initially at least in sympathy with Napoleon's reformist views, although he may well have played a double role after his mistreatment by the Napoleon's Army. This comment suggests a family division which echoes the one between Eugenio, Count de Montijo, and his younger brother Cipriano, Count de Teba, a Colonel in Napoleon's Artillery.

When William and Fanny's daughters returned to Málaga from Paris they were clearly the toast of the foreign community even if their French associations, manners and schooling kept local Spanish suitors away. *The Gentleman's Magazine* of July 1818 reported a marriage which occurred "lately" between Thomas James Kirkpatrick and Carlota

Kirkpatrick at Gibraltar, and "at Málaga, Cipriano Palafox, Count Jeva, *sic*, to Mariquita Malvina, eldest daughter of William Kirkpatrick, Esq. Málaga." Witnesses at Cipriano's marriage to María Manuela in 1817 were a Jaime Seta, Colonel Antonio Diaz, Enrique Grivegnée and Enrique Neumann, all of Málaga.[63]

Prosper Mérimée describes María Manuela thus: *C'est une excellente femme qui a toutes les qualités solides d'une femme du Nord, avec la grâce et le sans-façon de son pays.* Clearly William had had a strong influence on his brilliant daughter even if their later relationship was more distant.[64]

María Manuela Kirkpatrick y Grivegnée, Countess de Montijo

William Kirkpatrick's favourite daughter seems to have been Carlota Cantalona, who married her cousin, Thomas James Kirkpatrick, the son of John Kirkpatrick of Ostende, and had five children.[65] Thomas was associated with Motril, but became British Vice-Consul at Adra.[66] Thomas and Carlotta and their family accompanied William as he moved from Málaga to Motril and then to Adra. Her death in Adra in 1831 must have moved William greatly and strengthened his affections for her youngest son Alejandro.

Thomas became deeply involved in the administration of William's legacy and the management of his lead mines but appears also to have been bankrupted on at least two occasions.[67] He played a supplementary role to his older brother John, who had also been with the British Commissariat in Wellington's Army and later became a banker in Paris and maintained a connection to Le Havre where their mother lived. Their brother, another William, settled in Brussels. John helped finance the development of the mines and paid for the education of Alexander, Thomas's son, who after the death of his mother in 1831, spent some years as a boy living with William in Adra.

William was also greatly attached to his third daughter, Henriquita, who married Dominique Cabarrús y Quilty, the son of Count Domingo Vicente Cabarrús. The Cabarrús connection with the foreign residents of Málaga is another example of the integration of the leading commercial families with progressive elements of more established Spanish families. Henriquita is described as the "calmest" of the three sisters and enjoyed "possibly not the least happiness" at her husband's large sugar plantation near Velez Málaga close to Torrox.[68]

Dominique Cabarrús was the grandson of the Frenchman, François Cabarrús, director of the Bank of San Carlos and the largest single stockholder and a founding member of what became the National Bank of Spain.[69] Domingo was the nephew of the notorious Térésa, who ended a fabulous succession of marriages and liaisons as the Princesse de Chimay.

Domingo Vicente Cabarrús moved to Málaga and lodged at the house of Thomas Quilty, a wealthy merchant of Irish origin who was an advisor to the Spanish Treasury and an elected Official of the Andalusian Government and pioneer industrialist. In 1795 he married Rosa Quilty y Cólogan (1775-1811) the daughter of Thomas Quilty and his wife; she was a member of the Cólogan family of the Canary Islands who had strong banking connections in Madrid and London. Thomas Quilty, (1739-1804) "bought two sugar engines to Málaga and revitalized the industry with the introduction of the mineral coal and the renovation of the machinery".[70]

Domingo Cabarrús inherited the title of Count de Cabarrús on 27 April 1810 on the death of his father the banker Francisco de Cabarrús, the first Count. He also inherited the extensive salt marshes near Valencia which his father had reclaimed and turned into productive agricultural land. He became a prosperous sugar planter and lived in some style in Velez-Málaga some miles to the east of Málaga city.

Don Domingo Cabarrús and Henri Grivegnée were named in the Málaga Municipal Council session of 17 February 1810 as having represented the Royal Commercial Council among the group of gentleman who travelled to Seville to send compliments to King José I, otherwise known as Joseph-Napoléon Bonaparte, the brother of the Emperor Napoleon, who had appointed him as King of Spain in June 1808.[71] They braved the brigands on the roads who did not hesitate to plunder those they suspected of collaborating with the French. In 1810 a similar deputation from the Ayuntamiento of Alcaudete, north west of Granada, on its way to congratulate Joseph Bonaparte on his conquest of Andalusia, was held up and "stripped of it horses".[72]

The wider de Grivegnée family was heavily penalised for their pro-French actions after Joseph Bonaparte's retreat to France in June 1812. They were eventually bankrupted by a series of court actions and were in desperate straits. Cipriano, Count de Teba, was also caught up with the French withdrawal from Spain in 1813. As a colonel in the French controlled Royal Corp of Spanish Artillery, he was obliged to accompany his Spanish unit on the long march back to Paris.

These families were tied by numerous bonds of consanguinity giving them cohesion and resilience. These links were reinforced by the legal ties of marriage contracts, interfamilial business and dowry guarantees, and testamentary settlements. Although these were a source of strength and capital in the earlier days, it was these very arrangements that led to the actual bankruptcy or near ruination of swathes of the family after Napoleon's despoliations.

# 6. The Kirkpatricks Abroad

Romantic legends give varying accounts of the Kirkpatrick brothers' departure from Dumfries and their scattering around the margins of Europe. These often reflect a Victorian fascination with the story of Bonny Prince Charles Stewart of Scotland embroidered by the novels of Sir Walter Scott. But the extent of the Kirkpatrick diaspora sets the international context for William Kirkpatrick's Málaga enterprises. It shows that María Manuela and her sisters started life with wide horizons which reached well beyond the narrow streets of old Málaga. Eugénie's startling rise is less surprising when we consider her family origins.

The following small vignettes, of life in those times, illustrate how people lived and travelled and made their way in a Europe that was soon to endure Napoleon's despotic rule.

> "The Empress Eugénie's great-great-grandfather joined the standard of the Pretender in 1745, and being taken prisoner, died on the scaffold. His son left Scotland, and settled at Ostende, whence the family emigrated to Spain."

Antiquarians like William Anderson,[73] quoting as above from Charles Hoddam Sharpe, explains the Kirkpatricks emigration by stating that they fled abroad after Robert was executed as a Jacobite in 1745. This was later taken to refer to the children of William of Conheath.

New evidence shows that this forced emigration refers to the children and the brothers, of the Robert Kirkpatrick, who died a martyr to the Jacobite cause, and not to his grandchildren. This also appears to be an echo of an earlier dispersal after the rebellion of 1715 which may well have sent a prior group of Kirkpatricks to Málaga and Ostende and even as far as Charleston, South Carolina.

Other less romantic family activities seem to have been conveniently lost to time. Recent research has revealed that the Ostende operations were deeply involved in smuggling and the contraband trade.

A Juan Kirkpatrick was in Málaga as early as the 1730s and there were Kirkpatricks in Ostende from 1739, six years before Robert was executed in Scotland. These Kirkpatricks would have been of Robert's own generation or that preceding it, and must have been his siblings or cousins or uncles. Doubtless, his children went abroad after the arrest of their father. But they left to join family members who were already settled and established in trade in cities where Kirkpatricks of succeeding generations were to make or lose their fortunes.

Family mercantile networks were a feature of the growing trade on the Atlantic seaboard. Close relationships established trust and facilitated credit and communications. Expatriate Scots and Irish families, escaping difficult conditions at home, were a significant and under recognised element in the internationalisation and the growth of commerce in the seventeenth and eighteenth centuries.

In the 18th Century, Ostende flourished under Austrian rule, and some two thousand British merchants and artisans and their families brought their own way of life along with their English Church which was established in an old barn in the 1780s. The French Revolution forced most of them to leave and they did not return until 1817. The English Church in Ostende records a Kirkpatrick birth in 1739, another in about 1743 and a marriage in about 1764. A John Kirkpatrick was born in Ostende in 1765. But this way of life was brought to an end by the events which followed the storming of the Bastille on the 14 July 1789 and the onset of the French Revolution and the fall of the Bourbon Monarchy. Those who remained were held under a form of loose house arrest and had difficulty obtaining passes to travel.

The John Kirkpatrick y Wilson who was William's older brother settled in Ostende in January 1788 and by the 18th of the same month he was a burgess or citizen of the town. His place of business was on the corner of St. Jozefstraat and St. Thomasstreet.

John Kirkpatrick's Business House on Sint Jozefstraat in Ostende.
This side is 136.5 metres wide.[75]

He also owned a country estate at Meickleculloch, now Meikle Culloch, 16 Km south of west from Dumfries, which he sold in 1791 for the large figure of £4,266. He sold an estate named Lainfils, near Stirling in central Scotland, for £910 during this period. These sales, which may have been of property belonging to his wife Janet Stothert, were to fund his purchase of the family estate of Conheath from his father's creditors for £8,100. By the 20 January 1795 he had become a burgess of Vlissingen, on the mouth of the great Schulte River, the day after Holland was taken into Napoleon's grasp as the Batavian Republic with a new constitution and government which was to run through to 1806, when Louis Bonaparte was placed on the throne of the Kingdom of Holland.[74]

Jan Parmentier of the University of Ghent has shown that his success was due to more than straight forward trading activities. John Kirkpatrick and his brother Thomas were actively engaged in the smuggling business. But their role seems to be that of promoter, ship owner and wholesale provider of contraband rather than desperate landings and running engagements with armed revenue officers.

These activities may have been more of a commercial effort to avoid government imposed sanctions and trade embargoes than really criminal activities, although the penalties for capture would have been severe.

John Kirkpatrick's main smuggling activities were centred on Guernsey in the British owned Channel Islands. These illegal cargoes included tobacco, Dutch gin, tea and brandy. He regularly sent as many as three or four shiploads to the Island at a time. Given the small population of the Island these goods must have been transhipped and passed on to other carriers perhaps for trade or smuggling into mainland Britain. But he is also reported as having been smuggling into Ayr on the west Coast of Scotland although this may been through a third party.

His more legal shipping activities were on an extensive scale with small vessels sailing to Dumfries where they were doubtless supplying wine, brandy and Mediterranean produce to his father's company, Riddick and Co, and the Gatehouse Wine Merchants. His sloops and cutters also off loaded at Ayr, Kirkcudbright on the Solway Firth, and Stranraer at the head of Loch Ryan. They were also trading tobacco with the Faerøe Islands well to the north west of the Shetlands and Orkney. This connection shows that the Kirkpatrick vessels took the northern course round the top of Scotland and then down through the Hebrides to the west coast near Dumfries. This track may seem to take them far out of their way, but if there were cargoes to be had and goods to be sold it must have paid its way. There may also have been good seamen to recruit in the Shetlands and Orkneys who knew the northern seas and may not have been too concerned about their cargoes. This was also a route which took them far from the fast offshore Revenue Cutters of the English Coast Guard Service which patrolled the English Channel and the Irish approaches.

John Kirkpatrick y Wilson's worldwide network of suppliers and customers formed a web of commercial activity which linked back to Málaga and Spanish suppliers and markets. Jan Parmentier has revealed an 18th Century system of shipping business which gives an insight into the activities of shipping agents, ship owners, and importers and exporters like Henri de Grivegnée, and William Kirkpatrick and his predecessors, at the House of Kirkpatrick and Escott and in London too. London was a vital part of this web providing banking and discounting facilities and thus the trade capital for these activities.

During the 1790s John Kirkpatrick regularly imported shiploads of St. Dominique coffee and sugar and cotton from New York. He also bought tobacco and rice for the South Netherlands market from St Petersburg in Virginia and Charleston, South Carolina.

John Kirkpatrick had commercial contacts with Salem in Massachusetts. The return cargo for the American trade consisted primarily of brandy, Spanish wine and Madeira. Each year his Ostende house ordered several cargoes of both dry wine and Pedro Ximenes dessert wine from Henry de Grivegnée in Málaga. In the 1770s this John was part of the mercantile House of Grivegnée, Kirkpatrick, Escott y Cíe. of Málaga. For Madeira wines he dealt with the House of Scott in Funchal, the capital of the Island of Madeira. Catalan wines were bought from his former partners, Nicolas Reserson and William de Vic, Tupper who had settled in Barcelona. His brother Thomas Kirkpatrick y Wilson acted as the manager of the Dunkirk branch before he moved to Hamburg and then to Málaga.

His trade was geographically extensive. From Lisbon he bought dry hides and from Tuscan Livorno, he ordered juniper berries. He occasionally ordered rum directly from the Danish island of St. Croix in the West Indies. He also participated in the British East Indies trade using Ostende as a base.

Much of this trade was carried on John Kirkpatrick's own vessels as he had extensive shipping interests, owning or part owning six smaller craft in the period up to 1793, when he sold these ships and bought the new brigantine *Trinity*, 200 tons and the sloop *Black Prince*, 60 tons. In 1791-92 he used dry bulk contracts for part of the outward cargo for the Bengal trade with the Danish flagged *Flora*, Captain Ole Holmstrom and for the Madras trade the vessel *L'Aquila*, Captain Luigi Fortunato Goreni sailing under the Genovese flag. He also acted as port agent for captains sailing to Scotland, America and Málaga and Madeira, and as agent for numerous mainly Anglo-Saxon mercantile houses. This included acting as proprietor of a Genovese East Indiaman, the *Justina*, 400 tons which belonged to two English ship owners who doubtless wanted a neutral to take over the vessel during a difficult political period. (see list in Appendix Nine). These activities reveal for the first time the details of the Kirkpatricks' extensive trade and show the reach and volumes involved.

A very immediate sense of an encounter with the Kirkpatricks of Ostende and what it was like to travel in Europe in that period is found in the diary of a lady of that era.[76]

> *"This story is from the journal of Mary Westwater Campbell and is a true account using her words in the speech of the time. It takes place in Europe circa 1792 or 1793, during the turbulent period leading up to the "Time of Terror" of the French Revolution (1789 – 1799)."*

> "Left Leith on board a Trader bound for London on Christmas Day, either of the year 1792 or 1793; in charge of two nieces whose mother, my half sister, was dead. Their father, Lieutenant & Quartermaster Douglas of the 53rd Regiment, was at that time in service abroad, and wished his daughters to be placed in a Convent for their education and also that he might have a chance of seeing them sometimes. We arrived in London after a passage of a fortnight; which was about the usual time in those days. There were several passengers on board, among them was a foreigner who fell or pretended to fall in love with me and although I had scarcely spoken to him, insisted, upon leaving the vessel, to get a lock of my hair – which I was obliged to give to get rid of him.

> The Captain of the ship took us to an Inn where we refrained for three days. I saw little of London as I was scarcely out, unless at the offices of the agents of the Regiment – Greenwood Company, which I think was in or near the Exchange. Left London, for Dover by stage, nothing occurred remarkable

during the journey. We sailed at night from Dover to Ostend by the passage boat. Had a most fearful, stormy passage, none on board ever expected to see land. A lady and her two children were in the cabin with me. We could hear an officer who was going to his regiment, cursing at a fearful rate. It was awful to hear him and would have been so at any time, but it was more so when we were all thinking that every minute might be our last. We reached Ostend at last, for which we were very thankful.

We had letters of introduction to a Mr. Kirkpatrick, the British Consul at Ostende, who, with his wife, received us very kindly. He was from Dumfriesshire, and I think must have been Grandfather or Granduncle to Eugénie, Empress of France. We remained with them a few days. They live in good style. They had one son, a little boy, who always gave us his toast, "The Duc-de-York." They played cards on Sunday and were not pleased that I would not join them in the game. They would have gone to the "Theatre" had it not been a bad day. They taught me on the other evenings to play vingt-un at which I gained.

We left Ostend for Ghent, by barge, which is a very pleasant way of travelling, one would not know one was moving. The barge was a very handsome one and we had a grand dinner on board. We went the first day to Bruges where we were to stay overnight. Upon going to the hotel to which we were directed, we could not get admission as it was quite full, but the people sent us to another where we were pretty comfortable, although we had to share a room with another lady.

Went on board the barge in the morning and reached Ghent in the afternoon. We had a letter from Mr. Kirkpatrick to the Hotel Royale, where we went on arrival. It was a very fine hotel, situated on the Grande Place. While there, we saw from the window, a large body of troops reviewed by the Duke of York. There were several bands of music, which was delightful. We dined at the Table d'Hotel, which was generally very crowded.

Upon hearing that the 53rd Regiment was at Oudenarde, - we set out for that place by stage – when about halfway we met Mr. Douglas coming up to Ghent – when we turned back along with him. We had lodgings in the house of a Madame Willard. She had a great many lodgers, but though we had rooms to ourselves, we all dined together. She had a billiard table."

This reference to John and Janet Kirkpatrick y Stoddard suggests that he was at that time acting or honorary British Consul. This is surely an extraordinary official post for a merchant so involved in illegal trade?

Despite his income from his irregular activities John Kirkpatrick was declared Bankrupt in 1805. This was probably due to the general collapse of the export and import trade following Napoleon's restrictions and British counter sanctions. Jane Kirkpatrick had to pledge her family property and offer part of her Tarscreechan estate as security in settlement of a bond for £900 which they had taken out previously. By June 1813 his son William Escott Kirkpatrick was able to take over the burden of undischarged debts of £2,000 and £1,000.[77] These events illustrate the continuing ties between the family and Dumfries. This bankruptcy must have caused financial and trading difficulties for the Kirkpatricks in London, Málaga and Hamburg.

But there was another side to the Kirkpatrick's activities which shows that they had contacts with English officials too and may explain his Consular role. The British Government had been alarmed by many aspects of the French Revolution and supported some fractions among the émigré Royalist resistance, but was wary of others who may not have been able to obtain popular support in the French countryside.

In 1793 Evan Nepean, an under-secretary at the British Home Office and later at the Admiralty, contacted Gideon Duncan, the British Consul in Ostende, with a request for a small ship to carry out intelligence work on the blockaded coast of Revolutionary France. Nepean was an "able professional administrator" who controlled the budget for British secret service intelligence gathering in France.[78]

Nepean's principal Intelligence interest was in the deployment of the French Navy but he had heard reports of an uprising in the Vendée led by the legendary General Gaston. Britain had been considering giving military assistance to the Royalists and Gaston's army, which was rumoured to be 200,000 strong, and was thought to be a potential asset. Nepean hoped to work through contacts between the French mainland and the Channel Islands. The British urgently needed to establish relations with Gaston and verify the reports and see what help he needed.[79]

Nepean asked Gideon Duncan to hire an "American Schooner" to go up the coast of France, and learn what Gaston was doing. The Consul recommended the *Lydia,* owned by John Kirkpatrick and Co., which was charted on 16 May 1793 for £150 per month. It is unclear whether this Company was named for John Kirkpatrick of Ostende, the older brother of William, or the John Kirkpatrick born in that city in 1765 or an even earlier Kirkpatrick enterprise.

The historian Alfred Cobban tells the story:

"The supercargo, a Milanese named Madeny, was to be the only person on board who knew the real object of the voyage. 'For cover the *Lydia* was cleared out for Lisbon, and to call at Nantes by way of looking for freight; whatever information she could pick up she was to deliver to the Government of Jersey or Guernsey, and all the English men of war had notice of her, that she might not be molested.' Arriving at Nantes, the *Lydia* at once found herself under embargo with all the other ships in the port. She subsequently forgot the mission she had been hired for, and engaged in trade between France and America and Hamburg, until she was seized in the Channel with a cargo from Holland to Bordeaux, by a British warship. Duncan thought there had been conclusion between Kirkpatrick, Madeny and the Captain, and Nepean evidently got no information for his money."

These excerpts are given at length, as they are the only significant references we have to the Ostende Kirkpatricks. The Juan Kirkpatrick who was in Málaga in 1730 was part owner of a ship which brought in flour to the relief of the inhabitants. This, linked with the reference to trading with Hamburg, shows that these Kirkpatricks owned or part shared merchant vessels or bought and sold them with their cargos, as was a normal trading practice. Consul Duncan's view, that the failure of the plot was due to collusion, is explicit, but whether this was deliberate sabotage on the part of Madeny or Kirkpatrick, or just the pressure of French regulation and commercial events, is unresolved. Madeny may have heard of Gaston's fate. He was captured and shot in April 1793; his army had consisted of no more than a few hundred peasants. But this may be a hint that Kirkpatrick, despite his reported Consular Status, was not the British patriot Duncan had taken him for.

William's older brother John Kirkpatrick married Janet Stothert (also spelt Stothert), an heiress in her own right to the estates of Tarscreechan.[80] A transcription of the register of the English Church of Ostende,[81] shows a son, Thomas James Kirkpatrick, born to John Kirkpatrick and Janet and christened on 2 August 1791 at Ostende, West Vlaanderen, Belgium. This son married Carlotta Catalina, the second daughter of William of Málaga, in Gibraltar in 1818.

Another son of John of Ostende, also a John, is described as having being very useful to the Duke of Wellington's Commissariat up to 1814.

He is then reported as banker in Paris. He is an example of the extent to which the family found itself on opposing sides during the Napoleonic Wars although their ultimate allegiances now seems to have been firmly to the British cause.[82] Their daughter Maria Isabella Kirkpatrick, born in Ostende in 1792, married Joseph Kirkpatrick of the family that settled in the Isle of Wight. This long separated branch of the Dumfries family had prospered in the south of England and owned the Kirkpatrick Bank that operated on the Island.[83]

These marriage alliances between widely dispersed cousins show the longstanding cohesion of the extended family and may indicate that the Bank also played a part in John Kirkpatrick's trade and the Málaga operations.

Janet Stothert Kirkpatrick died at Harvé on the 22nd February 1846, the relict of John Kirkpatrick, Esq., late of Conheath.[84]

### A Kirkpatrick Memorial

*"in the churchyard of Caerlaverock, some six miles below Dumfries, — at no great distance from this memorial stone (for Old Mortality) appears an enclosed space — which contains the remains of the Kirkpatricks of Conheath, ancestors of the Empress Eugénie. The following inscriptions are found on it:- "*

IN MEMORY OF WILLIAM KIRKPATRICK, LATE OF CONHEATH; -
MARY WILSON, HIS SPOUSE; ISABELLA, ALEXANDER,
AND ELIZABETH KIRKPATRICK, THEIR CHILDREN.
ROSINA KIRKPATRICK DIED AT NITHBANK THE 5TH DAY OF
APRIL, 1833.
JANE FORBES KIRKPATRICK, THE LAST SURVIVING DAUGHTER
OF THE ABOVE WILLIAM AND MARY KIRKPATRICK, BORN THE
18TH OF SEPTEMBER, 1767; DIED THE 21ST DECEMBER, 1854.
ERECTED BY JOHN KIRKPATRICK, MERCHANT IN OSTENDE,
ELDEST SON OF DECEASED WILLIAM KIRKPATRICK, APRIL 1788.[85]

Although there were claims about William's Irish background, he was clearly of Scottish origin. His great uncle, George Kirkpatrick, an officer with William of Orange, went to Ireland in 1719 and prospered there. This shows an interesting political pragmatism in the extended family of the period. Some members supported the "Bonny Prince", others the new Orange Protestant order, implying a Protestant allegiance. But William of Málaga was not from that Irish line although he maintained contact with his Dublin relations. On 26 October 1814, he sent them boxes of Spanish Muscatel raisins, some almonds and two boxes of grapes in the care of Captain Fox of the brig *Mary*. He also canvassed their support for his business. He signed himself "Your most affect. C.G. (Cousin Germane) William Kirkpatrick, Kirkpatrick & Grivegnée." See Appendix Six.

His younger brother, Thomas Kirkpatrick, having served his apprenticeship in the Kirkpatricks' Dunkirk office, was to become a prominent member of Málaga's foreign community. He was appointed Málaga Consul General of the small North German Duchy of Oldenburg in October 1807, which office he kept until at least 1817. Some of his correspondence survives in the Oldenburg State Archives.[86] He was later the Málaga Consul for the Grand Duchy of Hanover, in which city state he is reported to have spent the years from his departure from Scotland to his arrival in Málaga.

Thomas Kirkpatrick was married to Dona Juana in Málaga on 10 October of 1810. She was the daughter of Isabella Nagel and Nicholas Plink. Plink was originally from Hamburg and was Hanoverian Consul in Gibraltar in 1812.[87] Kirkpatrick family records say that Thomas was first married to a Dorothea Kilbi of Dumfries. [88]

Another source says that Thomas married a "Swedish lady of rank" and became Swedish Consul,[89] yet another that he was the Russian Consul. Other reports say that Thomas went to Sweden where he married a Swedish lady who had British parents. He then moved to Málaga as Swedish Consul.[90] However, the records of the Kingdom of Hanover confirm that Thomas Kirkpatrick was their Consul General in Málaga from at least 1818 to 1837.

In a letter written on the 12 February 1808 from Hamburg Thomas says that his brother, William Kirkpatrick, the America Consul, has told him that the uniform that the Oldenburg authorities sent out to him had arrived, but that it was not regarded with respect in the country where it is necessary to walk with "le Pomp". He asked that his Serene Highness the Duke be approached for permission for William to carry two gold epaulettes.

This letter is difficult to read, but it shows that William was acting as temporary Consul for Oldenburg until his brother's return to Málaga. This was a long-term arrangement, explaining some of the confusion over the brothers and their various consular posts. This also explains why, when William was detained by the Paris Police in 1808, they recorded that he had been appointed Consul at Hamburg by the Grand Duke of Oldenburg. However, Thomas was in Paris in May and August 1808 so there may have been some confusion over the foreign names. From this statement we can assume that William visited Hamburg to see his brother, and obtained official approval of his role as his brother's deputy during his absence. Thus he was appointed in the city of Hanover but the Consularship was that of Málaga. A well informed but anonymous diplomat, in his 1865 biography of Napoleon III, says that William's brother Thomas, "was intimately connected with Hamburg, as he was in business there up to 1815, and many persons still remember him, and the house he occupied — No. 92 Reichenstrasse."[91]

Napoleon's long reach had extended to Hamburg which his forces occupied twice. In 1804, his officers abducted the British Minister Sir George Rumbold from his home in a village outside the city. The second occupation between 1811 and 1814 culminated in a long siege which finished with the surrender of Marshall Davout. This ended his repressive and stern rule which had resulted in the loss of Hamburg's commerce and half the population. These misfortunes may well have prompted Thomas Kirkpatrick's move to Málaga where his brother had re-established his businesses.

There is also a letter signed by John Kirkpatrick Maxwell, written in Hamburg in November 1807, addressed to Krammas Rolf Mentz, the Secretary of State for the principality. This shows a further Kirkpatrick link with Hamburg and is an interesting continuation of the family's custom of including Kirkpatrick in the names of members of other families which they married into. This is surely a symbol of the strength of the Kirkpatrick name when it came to trade and influences. Further connections may come from the William and Elizabeth Ann Kirkpatrick who registered the birth of four children with the British Chaplain in Hamburg between 1820 and 1830.[92]

Thomas is shown in the official Handbook of Hanover as their Consul General in Málaga from 1818 to 1837. It also records that he was Consul General for Oldenburg, the neighboring State from 1818 to 1823. The shipping records for Málaga show that the Consularship of Oldenburg was hardly a busy post, but the addition of the port city of Bremen and sea trade from Hamburg, would keep a German-speaking Consul busy in Málaga. In a testimonial he wrote for his bother William on the 12 February 1818 he signs as Consul and Commercial Agent of His Most

Serene Highness the Duke of [Berwick], Holstein, Oldenburg, Prince Regent of Lubeck, for the city of Málaga and the Kingdom of Granada.

When Thomas moved to Málaga, he lived at no 2 Alameda, in the City's main thoroughfare. This must have been a substantial property as it was valued at over 32,000 Reales and taxed at 563 Reales, a large figure in comparison to other properties recorded in the 1818 tax lists.[93] Antonio Gallegos, the grandfather of Fanny Kirkpatrick, was taxed at the same time, his property being worth rather less.

Clearly consular level contact with government officials and local Spanish society was vital to the family's business interests and they went to great lengths to maintain their diplomatic status. William's concern about "le pomp" reveals laconic Scots humour combined with a desire not to be over looked amid the glitter of civic receptions, sprinkled with flamboyant military uniforms and even finer official court dress.

# 7. A Family Business

When William Kirkpatrick stepped out on the long road to Málaga and fame and fortune, he would have known that all he had was his native wit, his good name and his family, to help him on his way. There would be no inheritance of wealth, land or titles. He came from that section of the Scottish landed classes who required its sons to go forth and seek their destiny as best they could. In England in that period younger sons of even minor country gentry would enter the military services, the church, law, the civil service or any profession rather than trade.

But Scotland was different. Roman Catholics in particular could not obtain Government appointments. North of the border prominent families found it socially acceptable for younger sons to go into business by way of established merchant houses. The Honourable East India Company was the preferred route to fame and fortune. Others entered the West Africa Company or the Hudson's Bay Company.

Numerous Kirkpatricks distinguished themselves in the East India Company and later in the service of the British Empire. The most noteworthy of these were the sons of James Kirkpatrick of Keston near Bromley in Kent. Their story, as told by the historian William Dalrymple in the *White Mughals* [94] is a fascinating tale of the Raj before the Memsahibs came to India and spoiled the fun.

There has been some confusion over the relationship between these Keston Kirkpatricks, and the Closeburn family of Dumfries. It was thought that the James Kirkpatrick who founded this Indian line was a brother of Robert, Abraham and John Kirkpatrick of Dumfries, and thus the son of James who originated in Glenkiln. But it is impossible to reconcile the medical doctor and poet of Charleston and Keston with the James Kirkpatrick of Cullompton in Devon who was a Lawyer and Town Clerk in Devon and Bristol.

This uncertainty has recently been clarified by James Pearson who edits *The Chronicles of Clan Colquhoun*.[95] He has shown that the James Kirkpatrick who was said to have fled the Jacobite rebellion of 1715 and settled in Charleston, South Carolina, was from Ireland and not Glenkiln or Closeburn, although he may have had earlier family roots in Dumfriesshire. In his earlier days he spelt his name Kilpatrick but later changed to Kirkpatrick.

James Kirkpatrick, the father of the Handsome Colonel of Dalrymple's story, was born in Ireland, perhaps in Carrickfergus in the 1690s and attended Edinburgh University between 1708 and 1709 leaving without taking a degree. He returned to Carrickfergus but emigrated to Charleston in South Carolina 1717 to join relations. Here he prospered practising medicine and dispensing drugs. Records in Charleston show that in 1725 he married Elizabeth, the daughter of Thomas Hepworth, the Secretary of the Colony of South Carolina, and had two sons[96]. In 1738 he was instrumental in using early inoculation techniques to treat 437 smallpox patients of whom only sixteen died.

James and his two sons returned to England although there is no record of Elizabeth's fate. He built a fine house named Hollydale on Keston Common near Bromley, Kent which became the family seat for some generations. His son James Kirkpatrick, and in turn his sons, James Achilles and George plus an earlier son, William born in Ireland of a Mrs Butler, all served in India. William Kirkpatrick became a General in the HEIC Army in the 1780s and 1790s; James Kirkpatrick was Acting Resident at Hydrabad, while George was a civil administrator and Collector for the Company.

James's daughter, Kitty Sahib Begum or Katherine Aurora, whose mother was the Indian princess Khir un-Nissa, greatly attracted the historian, Thomas Carlyle. In 1829 Katherine married Captain James Winslowe Philipps of the 7th Hussars and produced seven children.

There appears to have been no connection or association between the two Kirkpatrick families although service in India was a common thread in the lives of their descendants as was a tradition of a Scottish link.

Francis Kirkpatrick Aiskill, the son of Francis Aiskill, British Consul in Málaga, used the promise of his very large inheritance from Robert Kirkpatrick to buy a cadetship with the Company's Army. This legacy was to result in a legal battle with John Kirkpatrick Escott, the residual legatee, and James Kirkpatrick of Bristol.[97]

The Aiskill case, some twenty years later, shows how entry to the HEIC Service required money and social connections which were not available to William Kirkpatrick in 1780. He had to use family links to obtain a post within the long established trading partnership of Robert Kirkpatrick, John Kirkpatrick Escott, James Reed and Jeremiah Parkinson.

We can imagine the raw young Scotsman climbing down from the roof of the Scottish Post stagecoach, after the 36-hour journey from

Dumfries,[98] and making his way to number 5, Lime Street Square, in the heart of the City of London. There he would meet his older cousin John Kirkpatrick Escott,[99] the son of Robert's sister Elizabeth Kirkpatrick. Jeremiah Parkinson would also have been in the office at 5, Lime Street Square and other family members would have called in on business. William would have visited Woodford in Essex to see his aging cousin, the head of the house, Robert Kirkpatrick y Capper of Málaga. Robert died on 14 April 1781. Although William does not feature in the old man's Will, he had given William a gold ring which William left to his nephew Thomas Kirkpatrick. This was surely a signet ring, with a seal or crest, and a symbol of the transfer of the Spanish interests to William.

A note on a personal record card in the US National Archives clearly links William Kirkpatrick to the London trading house of Robert Kirkpatrick and Messrs James Reed and J. Parkinson. Their "Patron" was John Kirkpatrick Escott, the principal heir of Robert Kirkpatrick of London. These gentlemen are listed as the Principals of the Málaga House referred to in George Cabot's letter to the President. [100] John Escott was in correspondence from Málaga with the 2nd Baron Grantham in 1775 showing that the family were residents of Andalusia up to this point.[101]

Robert was born in 1717 and died in Woodford, Essex on 14 April 1781. Blackwood's describes him as "a very confidential agent in the Spanish trade".[102] Burke's Peerage says he was a merchant in Spain. His Will, details numerous substantial legacies to his extended family, his friends and his servants amounting to some £15,000; a very large sum for those days. Jeremiah Parkinson received £500. He left the remainder of his fortune to his "dear sister" Anne Kirkpatrick and to his nephew John Kirkpatrick Escott who, with James Kirkpatrick of Bristol, he also appointed as his executors. Witnesses were James Reed and also a Sarah Reed and an Ann. This must be the J. Reed mentioned in the note attached to George Cabot's letter,[103] and the James Reed who was a director of the Bank of England.

James Reed and Robert Kirkpatrick Escott fell out in 1809, and appear as plaintiff and defendant respectively, in a case heard in the Chancery Court in London.[104]

London trade directories show that Kirkpatrick, Escott & Reed, Merchants, were trading at 5, Lime Street Square from 1765 through to 1785. The business had continued after Robert's death in 1781. There are no entries for Kirkpatrick in the 1800 Post Office directory. John

Parkinson is shown in partnership with Reed in 1791 and on his own account in 1792; all were trading at 5, Lime House Square.

Robert Kirkpatrick's Will gives us a clear view of the scope of his business and its family connections. There were Kirkpatricks or relations in Ostende, Hamburg, Brussels, Bristol, London, Málaga, Adra, Tobago, and in Richmond, Virginia, and Charleston S.C., and Wilmington, N.C. As late as 1864 a Thomas Kirkpatrick was US Consul in Nassau, New Providence Bahamas, and Edward Kirkpatrick, a descendant of the Ostende family, was British Consul in Honduras a few years later.

Both Robert and John Kirkpatrick Escott had lived in Málaga for some thirty years but returned to England on the outbreak of the hostilities with Spain in June 1779 related to the War of American Independence. They left their Spanish business in the hands of Henri de Grivegnée who acted as their agent. We don't know how long the young William was in London but reports suggest that he soon made his way over to his brother John in Ostende, where he remained for some years. This would have been a period of instruction and familiarisation, and a time to improve his French. It would also have been his first exposure to a largely Roman Catholic environment. We cannot tell whether this challenged his Scottish Protestant beliefs, but at some point between his time in Ostende and his marriage in Málaga, he converted to the Roman Catholic faith.

Some Protestants were accepted in Málaga society and flourished in the export trade as is shown by the local bequests of John Kirkpatrick Escott, an "Englishman" and a Protestant. In a hand written addition to his Spanish Will of 1766, he left legacies of 200 pesos to the Capuchins, and 600 pesos to the Arch Priest of the Sagrario Chapel of Málaga Cathedral, to be distributed among poor families. He also left 500 peso to the Notary Public as a token of his friendship and affection.[105] If this is the same man who died in Ongar Hill in Essex in 1799 he would have been 38 at the time he made this Will. Perhaps he went down with one of the frequent fevers which plagued the area and feared for his life. There is no indication that the good people of Málaga benefited from his English Will. His son, James Kirkpatrick Escott, was later head of their London trading house, but became involved in a legal dispute with his partners.

The Catastro [Census] de Marquées de la Ensenda in the Municipal Archives in Málaga shows that a Robert Kirkpatrick and a Juan Kirkpatrick and a Juan Escott were among the foreign merchants resident in the city in 1754. William Escott's son, John Kirkpatrick Escott added the surname of his mother Elizabeth Kirkpatrick, in the Spanish style, and kept the usage when he returned to London to show his link to the Merchant House of Kirkpatrick.

But two John Kirkpatrick Escotts died in England in the 1790s. Both left Wills and one left a memorial. These men of the same name and generation were connected to each other and to the other Kirkpatricks in the Málaga trade and London Merchant partnership. Evidence from their Wills suggests that they were cousins, both with Escott fathers and Kirkpatrick mothers.

The Will of John Kirkpatrick Escott, Gentleman, of Bristol is dated 1798 (the 8 is unclear). He is clearly part of the extended family and perhaps of the trading partnership in London. He is linked to the John Kirkpatrick Escott of Ongar Hill whom he called his "friend" and to whom he left £100. The rest and residue of his estate went to his devoted mother Mary Escott and to his Aunt Sarah. Also he left £10 to his "friend" Abraham Kirkpatrick Wilson of London. This linking of Kirkpatrick and Wilson implies that the mother of Abraham Kirkpatrick was a Wilson but seems to be an error. The wife of James Kirkpatrick of Cullompton was Elizabeth Capper.

> "Over the foregoing is an elegant memorial of white marble, on a
> dove coloured ground, surmounted by a sarcophagus and urn, for
> John Kirkpatrick Escott, esq., of Ongar-Hill in this parish, who
> died on the 16th February, 1799, (aged) seventy one. It records,
> also, the interment of *Mary Jane*, his youngest daughter, who died
> at the age of twenty-one, on the 12th of July, 1817; and of *Deborah*,
> his widow, who died April the 22nd, 1818, aged sixty-one.[106]

The Will of John Kirkpatrick Escott of Ongar Hill is much longer and more difficult to read, but shows that he too was connected with the London partnership as he leaves £25 to Mary Parkinson. He also leaves the much larger sum of £500 to his cousin Francis Aiskill. Perhaps he hoped that the young East India Company cadet would marry one of his daughters. It also implies that he was close to the Francis Aiskill who was British Consul in Málaga in the 1730s. The residue of his estate went to his son Robert and his daughters Elizabeth and Mary Jane Escott.

Other British and Irish merchants were long-term Spanish residents, including Thomas Quilty, whose daughter married into the Cabarrús y Kirkpatrick family, and the Lovelaces, and the Lorings. Guillermo

Reille and Gabriel O'Reilly y Falon are also listed in the Catastro with some three hundred other foreign merchants and artisans in Málaga at that time. [107]

Establishing Robert Kirkpatrick y Capper's connection to Málaga is important, as it shows that he is the same Robert Kirkpatrick who was later the prosperous merchant in the City of London and was the guarantor and supporter of William Kirkpatrick's application for the US Consulate. This Robert seems to have been the quiet force behind the success and prosperity of the family.

Clearly William was trained in the ways of their trade and then moved to Málaga to represent the partnership founded by Robert and continued by his second cousin John Kirkpatrick Escott. In the days when Bills of Exchange were the only means of commercial payment, traders or négociants relied on their good name to have their Bills accepted at reasonable interest or discount rates. Family connections and recommendations were essential.

In 1782, William joined his older brother John in his trading concern in Ostende. From the Atlantic coast William went to Barcelona for almost three years to learn the trade from his brother's associates, Nicolas Reserson and William de Vic Tupper who had settled in Barcelona. He then moved on to Málaga in 1788.[108]

There were at least four other Kirkpatrick y Wilsons in the Málaga area some fifty years later in the 1800s. William's sister Harriet Kirkpatrick y Wilson, who lived for a while in Honfleur, probably with her brother John, died in Málaga; another sister, Janet Kirkpatrick y Wilson, died in Spain in 1817.

William's younger brother Thomas was apt to stand on his dignity as the Hanoverian Consul in Málaga and to write peremptory letters to the British Embassy in Madrid. His attitude is shown by a letter in the National Archives in London dated 22 June 1822, when William Laird was the British Consul. It reveals the complexities of Hanoverian rule in England at that period. Thomas was receiving letters from the Customs House in Málaga as Consul del Hanover, and was requesting help from General Meade, His Majesty's Consul General at the British Embassy in Madrid. Thomas was representing the commercial interests of the "House of Kirkpatrick" and the shipping interests of all his Hanoverian Majesties' subjects. His letter explains the situation.

Dear Sir                                    Málaga 22 August 1822.

By the post on Thursday I have received the letter you did me
the favour to write under date 1st of this month and in answer
to the doubts you express as to being authorised to interfere in
[unreadable] these regarding His Majestys Hanoverian subjects
I beg leave to inform you that by my instructions I am directed
to apply to the British ambassador in cases where there is no
Minister appointed expressly for the Kingdom of Hanover
which is the case at present in the court at Madrid. I am
therefore obliged to importune you again with the case of Capt.
Jacob Lietjen[?] of the Hanoverian Galid *Elizabeth* which vessel
is at present detained  here by order of the Administrator of
the Customs House. Further motive explained in the enclosed
Memorial.

I entreat your kind exertions may be immediately used in
favour of this.                                    Signed

Thomas Kirkpatrick

To Lionel Hervey Esq., H. B. Majesty's Minister Plenipotentiary,
Madrid.[109]

By 1863 the Hanoverian and the Oldenburg Consuls were still listed
separately in the City's register of consuls and vice-consuls.[110]

William's nephew, John Kirkpatrick y Stoddard, was Honorary
British Vice-Consul at Adra from about 1834[111] and continued with this
post to at least 1857.[112] This John was involved in managing William
Kirkpatrick's estate. His Consular post was unsalaried although he
would have earned fees dealing with shipping documentation. William's
other nephew, Alexander Thomas Kirkpatrick y Stoddard, is shown in
1856/57 as Honorary British Consul at Garrucha, the port for Vera, east
along the coast from Adra.[113] The Kirkpatrick's long association with
Spain continues to this day in the form of a firm of lawyers named Trías,
Kirkpatrick y de Grivegnée in Marbella. Members of the Kirkpatrick
family still play a major role in the government of Spain.

William Kirkpatrick's defining role in Málaga was that of United
States Consul in Málaga. It established his place in the city and
determined his friends and trade connections. The official documents
recording his appointment reveal a wide set of commercial relationships
and throws light on a system of personal business now overtaken by
global corporations.

He was Consul for the newly independent and fiercely Republican
United States of America. As far as we know, he was never a naturalised

American citizen and thus as a Scotsman he remained a native-born Briton. His U.S. Consular record shows a blank under "Allegiance". The United States were at best neutral during the Napoleonic Wars, and revolutionary sentiment favoured the French cause, although some old "Tories" preferred the British to the French. Some American consuls and diplomats favoured Napoleon and there are reports that Kirkpatrick was among their number.

In 1791, George Cabot, the great American legislator, wrote:

To: President George Washington

Beverley, January 1791

"Sir, - Mr William Kirkpatrick, a member of the house of Messieurs Grivegnée & Co. of Málaga, wishes to have the honour of serving the United States in the character of consul for that port. Should it be thought expedient to institute such an office, it may be found that Mr Kirkpatrick's situation, as well as talents and disposition, peculiarly enable him to fill it with propriety. Permit me, therefore, sir, to request that, when the qualifications of candidates are under your examination, his also may be considered.

"If any apology is necessary for this freedom, I hope it may not be deemed insufficient that, having been led by my profession to make frequent visits to Spain, among other intimacies I formed one with the principals of the commercial establishment to which Mr. Kirkpatrick belongs: that these have desired my testimony on this occasion, and that my experience of their integrity and their friendship to the people of this country constrains me to think well of a gentleman they recommend, and to confide in one for whose faithfulness they are willing to be responsible.

I am, with most profound respect, sir, your most faithful and obedient servant, George Cabot, Senator for Massachusetts."[114]

It took some nine years for Cabot's recommendation to come into formal effect. It was not until 1 January 1800 that his appointment as replacement for Michael Murphy was laid before the Senate and approved by President John Adams. Cabot had a lively early life as a ship's master and international merchant before becoming a legislator. During the War of Independence he guarded his capital by using banks in Bilbao. He would have encountered Robert and Juan Kirkpatrick during this period, and may have owed them a favour or two for protecting his ships and cargoes from forfeiture by the British Navy.

Note in the National Archives in Washington DC:
William Kirkpatrick 1814.

William Kirkpatrick was born at Dumfries in Scotland in 1764 – has had a liberal education and in 1782 went in a mercantile capacity to Ostende where he remained 3 years from there to Barcelona where he resided nearly three more and then to Málaga where he remains – his patrons in London are Messrs James Reed and J. Parkinson and their Patron is my old friend John Kirkpatrick Escott who with his deceased Uncle old Rob. Kirkpatrick of London and another principal London house are the Principals of the Málaga House referred to in my letter to the President.[115]

This was an active post and William Kirkpatrick, described as consul for the United States for Málaga in the Kingdom of Granada, asked Madrid for Royal approval for the appointment of vice-consuls in Marbella and Estepona and Almíera in 1801, and in Vélez-Málaga in 1807.[116]

William must have first applied for the Consulate some time before George Cabot's letter of January 1791, but instead Michael Murphy was appointed on 2 March 1793. There appears to have been real competition for these posts and William tried for the vacancy and lost to his rival.[117] US Consular establishment records show that he was US Consul from 8 January 1800 to 11 December 1817, when he was superseded by George G. Barrill of Massachusetts who took charge in June 1818 and served through to the end of 1837.[118] On 4 September 1817, Oliver H. Perry wrote to James Madison recommending that William Kirkpatrick be continued as Consul at Málaga.[119] He survived for a few months but was obliged to give up the post in June 1817.

Relations between the British and American Consuls continued on a friendly footing and William Laird's Consular accounts were checked and signed off by William Kirkpatrick's replacement, George G. Barrill. This is an early example of Anglo American co-operation, despite the difficulties of the 1812 war and the long term British blockade of European ports and tensions over the United States' own Embargo Act of 1807 which had led to the Anglo American hostilities.

# 8. Consular Life

The day-to-day affairs of a Consul in a busy port are aptly if imaginatively summed up by the Hon. Mrs Caroline Norton in a petition she wrote to Queen Victoria in 1855 seeking her support for more liberal divorce legislation.

> "When Mr Kirkpatrick, a Scotch gentleman, was doing duty as Consul at Málaga: worried with the petty details of his consulate position; clash of mercantile interest, the perplexities of international law, the claims of mariners, the jealousies of residents, the broiling heat of the southern climate, and the disputes about nothing, which are always, in all consulates, arising about twice every month, and are always said in the most immanent degree to threaten ... the flag."[120]

Although Mrs Norton seemed to believe that Mr Kirkpatrick was the British representative, she had a very clear vision of the life of a Consul as is confirmed by the letters to Mr Kirkpatrick by the actual British Consul in Málaga transcribed in Appendix Two. These bring a sense of reality to Mrs Norton's vivid picture of the daily world of a port consul of the period.

On taking post, William purchased the Arms of the United States and the Consul's seal from the widow of his predecessor Michael Murphy, who had died in post. These were important symbols of his post, but he was unsure as to whether the United States government would re-repay this expense. He also procured a portrait of George Washington which survived the events of the following years, to grace his house in Adra until his final days.

During a large portion of his time in Málaga, William had to find ways of circumventing the British blockade of Spanish ports and clamp down on Spanish trade with her rich colonies in the Americas and also the French embargos. Spain was at war with Britain from the end of 1796 until the peace which followed the Treaty of Amiens of March 1802. These hostilities, mainly conducted at sea, must have put him in a difficult position, and may have prompted his application for the consular post. His situation was complicated. William was a British subject and as such his trading activities were constrained by the regulations laid down by the British government restricting commerce with enemy states. During most of this period he enjoyed the privileges of being a US Consul, but this had to be conducted as a separate function from his business affairs. This gave him influence and shipping business, and social contacts, but it would not have given his personal trade any form of official immunity.

Another source of difficulty for Kirkpatrick was the British Royal Navy's insistence in "pressing" or forcibly conscripting to its ships, any "English" sailors it could lay hands on, including the crews of American registered merchant vessels. As the Navy's interpretation of the term English in this context was very wide, this was a continual source of friction between the two English-speaking nations, and was to be a prime cause of the war between them in 1812.

A letter from Frederic H. Walloston, the U.S. consul in Genoa, of 8 December 1800, is an early example of the effect of the British blockade of continental ports. Walloston relays the news that the Port of Leghorn in northern Italy had been issued with an official "Information from a British Naval Officer" stating that the Port was Blockaded and that all neutral ships had to quit the place within eight days or they would not be allowed to sail or depart. Two American ships and two Danish ships had already been turned away by an English Ship of War. Genoa port still remained open at that point.

The trade routes over which William Kirkpatrick watched as Consul for two countries and used for his business affairs were also threatened by Corsairs or raiders from the Barbary Coast States on the southern shores of the Mediterranean. Although these were nominally still under Turkish sovereignty, they were manoeuvring for greater autonomy. Much of his Consular business dealt with attacks on shipping from this source and he was continuously urging James Monroe, the United States Secretary of State, to dispatch a Naval Squadron to the Mediterranean to defend American vessels. On the 22 April 1801, writing to The Secretary of State, James Madison (although he may not have known of his appointment at the time of writing) Kirkpatrick warns of reports from the Consul in Tripoli, that the "Bashaws were acting in a hostile manner against the United States" As there were many American vessels then in the Mediterranean he feared for their safety.

"I sincerely hope a few frigates are now on there way for these Seas, a Small force would be sufficient to block the Tripoli Cruisers in their Ports, and oblige them to admit of conciliatory measure, indeed there should always be some on this Station, for the Protection of our Navigation which, up the Mediterranean, is very extensive, and must till then be constantly exposed to the Caprice of all the Barbary powers: - I never expected they would have remained so long on a good footing with the U.S. for scarcely a Year passes without some one or other of them making depredations on the Commerce of Denmark and Sweden."

He was "particularly attentive" to ensuring that copies of a further warning from Richard O'Brien Esq., the consul at Algiers, were circulated around the ports of Europe including France, London and Hamburg "in order that American Captains may be on their guard and abstain from going up the Mediterranean till matters are arranged, as the Tripolitans have I understand only five or six Cruizers of no considerable force, they seldom come this side of Alicante, & I believe have never doubled Cape de Gat."[121] Other letters show that he was used as a transit point for letters from the U.S. Consul in Algiers and the other north African port as he was able to send dispatches overland to Gibraltar by "Express". There they were more likely to find a carrier for Europe or to take them to the Secretary of State in Washington and distribute them to other Consuls around the Atlantic freeboard.

Tunisian Corsair boarding the *Mercury* of Boston

On the 21 May 1801 the Secretary of State circulated all the U. S. Mediterranean Consuls notifying them that a U.S. Navy squadron of three frigates and a sloop of war, under the command of Commodore Dale, was preparing to sail for Europe. The squadron would cruise the Mediterranean and venture as far as the Levant and Constantinople if time permitted before returning home. They would thus show the flag and be in position if war should really break out with the Barbary

Powers. They would also block the Tripoli cruisers in their ports and force them to conciliatory measures. The Secretary comments that there should always be some ships on this station for the protection of our Navigation. He also notes scarcely a year passes without attacks on the commerce of Denmark and Sweden. (This is in spite of the huge subventions these countries paid and the agreements then made for the protection of their shipping).

> "The United States being also happily at peace with all the
> Powers of Europe, the moment is the more favourable in every
> view that can be taken of it."[122]

The Americans, who were keen to increase their Mediterranean trade, and the French, British, Spanish and other European powers tried negotiation and bribery. The rulers of Algiers, Tunis and Tripoli aimed to develop their autonomy from the Ottoman in Istanbul, by exerting their power over European and American shipping and exhorting protection money from Western merchants and governments. There were considerable sums involved. In 1801, when the total United States Government budget totalled about $10 million, Tripoli alone demanded quarter of a million dollars. Algiers and Tunis also exhorted similarly large sums constituting a considerable proportion of the governments' budget. The Corsairs ranged up into the Gulf of Lyon and commercial shipping was sometimes confined to ports as far north as Barcelona waiting for months for the protection of escorted convoys.

On the 28 May 1801 Kirkpatrick was again writing to the Secretary of State reporting that 26 American vessels were detained at Barcelona for fear of Tripolitan Cruizers and hoping that some Frigates may already be on their way to "prevent depredations and at the same time to force the Bashaw to come to an amicable accommodation". At the same time the American Secretary of the Navy was urging his captains with all his powers, to get on board their vessels and set sail for the Mediterranean with all haste.

Kirkpatrick then explains lengthy dealings with some American sailors who were involved in a mutiny on board an English ketch. He had to regret that he was unable to alleviate the rigorous Quarantine which had been imposed on American vessels and its effect on trade. He also reported a successful outcome to a dispute with the local Collector of Customs. Citing the helpful intervention of the American Minister in Madrid, with whom he was in close contact on this and other matters, he had been able to get some $65,000 of back duty refunded to local trading houses which had been wrongly charged in arrears on imports of Spanish colonial Produce by American vessels.[123]

Commodore Dale, United States Navy.

By the beginning of August 1801 he had the "Satisfaction" of hearing about the dispatch of Commodore Dale and three frigates, the *President*, *Essex* and *Philadelphia* to the Mediterranean, which he considered a "very Judicious, and well concerted Plan" and hoping that "some force would be retained in the area as little dependence can be placed on any of the (Turkish) Regencies remaining on Good Terms with any Nation" He was also very careful to note that he would properly explain the object of the force and the "desire which (the U.S.) Government persists in, of living in Peace & Friendship with all nations." [124] This is an early example of a public relations exercise being used to win "hearts and minds."

On Tuesday 25 August 1801 Kirkpatrick had the further satisfaction of going on board one of the U.S. warships for which he had been campaigning. Captain Bainbridge had entered Málaga Harbour, which he describes thus:

> "At 1/2 past 8 came to in 25 fathom water, the large church bearing N N W. & the signal tower N E by N, distance about 3 miles from the Mole. The bay of Málaga is a pretty good one, on account of its gradual shoaling and good ground. It is exposed to the Sea Winds from S W to East, but I presume a vessel well found in ground tackle would ride any gale out, the mole is large, 7 fathom water at the entrance, & shoals on to 3 fathom sufficiency of water for any Frigate."[125]

At this point Lt. Stephen Decatur was sent ashore where he must have met William Kirkpatrick as he obtained "pratick" or port clearance, for which he needed the Consul's help. Stephen Decatur became the hero of the Barbary Wars when he went into Tripoli harbour at night to burn the *USS Philadelphia* which had been captured after running aground in 1803. In the war of 1812, commanding the *USS United States*, he was further celebrated when he captured the British frigate *HMS Macedonian* after a classic duel off the Azores. Later when Decatur was at the embassy in Madrid he is said to have met the Empress Eugénie and told her stories of his earlier adventures, and of his visits to Málaga.

But the Tripoli Cruisers also had difficulties and John Galvin, the US Consul at Gibraltar, wrote to William Kirkpatrick in August 1801 reporting that two Corsairs had to haul into the new mole and lay up for want of adequate crews following desertions. Four hundred of the crew had fled to the Barbary shores following a mutiny and the Corsair Admiral had offered to sell his remaining vessels, but they were unsaleable.[126] Kirkpatrick also reported this incident and added that the two ships were blocked in Gibraltar by the Frigate *USS Philadelphia* and that the Sultan of Morocco was providing some supplies to the starving crew. By this time the *USS Essex* had escorted 23 merchant ships from the coast of Catalonia and intended taking them in convoy to the "Gut" or narrow straights between Gibraltar and Morocco and thus see them safely on their way to America and Northern Europe. Clearly the Squadron was having the effect Kirkpatrick had hoped for and trade routes had become relatively safe again. But the supply position was difficult and by September 1801 he had to tell Captain William Bainbridge that while he could obtain bread and fresh meat, there were no salted provisions to be purchased in Málaga.

U. S. SCHOONER ENTERPRIZE CAPTURING THE TRIPOLITAN CORSAIR TRIPOLI, 1 AUGUST 1801.

US Schooner *Enterprise* captures the Tripolitan Corsair *Tripoli*, 1 Aug, 1801

In October, the U.S. Minister in Madrid advised William that a Tripoli cruiser had left the port of Mahon, in the Balearic Islands, with a Minorcan crew under English colours. He added that two more Corsairs were preparing to sail under English documents and that all three ships were planning to avoid in this way, the searches of the American Warships, however "illegal, extraordinary or almost incredible such conduct (by the Corsairs) might be".[127] Captain Richard Dale of the *USS President* quickly investigated this report.

William Kirkpatrick also had his informants and was able to tell Captain Dale that he had a statement that the three vessels had been bought by the Mahon agent of the Bey of Tripoli and that they were to be delivered to Tripoli by the person who sold them. One of the ships mounted 36 guns, a cruiser taken from the British by the Spanish. Captain Dale was more afraid of the Dey getting "a number of renegades of various nations into his Service" than he was of the vessels.

William comments that these foreign crews would enable Tripoli to keep the cruisers at sea during winter when it is impossible to keep a convoy of merchant ships together. He also warns that a stronger force was needed if the Dey of Algiers, the Bey of Tunis and the Emperor of Morocco intend to take common cause against the United States. He reports that he has been told that Tunis is willing to do so, and he hopes to find out more on his visit to Algiers.[128] This is the only mention of William Kirkpatrick visiting Algiers so it may not have happened.

However, when Captain Dale of the *USS Essex* visited Mahon in December 1801, he found that the reports of the three Tripoli cruisers seemed to be groundless. The three ships were Xebecs or lateen rigged vessels and the governor assured the Captain that he would not let them leave port without sureties that they were not for the Bey of Tripoli nor bound for Tripoli. However, the local Mahon Pilot had guided the *USS Essex* onto to a rock, badly damaging her keel and putting the vessel out of action for some time. Perhaps Mahon was playing to different rules.

The Corsair threat was ever present although outright warfare was limited to the periods when the United States dispatched strong naval units during the First Barbary War between May 1801 and June 1805 and the Second Barbary War in 1815. The Ottoman Regencies of Tunis, Tripoli and the Dey of Algiers had significant fleets which continued to prey on shipping until the French colonised Algeria in 1830. William Kirkpatrick was in post for both these conflicts during which the U.S. Navy developed its new role in force projection. He had personal dealings with Commodore Bainbridge, the commander of the group of powerful new style American frigates sent to deal with the demands of the Pashas and to make whatever agreements were possible to safeguard American merchant shipping and thus the vital export trade of the new nation. (See Appendix Ten for a vivid account of Commodore Bainbridge's exploits.)

The United States Consul was also deeply involved in matters arising from the ebb and flow of war between Spain and England and the conflicts with Revolutionary and Napoleonic France. Further hostilities between France and Britain followed in 1803 and Spain again declared war on Britain in December 1804. This time the war was prolonged and multi-sided with numerous land actions, and peace was not really restored until the French were driven out of Spain by the combined efforts of the Spanish and the Duke of Wellington and their Portuguese allies in June 1813.

During the Anglo-American war, which lasted from 18 June 1812 until 23 March 1815, William Kirkpatrick, a British subject, was the Consul of an enemy power resident in Spain, parts of which were allied to Britain in its War of Independence against Napoleon. Quite how he reconciled these conflicting loyalties is unclear today. If he needed clarification for the safety of his cargoes, the British Admiralty Courts of the time would have known only too well. They were past masters at resolving exactly that sort of complex issue and would have adjudicated with precision and clarity. Enrique Kirkpatrick Mendaro supposes that it was William's American post that gave him some protection against the Spanish "Patriots" when the French forces departed in 1812, and that his bother Thomas took the post of Hanoverian Consul for the same reason. This is confirmed by letters William wrote to the Málaga authorities complaining bitterly of the terms of his detention when he was held in military Barracks during this troubled time.

Consular letters in the U.S. National Archives at College Park, Maryland, include a significant number of dispatches from William Kirkpatrick to the Secretaries of State of the period including James Monroe, later the Fifth President of the United States. Monroe was United States Minister to France between 1794 and 1796 when he expressed strong sympathies for the French cause. His attitude may have influenced Kirkpatrick's initial reaction to the French occupation of Málaga.

William's correspondence covers the usual Consular work with ships and their captains, crews and cargoes. He also sent regular returns of United States shipping arrivals and departures at Málaga with details of cargoes, customs duties and export totals. These were very similar to the returns found in the British National Archives relating to William Laird's tenure as British Consul in Málaga a few years later. As early as 25 August 1800 he was active certifying shipping letters. The letters he wrote in French which were copied to Washington appear clear and fluent suggesting he had good French, or perhaps he had a clerk who wrote them for him, or his wife Fanny helped him.

> Sir, Having purchased, as an American Citizen, the Brig *Active* now lying in this port, [Málaga] I take the Liberty of requesting you to appoint two captains of vessels to go on board to take

an exact measurement of her burden. At the same time Sir, be pleased to furnish me with all the necessary papers for the Brig, the bill of Sale of which, in the Spanish Language, I send you herein for your Inspection and Legalisation.

The Capt. & Mate as well as the sailors are already on board being all Americans & I shall go myself to Philadelphia in my said brig.

With the greatest respect & Consideration, I remain

Sir,   your very Obt. & Hble Servt.  Signed Joseph Bavara

A True copy signed Willm. Kirkpatrick.

Captain Bainbridge Pays Tribute to the Dey

A letter dated 5th January confirms that the *Active* left Málaga that September with such ships papers as William judged she needed to navigate to Philadelphia. Clearly this second letter, with a validated true copy of the first letter of August, was intended to find its way to the right authorities in Philadelphia in case *Active's* Málaga papers raised any suspicion. Ships had to be fully documented and any discrepancies raised serious doubts and could lead to delays or fines, or an excuse for a lively privateer or warship to seize the vessel as a prize, and thus make it a total loss to the owners. The *Active* would have made a valuable prize as it had on board a cargo of wine and fruit.

American seaman had to be dealt with as well. They sometimes arrived in port as released prisoners or runaways from British warships, who made a point of pressing American seamen, and forcing them to serve with the Royal Navy, which was desperately undermanned during the Napoleonic wars. As many as a dozen or more men would arrive with only the clothes on their backs, penniless, without shoes or stockings, facing a Spanish winter before finding a berth on a ship home. The Consul was expected to ensure that they were given a small amount of cash to see them through. This could then be claimed this back from Washington as expenses. The Málaga Consul's total disbursements from the Public Fund for 1801 were $1,125.60.

Most of his letters report details of the current official quarantine regulations and, in some cases, the daily list of the number of deaths from Yellow Fever and other contagious diseases. This was vital information for seafarers as quarantine could delay ships in port for many months. He also accounts for his Disbursements for the Public Service and notes bills for his expenses which he has drawn on Messrs Head and Amory, shipping merchant of Boston, who had regular business in Málaga.[129]

William Kirkpatrick's dispatches also contain political and military news. He reported Spanish decrees, the actions of the local Governor, and the movements and success and defeat of Napoleon's forces and the return of King Ferdinand VII.

By 1808 the threat from the North African states was somewhat reduced by American diplomatic negotiations and large payments.

EXTRACT OF LETTER FROM WILLIAM KIRKPATRICK, CONSUL OF THE UNITED STATES AT MÁLAGA, TO SECRETARY OF STATE, JANUARY 5TH 1808.

"By my last letter of the 15th December I enclosed copies of information I had received from Barcelona and Marseilles, regarding the hostilities commenced on our commerce by the cruisers of the Dey of Algiers, and I am now happy in having it my power to transmit a copy of a letter I have just received from colonel Lear, under date 16th and 17th December, (1807) with the pleasing information that he has succeed in adjusting matters with the Dey, and that the vessels captured had been set at liberty, which I hasten to communicate to you by a vessel on her departure for Salem."

On the 18th April 1809 he was in Málaga and wrote to the Secretary of State:

"No opportunity having offered from here to your continent since the date of my last 12 January by the *Leonides*, I have been prevented from writing to you and to transmit the return of Arrivals at this port from the 1st July last 'till the end of the month. You will now find it enclosed as also a sett of our daily publications, from which you may collect some information on what is passing in this part of the country. We are informed from Catalonia that the French have completely invaded all the Country on this side of Tarragona, and it is said the Marquis de la Romana has joined the Asturian Army and that they muster strong. We have no late Accounts from Portugal of an Official nature. The control Board remains steady at Seville.

I am, very respectfully,

Sir, Your most Obedient and Humble Servant,

Willm. Kirkpatrick."

These letters show William as a worldly man of business, knowledgeable about events around him, politically aware and in contact with local Spanish officials and affairs of Court. During some of the period he was Consul he had vice-consuls to help him with the more mundane tasks connected to ship inspections and cargo handling and Customs and Quarantine matters. He has a precise style which hints that he was writing quickly to catch a departing vessel or messenger.

Having previously complained of false ships papers he had again suspected forgeries.

EXTRACT OF A LETTER FROM MR KIRKPATRICK, CONSUL OF THE UNITED STATES AT MÁLAGA, TO MR SMITH, SECRETARY OF STATE, [WASHINGTON] DATED NOVEMBER 25, 1809.

"A few days ago the brig *Usforsight*, Christian Boden, master, arrived here from Poole, with a cargo of bale goods and fish. Although her papers appear to be in perfect order, some doubts exist in my mind of their legality. I have consulted with some citizens of the United States actually here, and they agree with me in opinion, that the signatures of the President, yours, collector of New York and of Joseph Nourse, are so well done. That it is impossible to discover any difference. Under this impress, I have determined to pass you a note of the ship's papers, that if they are false, you may consider proper for having them seized on by the consuls of Europe, where the vessel may be found. [130]

Note – The ship's papers alluded to, are found to have been forged."

A significant letter giving some explanation of his situation and relations with the French was sent to the Secretary of State.

Málaga on 24 October 1812.

"Sir,

My last letter to your Department a year [was] 23 May. I have since not had the honour of receiving any communication from you. The beginning of June last I was arrested by order of the French General Maranzin at the instigation of the French Consul to whom my House of Trade was owing a sum of Money, and went up to the Castle of Gibralfaro I exclaimed at such a violent processing which at the same time deprived me of my Liberty and Property as you will observe from the enclosed Letter to General Maranzin 1. of his answer No. 2. of mine No 3. and also of - -[ Ours] no 4. I addressed to his Excellency the Marshall Duke of Dalmacia, Commander in Chief of the French Armies in the Andalusias, then in Seville. His Excellency after its receipt ordered me to be set at Liberty, and I am happy in having it in my power to inform you that on the [illegible] August the French Consul was paid off the amount of his claim on my House with the very funds I had tendered him in payment previous to his making application for my Arrest as you will see by the copy of the letter written by him to the President of our Chamber of Commerce. No.5."

This letter to the President of the Chamber of Commerce is signed by Proharam, Le Consul de France, and dated Málaga 25 August 1812. It refers to a sum of Rbs 1,614,557 from the Maison Grivegnée & Co. but does not mention Kirkpatrick.

The letter continues:

"On the same day, 27 August, all the French Troops evacuated this place in the greatest order, this prevented me making application for obtaining the Satisfaction I aspired after they retired by Antoguara to Granada from whence they proceeded on the 17 September toward the kingdom of Murcia, since that day we have had not certain Information of the Marshall's Movements.

On the 28 August some Spanish troops came in here and took possession of the City. Two days afterwards Colonel Alburguerque arrived as Governor. He has since been superseded by Brigadier Traille who remains with the Chief Command.

General Ballasteros entered Granada after the departure of the French Army, was there and in the Environs since remains with his Army.

None of our vessels have arrived or been brought into port since the date of my last, tho' on the 4 September Lionhariat Keaney

[?] of Georgetown & James Barnes of New haven are distressed Seamen, who had embarked on a Spanish Gun Boat at Hyencia for Cadiz, arrived here and having made Application to me for Assistance I furnished them with $10 as a Payment with which to proceed to Cadiz by Land (with) as expectation of meeting up with an Opportunity of returning home. This part of the Country Continues to enjoy the best Health no symptoms of the Yellow fever or any other Contagious disease have appeared tho they labor under it evil affect at Cartagena. And in some ports of the Kingdom of Murcia.

I am, with high Esteem, Sir. Your Obt. Servant
Willm. Kirkpatrick"

William then turns his attention to important political news and comments on the possible return to constitutional rule..

"James Monroe Esq.
Secretary of State of the U.S.       Málaga 14 May 1814
A conveyance offering from hence to Halifax I profit of it to inclose copy of my last dispatch to your Department of the 4 Oct last.

The sickness which had broke out in Cadiz, and Gibraltar terminated with the year, since then every place in this part of the Kingdom has been perfectly healthy, a rigorous quarantine has been laid on all vessels from the Eastward in consequence of the plague prevailing at Smyrna –

You may probably ere now be informed of the return of King Ferdinand, to his dominions, instead of going to Madrid direct, as was expected, he has made a considerable stay at Valencia, he only sett off from thence on the 5 inst. As he was accompanied by many troops; the minds of the people are materially agitated, many are of the opinion he will not conform to or swear the Constitution, which to a certainty will occasion internal dissentions, probably even a (Civil) war. Some symptoms have already in fact broke out, for at Seville an insurrection took place on the 6 inst when the established authorities, were divested of command, one or other placed in their stead after proclaiming Ferdinand with all the powers & facilities he was in possession of in the year 1808. The constitution of course at that city has been completely done away, it would appear that at Xirez, and St. Lucas scenes of a similar nature have passed. It is impossible to say or form an idea to what extent they may be carried. The point however must soon be decided for on the 11 of this month the King was to arrive at Aranjuez only 7 leagues from Madrid. There the grand question whether it is or not to exist, will be determined –

By next opportunity what further occurs in this important business I shall advice you.

I am etc. Wm. Kirkpatrick." [131]

As late as the 24 June 1816 Kirkpatrick is still reporting on the conflict between the U.S. Navy and the North African States.

Sir,

"It is with infinite Satisfaction I have the honour of announcing to you that three Spanish Boats arrived from the Eastward and this morning the Captains of which bring the very pleasing Information, that whilst at anchor at San Pedro, a small Harbour on the other side of Cap de Gat, they saw on the 22 instant the American Squadron come up with and capture after a considerable resistance Two Algerian Frigates. I have spoken to the Captains myself, and have no doubt of the circumstances having taken place. They further mention, that there were only Two in company, the Third and smaller vessels must have been sent to cruise in some other direction, and I sincerely hope maybe found out by the victorious commander. The moment anything further comes to me knowledge, it shall be participated to you, and in the mean whiles Request you may have the goodness to lay this agreeable Intelligences upon his Excellency the President."

Kirkpatrick retained his contacts with the United Kingdom and is reported as having seen old friends in London in 1812.[132] After he moved to Motril and later to Adra, he kept up his friendship with the British Consul in Málaga advising him on local consular appointments and difficulties with Mr John B. Roman, the British Vice-Consul at Montril. He also maintained contact with the British Foreign Office and asked the British Consul to forward a letter to Lord Castlereagh, the British Foreign Secretary and great European diplomat, who died in 1823.

To; William Kirkpatrick Esq. 28th February 1821
Motril

"My Dear Tocayo, By yesterday's post I had the pleasure to receive your letter of the 22 inst. Enclosing one for Lord Castlereagh which I forwarded to his Lordship this day" -.[133]

While it is tempting to think that this might have been about great matters of state, judging from Laird's correspondence at the time, it is more likely to have been a confidential report on Mr Roman. This letter does not seem to have survived in The National Archives in London.

# 9. Málaga Enterprises

The Málaga Municipal Archives hold some Port of Málaga Health Authority inspection reports relating to Henri de Grivegnée, dating from 1794. They mention a consignment of barrels to Philadelphia which had to be inspected by the port sanitation officials and certified in a long document, that prior to shipment, they had been correctly cleaned.[134] The good name of Málaga wine was vital to the city and the quality had to be preserved.

William entered into various trading partnerships, including Grivegnée et Cie, Kirkpatrick and Greignow[?] (Málaga, 1815) and Kirkpatrick and Grivegnee (Málaga 1816) and later, Kirkpatrick and Parkinson. Henri de Grivegnée was often referred to as "Baron" as he had been awarded the Order of Carlos III which carried high prestige and a large pension. He is also sometimes referred to as a Consul but this is a mistranslation of his position as a Councillor and member of the Consulate Court of Málaga.

But William traded on his Scottish family's land holding associations to promote his standing in Málaga and used qualification as a Hidalgo to further his business and social interests. William exploited his new status to introduce other foreign merchants to the City's authorities, thus enabling them to obtain licenses to conduct business. He must have charged large fees for this service, as the process was complicated. Each new application needed full certification of the applicant's status in his country of origin and also formal translation of all these certifications. William had to restate his qualification as a Hidalgo on each application and the translators had to provide fresh evidence of their qualifications too. He would have ensured that it was worth his time and trouble.

William Kirkpatrick, and his cousin John Kirkpatrick Escott before him, were assiduous at forwarding the interests of their trading concerns and the products of the region. A note in the Bedfordshire County Record Office records that, on 10 October 1775, John Kirkpatrick Escott dispatched two cheeses to Lord Grantham, British Ambassador in Madrid between 1771 and 1779. [135]

On 13 September 1803 William wrote to "His Excellency, Thomas Jefferson Esq. President of the U.S. of America". It is significant that Kirkpatrick choose to honour the new President in this way. Jefferson was a powerful advocate of liberty and sympathized with the Revolutionary cause in France. While he may have only been sending customary courtesies to the new President, William may also have been declaring his own views and beliefs, those of the new age of enlightenment and republican progress.

Sir
Málaga 23 Sept. 1803
A Vessel offering from hence for Alexandria (Virginia) at the opening of our First Season, for the first time, I have taken the Liberty of shipping on board her, a few of what the Vineyards of my Family produce, to the care of James Madison Esq. with a request to present them to your excellency in my name, as also a quart Cask and cases of the very best Old Mountain or Málaga Wine (being the Vintage 1747) that my stores can boast of.
I sincerely hope these trifling Objects may arrive in safety and be delivered in good condition to your Excellency, who I flatter myself, will do me the honour to admit of them, as a rarity not to be met with in America.
I profit with much pleasure of this Occasion to assure your Excellency of the high esteem with which I have the honour to be,
Your Excellency's most obedient & humble Servant
William Kirkpatrick"[136]

Jefferson may have eventually prescribed this wine for his daughter Mary's "stomachic" as it was so old and mild. James Madison paid the freight charges on 21 June 1804. [137]

On the 4 February 1805 William was again offering gifts to President Thomas Jefferson.

"Wm. Kirkpatrick requests the favour of consul O'Brien to take charge of the Box which the bearer carried on board the *Martha*. It contains six clay Figures made in this place.
Two representing a mantled woman dancing the Bolero, to the music of the Guitar, which is played by a third Person, A Smuggler and his Mistress, all five in their proper Spanish Dress which the People they represent wear on festival days. To make up half a Dozen Another common figure has been added. W.K wishes Mr O'Brien to have the Goodness to present them in his name to His Excellency Thomas Jefferson Esq. on his arrival at Washington. They are object of curiosity which he [hopes] will happily merit his Excellency's approbation." [139]

Today we can imagine these scenes all too easily, doubtless they were more exotic then. Clearly Carmen was alive and dancing in Málaga long before María Manuela told the story to Prosper Mérimée.

In 1814 William wrote to his cousin, Alexander Kirkpatrick, Esq. of Dublin, sending presents of almonds and fruit and canvassing his support for his "House", asking that Alexander recommend his trading house to his associates. (See Appendix Six)

In 1815 and 1816 the House of Kirkpatrick and Grivegnée was in correspondence with Messrs Robert Hooper and Sons of Marblehead, Massachusetts, who were in partnership with John Bryant, William Sturgis and a William Reed as merchants, including wine merchants and various shipping ventures. [140] These Americans were substantial figures in Boston society. Bryant traded lumber, tea, opium and sugar and many other goods. Reed was elected to the 13th and 14th Congress (1811 – 1815) and Sturgis was a member of the Massachusetts House of Representatives and a State Senator. In 1815 the Kirkpatricks were also trading with John Venning, Baltic timber merchant and famous Russian prison reformer in St. Petersburg. [141]

Barcelona négociants had found it difficult to re-establish trade with the Americas after the end of the era of Napoleon wars[142]. But the House of Grivegnée seems to have been able to make export sales even as their financial position was deteriorating. In 1816, Henri Grivegnée consigned 500 casks and seventy barrels of wine to Peter Kuhn in Philadelphia, on board the brig *Eliza* ex Málaga.[143] There were also twenty-five bags of soft-shelled almonds, four hundred barrels and six hundred boxes of sun raisins and some carpeting. William Kirkpatrick consigned only four barrels of grape hip which he sent to a Dr James Kerr.[144] There were also a number of passengers. This confirms that the Kirkpatricks in Málaga were in contact with Philadelphia prior to the de Lesseps appointment as Consul to that city.

Perhaps the Kirkpatrick family's most surprising commercial achievement was their contribution to the Australian wine trade. In 1831 James Busby Esq., the father of the Australian wine industry, toured France and Spain gathering very detailed information on the growing of vines and the production of wine. He spent some time in Málaga as a major wine growing area, and obtained valuable information from a Mr. Kirkpatrick. He also left him with the task of gathering a large number of vine cuttings for shipping to London at the appropriate time of the year.[145]

"Eventually Busby sent cuttings of some 678 varieties of European vines back to Australia, where 362 were successfully grown in the Botanical Gardens of Sydney. It was these vines which were to propagate the vineyards of Australia."[146]

James Busby calls this Kirkpatrick "the Hanoverian consul, a Scotsman by birth, who had resided 40 years in Spain, and whose kindness to travellers was proverbial." By 1831 William had been long resident in Adra, so Busby was probably referring to Thomas, the Hanoverian Consul. But there is general confusion over the consular posts held by the brothers, part of which arises from the historical relationship between the Crown of the United Kingdom and the Ducal House of Hanover, and part by the role William played as Acting Hanoverian Consul and Consul for Oldenburg, the neighbouring Duchy. While they were variously Consul for the Duchy, it may have been thought that they were also acting for the British. Indeed, given their long-standing and close friendship with the British Consul, they may have acted in his place during his absences thus adding to the confusion of visitors.

Mr Kirkpatrick arranged for Busby to visit local vineyards, and gave him detailed export statistics for local produce which he had obtained from the Port authorities and copied for the Consulate. Busby reports that Kirkpatrick had a hundred woman shelling "Jordan" almonds in his yard at the time of his visit. "The women use a little anvil, striking the shells with an iron rod. The shells are purchased by confectioners for fuel, almost paying for the cost of the shelling."

In October 1831 Mr Kirkpatrick also helped Busby with data on dried fruit production and exports.

"The following accounts of the exportation of fruits from Málaga were taken from detailed statements which had been copied from the custom house dockets, and were kept in the office of Mr. Kirkpatrick.

The boxes are partly *Bloom* or *Sun* raisins, but principally *Muscatel.* The barrels and frails (rush baskets) are chiefly *Lexias.*

In the spring, shipments are made for the Baltic, and small parcels are sent, at all times, in assorted cargoes. On the whole, Mr. Kirkpatrick is of opinion that from 20 to 25 per cent may be added to the shipments of the fruit season, to make up the whole export from Málaga. This would make the whole weight of raisins annually exported from Málaga from 4,000 to 4,500 tons."

A later writer, Malcolm Seeley, makes it clear that he believed that it was William, the grandfather of the French Empress, who helped Busby with the vines:

> "Here Berry was well looked after on the voyage to Málaga where, with the help of ... He was introduced to a man by the name of Kirkpatrick who became the grandfather of the French Empress Eugénie. This Hanoverian Consul from the Clan McPatrick gave Berry much help during his short stay. He was also a wine expert with his own vineyard and was to be of great assistance to James Busby when he made a tour of Spain and France in 1831."[147]

Busby also held detailed technical discussions with the Rein and Domecq families on their production methods for wine, fortified wine and various dried fruits and almonds. The scientific nature of his notes, and the degree of statistical analysis and detail comes as something of a surprise to modern eyes.

# 10. Churriana

The years from the 1790s to 1810 were busy and productive for Kirkpatrick and his enterprises. We have various snapshots of his life during this period. He had appointed vice-consuls in adjacent ports, which relived him of much burdensome paperwork while he retained the status and involvement with affairs of state that came with the post of Consul. He could concentrate on the political side of the Consulate and the financing and provisioning of the United States naval ships which used Málaga for re-supply, during their excursions against the Corsairs. The House of Kirkpatrick would have been engaged in finding ways to circumvent the on–off blockades and embargoes and difficulties with shipping routes. Despite the added diversions of a house full of daughters and nieces and all their friends, Kirkpatrick found time to pioneer developments in cotton growing and production and to expand into the spinning and weaving of cotton. In 1800 he bought land and property in calle Llana in Churriana with the intention of planting cotton and by 1810 he was also processing cotton yarn.

The noted traveller and observer William Maclure was born in Ayr in Scotland in 1763, but became a naturalised American in 1796 having connections to New York and Richmond, Virginia. Whether the two Scotsmen found common cause is unlikely. Both were from the south west of the Scotland and both were from similar backgrounds, but Maclure was an early socialist with idealist views of the rights of the working man drawn from the writing of Thomas Payne and other early social reformers. Kirkpatrick was of a more hard-headed breed, practical and pragmatic, but with his own set of ideals based on the earlier reformist policies of Napoleon Bonaparte.

Maclure toured Andalusia in 1808 and recorded that he visited the cotton plantation at Churriana belonging to William Kirkpatrick, who he regarded as a man of great initiative. Maclure also visited the sugar cane plantation of Henry Grivegnée and favourably compared their standards to those of best practice in the West Indies. These references to sugar and cotton plantation are noteworthy in the context of Kirkpatrick family connections in Tobago in the West Indies, and in the southern United States, through José Gallegos and their de Lesseps relations whose cousins in New Orleans, Louisiana, were plantation owners. Both Kirkpatrick and de Grivegnée had access to American expertise if this was needed.

After the disasters of the French occupation and its immediate aftermath, Cipriano Palafox y Portocarrero wrote numerous letters from Churriana.[148] Doubtless it was a place of retreat from the heat of the city, and a place of refuge and comparative safety in times when yellow fever and other plagues ravaged the streets of the old town.

Maclure also states that Kilpatrick (sic) and Grivegnée with a third partner, (Alberto Gil Novales gives this as Rersin), established a textile factory in Málaga in 1810. It seems likely that their partner was Zacarías Gaspar Reissig Kuniko-Osstin, the Danish Consul and progenitor of the family which became the leading industrialists in Málaga. The American comments that this was the beginning of the Industrial Revolution in Spain. He wrote,

> "But in 1811 Málaga was occupied by French forces. Kirkpatrick made the error of being their partisan. This marked the end of his enterprise but he was still in Granada in 1821 where he was dedicated to the mining industry". [149]

Maclure was in southern Spain 1808 when he wrote:

> "Málaga Thurs. 12 May. We went 1½ leagues to a village called Churriana. Here Mr Kirkpatrick has made a large cotton plantation and he has tried all kinds of seed. The plant is perennial and withstands the winter although they cut it short it sets out new shoots each spring. It seems to thrive best on sandy land but requires watering in this climate where in general no rain falls from May to October. The plains are rich, flat, and well watered. The hills to the west are calcareous with blue white marble with abundant large springs". [150]

Alberto Gil Noveles, draws on Maclure's papers in his *William Maclure, Socialismo, Utópica en España*. To gives some more details[151]

> "In Marbella, on the following day, he visited the sugar cane plantation of Mr. Grivegnée, which has approximately 200 áreas, and produces between 200 and 300 pounds of sugar of extraordinary quality, and as clean as the sugar of Havana. Mr. Grivegnée pays wages of 35 (Reales) daily. He also has cows, ewes and goats, that among others things produce "fiemo" or fertiliser that he regards as their main produce.
>
> On the 18 of May, Maclure dispatched a box of minerals including marble, alum, etc., via Mr. Smith, a director of an alum mine, to Mr. Grivegnée, so that he can dispatch it on

to Marseilles, and by the Rhone canal system to Paris and to Maclure's agent, William Gorman of Macdonald, Gorman."

This dispatch route may explain how the wealthier families of Andalusia travelled to Paris, an apparently daunting trip they seemed happy to undertake with young family including daughters and nieces. Passengers were transported in *coches d'eau* or water coaches, drawn by teams of horses, aided by sail when the winds were favourable. Regular steam services were started in 1829. This inland route avoided the dangers of Privateers in the English Channel and there were connections to the other great rivers and the canals of Northern Europe.

Sir John Carr, K.C. provides a snap shot of de Grivegnée's enterprise in his entertaining travel book about a journey through Spain in 1808:

> "In the neighbourhood (of Marbella) is an extensive sugar plantation and close to the town is an *ingenico* or mill belonging to Monsieur Gravigne (sic) which a West Indian (planter) pronounced to be superior to any thing of the kind in the West India Islands".[152]

> "A few miles before we entered Málaga, we passed through Churriana a beautiful spot where there are several country houses belonging to persons of distinction residing at Málaga" - - pp. 135.

> "In proceeding amidst this beautiful and sublime scenery to a cotton farm belonging to Mr Kirkpatrick we had a demonstration of the tremendous fury with which the Guadalmedina rolls its waters in the ruins of a prostrate bridge and the aqueduct which had been built by order of the Prince of Peace (Godoy) for the benefit and ornament of the city. Although sheltered in one of the rudest and heaviest carriages perhaps ever constructed we found the heat scarcely supportable and were glad to get refreshment of melons, wine and bread, in a cool room in a farm where we saw some fields of cotton, (monadelphia polyandria), which had only recently been cultivated by way of experiment, but had already answered the most sanguine expectations of the proprietor. Note price of labour 6 – 10 Reals or one shilling and sixpence to two shillings and sixpence per day." Page 143.

Henri Grivegnée's sugar mill was the El Prado factory described in Cristina González's *Marbella's sugary past:*[153]

> "The factory changed hands many times throughout the centuries, at times very profitable for its owners, but the most important change came about by the purchase of the factory

by a Belgian businessman named Enrique Grivegnée, who set about building an aqueduct in 1808 to carry water to the factory from the river. Another important owner was the Paris banker Juan Lesseps, (Jean Baptiste Charles Lesseps 1775 - 1857) who later established the sugar factory at Guadaiza."

From this it appears that Juan Lesseps purchased or inherited the factory from his grandfather Henri de Grivegnée. Dr Traill gives a further perspective on William Kirkpatrick's enterprise when commenting on the production of sugar cane in Spain in the proceedings of The Royal Edinburgh Society in 1842:

"The author's remarks on the Spanish cultivation of the cane were the result of his personal observations during a residence of some months in Spain in the year 1814 and of some statistical information afforded to him by the late Wm. Kirkpatrick Esq. of Málaga. 'There were many small sugar plantations and a considerable number of sugar mills moved by either water or mules'."

Professor Traill recounts that many of the sugar mills around Málaga were destroyed during the Napoleonic wars but that some were still operating in 1814 when he made his visit. He says that:

"the finest and most perfect sugar estate I saw belonged to Messrs Grivegny (sic) and Kirkpatrick of Málaga". He then goes into the full financial, managerial and agricultural details of the process they used for sugar production. He had extracted this information from the (account) books of his "excellent friend William Kirkpatrick of Málaga".

His paper reveals a sophisticated industry operating on a large scale to contemporary scientific principles. This is characteristic of William's methods and Professor Traill records that William Kirkpatrick was manager of the sugar plantations at Marbella in 1806 and that they had became the property of his father-in-law, M. Grevigny, by Royal Charter in 1800.[154]

"Between Plaza Ancha and Plaza Altamirano stand several refined and elegant residences, including the houses of the wealthy Enrique Grivegnée and Ferdinand de Lesseps." [155]

Another view of William's position is given by William Rhind in his encyclopaedic work *The History of the Vegetable Kingdom* of 1857. Here William Kirkpatrick emerges again as a partisan of the French who flourished under their occupation, at least until Paris queried the quantity of cotton being exported from Granada.

"About the commencement of the present century the cultivation of the cotton-plant had been introduced with success into the southern parts of Spain, by Mr. Kirkpatrick, while acting as Consul for the United States of America at Málaga. The environs of the village of Churriana, at the foot of La Sierra de Mijas, which before had been an uncultivated waste, was converted by him into a flourishing cotton plantation. Success in this apparently unpromising situation, caused the cultivation of the plant to be quickly extended from Motril to Almería, along the coast of the Mediterranean Sea; and the pursuit has become at once a beneficial employment for native industry, and a source of considerable foreign commerce. When the French armies occupied the southern parts of Spain, in 1810, the exportation of cotton was so considerable as to lead the French government to suspect that the whole of that which went under the name of Spanish cotton was not the produce of Spain. Orders were therefore received by the military authorities to institute inquiries concerning the cotton plantations at Málaga and to ascertain the quantity which these actually furnished.

Restricted in the exportation of his produce, the indefatigable Kirkpatrick transferred his energies to the erection of spinning factories, and 3,000 workmen were soon employed in a village, which only a few years before had been a miserable hamlet. But popular commotions, and the occupation by hostile troops, were not favourable to the continued prosperity of the peaceful arts; and so soon as the French troops had evacuated this part of Spain, the prejudiced populace, either instigated by a blind fury, or more probably incited by the agents of those who criminally indulged in political animosities, not only destroyed the factories, but even tore up the cotton plants, and thus, to all appearance, entirely dried up the source of prosperity to a place, which had only existed from the profitable employment furnished by this branch of industry.

Notwithstanding, however, its apparently total destruction, the cultivation of cotton had been found too advantageous to be altogether abandoned by those persons who had formerly prospered through its means; and as soon as the opportunity was offered by returning tranquillity, plantations again flourished on the coast of Granada, cotton being now produced in abundance and of excellent quality at Motril and through the surrounding country." [156]

There is a reference to William Kirkpatrick in the *American Cyclopedia* of 1858 under the heading Almería.

> "Cotton is raised to some extent along the coast, its cultivation having been introduced by Mr Kirkpatrick, US Consul of Málaga, many years ago." It is also noted that, "the lead mines of the Sierra de Gader yielded in 45 years 11,000,000, quintals (some 220,000 metric tons) of that metal".[157]

Yet another reference to Málaga's cotton states that, "During the reign of Napoleon I, he caused it (cotton) to be introduced into Corsica, Italy, and the southern regions of France and Mr Kirkpatrick cultivated it near Málaga, in Spain".[158]

William Kirkpatrick was clearly the man English-speaking visitors wanted to meet to learn about the economy of the region. He is shown as a man of the Enlightenment by the way he embraces modern methods. His experiments with a wide variety of seed and his carefully recorded results show that he was a man of the new age where facts and figures counted and science was taken very seriously. His enterprise and initiative combined with Baron de Grivegnée's local standing, enabled them to be at the forefront of the industrial revolution which was just beginning to emerge in the main cities of the Iberian peninsular. Maclure used their enterprise as a model for his own pioneering attempts at a socialist style agricultural utopia near Alicante, where he bought a house and two fincas in 1822. Despite their differences in political outlook, the two Scotsmen may have recognised a common pragmatic and practical nature which drew them together when it came to essentials.

# 11. Domestic Life in Málaga

Enrique Kirkpatrick Mendaro notes that William lived in the Plazuela de los Moros when he first settled in Málaga. In 1795 William and Fanny Kirkpatrick were living in the calle de Santo Domingo on the west side of the river.[159] Later reports have the Kirkpatrick y Grivegnée family living in a tall, yellow-washed house, on the calle San Juan, its long narrow windows protected by jalousies.[160]

No 36, calle San Juan , a tall yellow house

William and Francisca were married on the 2nd November 1791. They baptised their first child Antonia Maria Ann, and also later children, at the Parish Church of San Juan at the end of the calle San Juan. This shows that they were living nearby. This street runs through San Juan Parish in the old part of the city behind the market. Church records show that other prominent members of the City also lived in this Parish at the time.

El Barrio del Prevchel, old Málaga.

Today there are a number of houses in the calle San Juan which fit this description, but there appears to be no memory or record of which one may have been the Kirkpatricks'. One of these houses extends some two metres beyond the current building line and may well have belonged to a previous period when the calle was narrower. But the house is now much changed, and is too narrow and too shallow, to fit the description of a "luxurious home" which could also house a wholesale trading business. Another double fronted house at number 19 calle San Juan, dated to the 1790s, fits that description rather better.

It is likely that William and his family moved from calle de San Domingo to calle San Juan and then, during their period of greater prosperity, they enjoyed the luxurious house on calle Postigo de los Abades where the telephone exchange building now stands next to where the old Hospital de San Juan de Dios once stood. This was a short winding lane leading from the waterside to the Abbot's Gate in the walls of the Cathedral.

The calle San Juan de Dios by the Abbots Gate, under the walls of the Cathedral, in 1945.

Calle San Juan de Dios in 1945, close to the old Hospital San Juan de Dios.

Other sources place him in a "stately" house, No. 8, in the calle San Juan de Dios in the shadow of the Cathedral in what is now central Málaga. Their use of the local Parrish Church, the Sacristy Chapel of the Cathedral, for family rites of passage shows that they changed churches when they moved nearer the Cathedral. The more prominent names in the baptismal and marriage records of the Sacristy Chapel also suggests that they changed their social circle too.

A local newspaper lamented the loss of these old buildings with an elegiac piece by Narciso Díaz de Escovar, 1860-1935.

> *The demolishing mattock,*
> *That, slowly our old people's legends,*
> *Are changing into a modern city,*
> *With its attractiveness, the comforts and dangers,*
> *But the people do not do much.*
> *Time has turned into piles of rubbish, a building that in past centuries,*
> *Had historical memories written on its valuable walls.*
> *Its inner ornamentation reveals to us who live in the XX Century,*
> *The wealth and good taste of its possessors.*
> *That building existed in the Postigo of the Abbots,*
> *Against the side of the Cathedral, whose place is now partly occupied by*
> *The flame of which you have become so fond, the Public Telephone exchange.*
> *In that same house lived an illustrious family, who tell how their descendants included an Empress and how she bore a Prince of the throne of Napoléon I,*
> *There the family of Kirpatrick lived in the XVIII century and under those walls Demolished by the modernist eagerness of reforms,*
> *Was born famous Doña María Manuela Kirpatrick de Closeburn, Countess of Montijo. The Kirkpatricks were natives of Scotland and Dedicated to the important businesses they established in Málaga,*
> *Where they continued residing for many years.*
> *In the middle of Century XIX,*
> *Don Thomas Kirkpatrick who was the Consul of Russia later lived there.* [161]

Another surviving building is the nearby section of the Bishop's Palace which backs on to calle Fresca. It was incorporated into the bishopric in 1819 and now contains the offices of the Ecclesiastic Curia and the Courts of the Bishopric of Málaga. This fine traditional house, with an Italian style central courtyard, belonged to the Quilty family in the early 18th century but dates from the 16th century.

Old houses near the present Telephone Exchange where the Abbot's Gate
once stood.

The Empress Eugénie's grandfather, William Kirkpatrick of Málaga,
has been variously described as a wine and fruit merchant, wholesale
wine merchant, sardine exporter, *Sardinier*, and even wine bar owner.
His daughters were said to entertain his clients in the salon behind his
business premises. María Manuela was accused of seducing Cipriano
during one such entertainment. But these accounts are written by those
determined to discredit Eugénie and Napoleon III.

William Kirkpatrick was a much more substantial man than that as
his Málaga concerts reveal. He received many tributes for the musical
performances held at his "salon" in the period from 1800 to 1814. He
was well known for his enthusiasm for music and his famous concerts
which were held at both his town house and his Hacienda at Churriana.

These soirées included both traditional Spanish music, directed by the renowned composer and guitarist Fernando Sor, and also works by Central Europeans, probably Hayden and Mozart, and Italian composers like Boccherrini, and also the popular French compositions of the period.

Fernando Sor
From a lithograph M.N. Bates after Goubeau

The Archives of Málaga Cathedral have originals of two of the known religious works by Sor. One is a lamentation *del Jueves Santo* (1800) and the other his accomplished motete *O Salutaris Hostia* (c. 1809). Both works belong to his early life before he became famous for his secular music. Maria José de la Torre Molina comments that the musicians of the Cathedral of Málaga (in particular Joaquin Tadeo de Murguía) knew Sor from the events organized by William Kirkpatrick and they too had performed at his private concerts.[162]

Sor, a Catalan, and an Army officer, was both a composer and a performer who had benefited from the patronage of the Duchess d'Alba during his period in Madrid. He was appointed head of the small Royal Administration in Andalusia, but spent much of his time in Málaga between 1804 and 1808, prior to the French invasion, and is reported in the City again in 1809.

"About the year 1802 or 1803 (sic) when Sor was an officer in
the army and in the garrison in Málaga or very near that city, the
Austrian (sic) Consul Mr. Quipatri (sic), gave a grand concert,

to which came all the most elegant people in Málaga and all around. In this concert Sor played a solo on the double bass, with variations, which left everyone who heard him admiring and astonished, including the professional musicians who were present. This was told to me in a letter (which I still have) by D. Vicente Ribera, a fine trumpet player of much experience, who on that occasion was playing the serpent in the orchestra. The leader of that concert was D. Francisco Ibarra, who was also leader of the Málaga cathedral orchestra; the leader of the second violins was D. José Colocós, and the first trumpet was D. Vincente Leza, principal musician, it seems of the Aragonese Regiment." [163]

As Brian Jeffery points out in his translation, there are errors in this report by Baltasar Saldoni, of one of Kirkpatrick's concerts, but its immediacy gives an authentic flavour of these celebrated events.[164] Sor too was an *afrancesado* who continued in French service as principal commissary of police in Jerez. After the collapse of their occupying regime after the battle of Vitoria, he was obliged to leave Spain in 1813, ahead of Ferdinand's savage repression of both Liberals and French supporters. He was in Paris between 1813 and 1815 when Francesca Kirkpatrick and her daughters were living with the de Lesseps. It would be fascinating to know if he renewed his acquaintance with the family. By 1822 he had joined a thousand or more other Spanish refugee families in Somers Town in London.[165]

William may well have run a bodega, literally a cellar or vault, as a base for his wine merchant's business, in calle de Santo Domingo or on the ground floor of his tall yellow house in calle San Juan, in his early days in Málaga. But this was surely more a place of business, where wine was tasted and prices negotiated before export in the barrel or cask, than a place of entertainment. Wine cellars of this type, "Bodegas" were "one of the most important investments made by British residents in Spain, and the largest supplier of wine to the British market in the middle of the 19th century." [166] The Kirkpatricks followed the progression of foreign merchants and retailers from the older, even more closely built-up areas in the west of the City, to calle Nueva and calle San Juan behind the present day market and then on to tree lined avenue of the Almeda where Thomas lived. Calle San Juan Dios is very close by.

William doubtless mixed business with pleasure during the soirées which were revived by Fanny and their daughters on their return to

Málaga in 1814.[167] Their French education would have prepared them to perform in evening house-concerts. Sheet music and instruments were purchased when they spent six months in London in 1814. María Manuela was well known for her singing abilities.

In reality both William's local and international trading interests were much more extensive than any bodega, however cultured the music and company. His business affairs were conducted in what we would recognize today as a most professional manner. He was clearly familiar with accounts and statistics. The detailed import-export returns he provided to the US Government also guided his business activities and provided the trade figures he gave to interested travellers.

# 10. Politics and Reaction

William Kirkpatrick's letters to Washington reveal the complex and stormy waters he had to navigate. He was increasingly exposed to political and commercial risks by his growing prominence as a merchant and his role as Consul of a new nation learning to exert its naval power in the Mediterranean. These snapshots illustrate how he and his family, and their associates survived. The tactics Kirkpatrick adopted were driven by events. They were influenced in part by moral principle and in part by pragmatism, the need to keep the money flowing.

In the period 1779 to 1812, Spain was convulsed by a worldwide war, dynastic instability, civil wars and the struggle to regain independence from French occupation and Napoleonic ambition. In 1820 the Liberal or Constitutionalists' rebellion against the government in Madrid caused more internal strife and a counter reaction and another French invasion under Duke de Angoulême. Even more dynastic rivalry and insecurity followed in the form of the Carlist Wars. The history of this whole period will be familiar enough to Malagueños, but some historical detail helps explain Kirkpatrick's reactions to the disasters which overcame the City and its inhabitants during the French occupations.

William Kirkpatrick's personality is revealed by his responses to these tumultuous events. He lived with the intermittent war with Britain and consequent trade embargoes, and the raids on mercantile shipping from the North African states. These difficulties became a matter of normal trade and Consular business, as did his work for the United States Navy as it tried to counter the Corsairs. William seems to have dealt with the matters in a straightforward manner showing flexibility and initiative. There is some evidence in Consular correspondence from Gibraltar that the American Consuls worked closely with their British colleagues over the North African difficulties.

The Kirkpatrick's trading house tried to use neutrals to avoid trade restrictions. Such tactics must also have helped William balance his own business dealings and his British nationality with his important American post and his consular relationships with the North German States while Europe was under extensive French occupation.

There is a detailed example of the Kirkpatrick family's earlier attempts to mitigate the adverse affects of the Embargo, and turn them to their advantage using de Grivegnée's neutral role.

British Admiralty Court reports show that Henri de Grivegnée was appointed to manage the Kirkpatricks' business when Robert Kirkpatrick's nephew, John Kirkpatrick Escott, left Málaga before war with Britain broke out in 1779. William was sent to Málaga to re-establish the Kirkpatricks' control of their enterprise and that de Grivegnée, described as their agent, held only a caretaker role for the wider Kirkpatrick interests although he had substantial other interests of his own.

A series of London Court cases during the 1780s shows the way the family and its associates conducted business and explains Henri de Grivegnée's position. It also illustrates the complexities of the rapidly changing political and legal situation.

The report of the Escott Case in the British Admiralty Court Records has Henri de Grivegnée, a Fleming, initially as an employee or member of the firm of Kirkpatrick and Company and later as their agent in Málaga when hostilities broke out between England and Spain in 1779. This rather complex affair involved the shipment of wines and other merchandise which had belonged to John Kirkpatrick Escott while he was resident in Málaga. Some months before the outbreak of war he returned to England, leaving his goods warehoused under the care of de Grivegnée who was a neutral. Henri de Grivegnée had instructions to ship the bulk of the property to Ostende as soon as a suitable ship was available. He duly dispatched the cargo on the neutral Dutch ship *Louisa Margaretha* on 7 April 1780, but the *Louisa Margaretha* had to return to Málaga shortly after leaving that port. At this point de Grivegnée received fresh instructions from London instructing him to re-consign the cargo directly to London in the expectation that it would be safe under the provisions of the Levant Bill which was then being considered by Parliament. De Grivegnée was to receive 14% commission for his troubles.

The *Louisa Margaretha* sailed for England but was captured and made a prize by a British Privateer in the English Channel. The essence of the final Admiralty Court judgement revolved around the precise intention of Parliament when it passed the Act under which the ship was rendered a prize. John Kirkpatrick Escott lost the initial action. While the ship was released the cargo was declared a lawful prize. He also lost an appeal. This case was subsequently cited in other similar cases.[167]

For Spain and her merchants, the 18th century had been a period of generally increasing prosperity. Juan and Robert Kirkpatrick y Capper, and William Escott, and his son John Kirkpatrick Escott, enjoyed a period of relative affluence which allowed Robert and his nephew to retire in comfort to England. In 1765 the Bourbon King Charles III had opened the major Spanish ports to traffic with the West Indies and in 1778 they were permitted to trade with all the Spanish colonies in America except Mexico which remained a monopoly for Cadiz until 1789. Business also developed with the newly independent United States, providing a large new market for Spanish exports, especially wines and metal products.

On 3 September 1783 Count Aranda successfully negotiated the Spanish settlement terms for the Peace of Paris concluding Britain's war with Spain, France and America. The end of conflict opened the way for William Kirkpatrick to move to Barcelona in 1784 and on to Málaga some four years later. His move may also have been prompted by a dramatic shift in Colonial export trade from Barcelona to Málaga.

In the period 1786 – 1788 Barcelona's registered export balance fell by nearly 7 million reales while Málaga's rose by nearly 6 million reales. The fall was even greater in the period 1791-1793 when Barcelona's balance fell by nearly 20 million reales and Málaga's again grew by some 5 million reales.[168] These statistics illustrate the success of the Málaga authorities in stimulating the commercial life of the City by the formation of the High Maritime Council. Much of this increase was due to the changes in regulations which allowed outward-bound ships from Barcelona to collect produce along the coasts of Valencia and Catalonia, cargoes which were then registered in Málaga before sailing for the Atlantic. These vessels were still largely financed in Barcelona although Málaga exporters would have benefited from the increased port traffic and Customs clearances.

These changes must also have influenced William. He had a good head for figures and understood the significance of the raw numbers derived from the Port Authority returns. He would also have realised the commercial potential of the American Consulate as the volume of shipping documentation increased.

Peace with Britain in 1783 brought ten or more years of growing prosperity under the reforming rule of Charles III and his enlightened ministers, and the Kirkpatricks and their associate Henri de Grivegnée benefited with the rest of Spain. During this period Henri was able to provide funds for his brother-in-law, José Gallegos, to establish the famous Gallego flourmills in Richmond, Virginia. In the context of capital and production, Málaga produced sufficient surplus finance for capital to be an export commodity, at least within the family framework of the Gallegos, de Grivegnée and Kirkpatrick family business alliance.[169] This is highly significant and is evidence of the success of the reforms made by the Madrid government of this period.

Intellectual life flourished in Madrid. The salon of María Francisca de Sales Portocarrero y López de Zúñiga, 7th Contessa de Montijo, became a centre the of liberal thought and influence which formed the character of her second son, the young Cipriano, Count de Teba. But these developments were not enough to protect the Bourbon's *Antiguo Régimen* from the storm of revolutionary ideas streaming from Paris.

William Kirkpatrick arrived in Málaga during 1788, the year in which Charles IV succeeded his father Charles III, as King. He was just in time to enjoy the last years of stability. But he must have become increasing concerned at the political outlook during the following decade as he went about his business affairs, married, and when his children were born. His efforts to obtain the United States Consular post started at about this time and may have been prompted by a need to find security in a quasi-diplomatic status. Reports of William Kirkpatrick's growing wealth through to 1810 suggest that he was able to find ways to navigate these dangerous shoals.

To assess how he and his associates adapted to the changes which followed, we need to have a brief look at the events which shook the world, and saw the end of the *ancien régime* throughout Europe.

Although Charles IV retained his father's able chief minister the Count de Floridablanca, who had adopted many English liberal and reformist ideas, the new King was unable to preserve the successes of his father's enlightened rule. Concerned at the threat of French revolutionary ideas, Floridablanca banned French publications and censored the Spanish press, which were exploring the new concepts being embraced by enlightened opinion throughout Europe. But reaction set in as extreme revolutionary and republican sentiment in Paris alarmed governments around Europe. Liberalism and reform in Spain became discredited and conservative elements, including sections of the clergy, gained the ascendancy.

Louis XVI of France pressed his Spanish relation to announce Spain's approval of the new French constitutional monarchy. Floridablanca was dismissed in 1792 and the Junta of State was abolished. The veteran Count Aranda was named Chief Minister in the hope that he might be able to exert a moderating influence on the French.

Events in Paris then assumed a terrible momentum. Louis XVI was deposed in August 1792, and executed in January 1793. The declaration of the French Republic soon followed. His queen, Marie Antoinette, followed him to the guillotine on 16 October 1793. Many years later this event was to haunt Eugénie, William's granddaughter, as the Second Empire fell apart. When her husband Napoleon III was defeated and captured at Sedan in 1870, Eugénie was forced to flee from the Palace of the Tuileries, in a hansom cab, with the mob at its front gates.

Charles IV responded to the Revolutionary Terror and the brutal guillotining of the Nobility and upper Bourgeoisie in Paris by dismissing Count Aranda and appointing Manuel Godoy as first secretary. The good times were over, and the events of the next twenty and more years presented Spain and its foreign residents with many difficulties. These complex shifts between war and peace are well summarized by Richard Herr:[170]

"Godoy's first major challenge came from France. The French Convention, after executing Louis XVI in January 1793, anticipated the response of Spain and Britain by declaring war on them. The Spanish war was fought at both ends of the Pyrenees. A Spanish advance in 1793 was followed in 1794-5 by French invasions of Catalonia and the Basque provinces. Both regions organised their own defence, but Godoy, suspicious of their loyalty to Madrid, negotiated peace in 1795, ceding to France Spain's half of the island of Santo Domingo in return for French evacuation of Northern Spain. Charles IV rewarded Godoy with the title of 'Prince of Peace'."

Peace provided Spain only brief respite. Britain, still at war with France, suspected Spanish - French agreement, and its navy attacked Spanish shipping. Spain responded by signing an alliance with the French Republic in August 1796 and soon declared war on Britain. The (Bourbon) Family Pact had been revived, although the French branch of the family was gone. The treaty of Amiens of March 1802 ended the war of Britain against Spain and France, but a year later France and Britain renewed hostilities.

Charles IV attempted to remain neutral; however, Bonaparte demanded payment of a 'neutrality subsidy' and Britain renewed attacks on Spanish shipping. Spain once more declared war on Britain in December 1804.

"Seldom have wars that saw little open conflict been so disastrous for a country. The British navy cut off most trade between Spain and America. By 1798 the merchants of Cadiz were in dire straights. The cotton industry of Catalonia, unable to get raw material or reach its best customers, came to a virtual halt, and the workers turned to soup lines, provided by the captain general."

In 1800 Henri de Grivegnée had been granted under Royal Charter, a large property near Marbella where he grew and processed sugar cane under Kirkpatrick's management. This appears a practical response to these political events. Although the Treaty of Amiens of 1802 would have given their international trade a brief respite, it was unlikely that many cargoes got through before the renewal of hostilities with Britain at the end of 1804 which led to the re-imposition of the blockades and further loss of trade with America. British ships had attacked Spanish silver convoys on their way home from South America and made off with large quantities of bullion.

> "Charles IV was outraged on hearing news of the loss of his silver and issued Orders, dated 14th and 23rd November 1804 that the property of all English subjects in Spain should be sequestered in reprisal. These orders were rigorously carried out and on the evening of 21st November all the English ships in the port of Málaga and in the bay were arrested. The contents of the ships were seized, without exception, as were the contents of houses and warehouses of English people, which had been left unoccupied on account of the yellow fever epidemic".[171]

Kirkpatrick's Consular letters make frequent mention of the quarantine regulations imposed to restrict the spread of the yellow fever which had first reached Cadiz in 1800, and had spread to Andalusia. But he makes no mention of any reprisals against British merchants in Málaga. Perhaps being a foreign consul and "Scots" or "Irish" and integrated into the local community through marriage and church gave him protection. To add to the country's woes the harvests of 1803 and 1804 were ruined by excessive rain. By October 1805, when Lord Nelson defeated the combined Spanish and French fleets at Trafalgar, Charles IV and his minister Godoy were being blamed for the end of prosperity and the plight of the country. The Government in Madrid and the Court were impoverished by the loss of revenues from the American colonies and customs duties which had contributed half of the King's revenue in 1792.[172] These events would also have reduced Kirkpatrick's income from the charges consuls made for shipping documentation, and from his own overseas trade.

William's business association with the neutral Henri de Grivegnée and his own semi diplomatic status may also have helped him avoid the sequestration of English goods in Málaga. But further restrictions on foreign commerce must have prompted them to look for promising local enterprises, and they turned to growing cotton on land at Churriana in the valley of the Río Guadalhorce.

Political Spain was in turmoil. The court split into competing factions. Manuel Godoy, the power behind the weak monarchy of Charles IV, was at the centre of plots to take over the Crown, with his lover Queen María Louisa at his side. Napoleon was watching events in Spain with a close eye and moved quickly to take advantage of these intrigues.

In 1806 Napoleon entrapped Spain by persuading Godoy to join forces with France in a war against Portugal. Large numbers of French troops entered northern Spain en route to Portugal, which was overrun by November 1807. To the alarm of the Spanish, the French did not return home but poured more troops into the country on the excuse that they were to save the Infante Frederick from Godoy and his plotting. Before Spain had quite realized what had happened, the north and west of the county were effectively under French occupation.

Crisis point was reached in March 1808. With Napoleon's forces approaching Madrid, Ferdinand's supporters rose against Godoy who went into hiding. Charles then abdicated in favour of his son Ferdinand. Throughout Spain there was jubilation at the fall of Godoy and the accession of Ferdinand, *El Deseado*, 'The Desired One'.[173] Eugenio, Count de Montijo, Cipriano's older brother, was deeply involved in these events and played a leading part in supporting Ferdinand. Unlike his mother and younger brother, he was of a reactionary frame of mind, and had supported an aristocratic renewal plan in his youth.

Charles IV tried to revoke his abdication claiming that he had acted under duress, but it was too late and matters were out of his hands. Napoleon then effectively kidnapped the ex-King Charles IV and had his newly installed son, King Ferdinand VII, brought over the border to Bayonne. He then forced Ferdinand to return the Crown to his father, and in turn compelled Charles to transfer the Crown of Spain to Napoleon's older brother, Joseph. Initial disturbance in Madrid, the revolt of the Dos de Mayo, were brutally put down by French forces as is so graphically portrayed by Francisco Goya, but as Herr comments:

"A few days later the Council of Castile published the texts of
the change of dynasty. This time the people, suddenly aware

that they had been robbed of their young idol, would not be quietened. Despite warnings that Napoleon was invincible, crowds in Valencia, Zaragoza, Oviedo and Seville forced the hesitant officials to proclaim war in the name of Ferdinand VII. By June all unoccupied Spain was mobilizing for war."[174]

The installation of Joseph Napoleon Bonaparte, as King in Madrid, brought matters to a head. Spain had become divided into the areas occupied by France, where many Spaniards co-operated with the government of Joseph, and the unoccupied regions where local dignitaries formed provincial Juntas in the name of Ferdinand VII. The Supreme Junta in Seville mobilised resistance, and Britain set about organising military aid to unoccupied Western Spain and Portugal. When the French invaded Andalusia the Junta fled to Cadiz, which then became the centre of Spanish resistance.

Kirkpatrick had to find ways to continue his business in the face of these upheavals. At first Málaga may have seemed removed from the squabbles at Court and the plotting in Paris. There is evidence that both Henri de Grivegnée and William Kirkpatrick took care to arrange their affairs at about this time and make provisions to safeguard the interests of their wives, sisters and family as a response to the deteriorating political and security situation and Wills were drawn up.

On the 7 January 1808 Henri de Grivegnée and his brother William Grivegnée, a Marbella City Councillor, with William Kirkpatrick and a Frenchman, José Gemigniany, formed a partnership, Gemigniany and Company, for local soap manufacture.[175] William Kirkpatrick's interest in this factory was probably sold to Guillermo Enrique Huelín y Madly, the brother of Matías Huelín, in August 1821 when Manuel Muñoz Martín records that Huelín bought a soap factory from a don Guillermo in Alhaurín el Grande to the west of Málaga which had been founded in 1808. The Gallegos family which had married into the de Grivegnée family had been long established in that town.[176]

Two years later he was involved in the formation of a chemical company with Henri and with Don Domingo Díaz. While Henri de Grivegnée and his enterprises were doing well this would have been seen as a safe investment. But when the French occupation and its repercussions destroyed their company, the fortunes of the family were eventually wiped out too.

Intelligence from Kirkpatrick's widespread contacts would have revealed that Andalusia could not remain immune from these momentous political changes. He had to balance his personal position as a man of business with the foreign policies of the United States government which he represented. He also had to consider the differences in the approach of changing United States ministers, some pro French and supportive of Napoleon's reformist ideas, others, more Tory in outlook, concerned at the excesses of the Revolution and the new Emperor Napoleon's expansionist policies.

Kirkpatrick's local political position was clear up to 1807. He was well set up in a major city that enjoyed a Liberal reputation where his French sympathies and "modern" outlook would have matched those of the generally pro French foreign colony. His musical concerts cemented his social standing and also reveal the character of the man.

Fernando Sor was also a Liberal and the Kirkpatrick household with it internationalist prospective, would have suited his views. William would have done well enough under the rule of Charles IV and been in sympathy with the more progressive elements in the government. Spain was on the path to a modest degree of modernisation. In the face of the Revolutionary excesses in France the moderate stance of their Government would have suited the pragmatic foreign business folk of Málaga and Cadiz.

In the midst of these difficult times it is surprising to find Kirkpatrick in Paris in 1808. But he must have needed to respond to change and make new business arrangements wherever possible. Where better than the heart of the new power in Europe? He seems to have been able to travel within Napoleon's Europe and move from one occupied country to the next. Whether this was because he had diplomatic status or because he had means and connections is now unknown. He would probably have travelled to Marseilles and then taken the Rhone canal route to Paris. This would have avoided the danger of the Atlantic privateers and the alternative a long uncomfortable coach ride through northern Spain and most of France. French control was more pragmatic and less authoritarian than the mid 20th Century occupations which we know more about today. People with money, good connections and appropriate letters of pass and introduction moved fairly freely. He is reported as having been detained in France by the Paris police in 1808 but was released.

"Last but not least is William Kirkpatrick, a son of a Scottish (Closeburn) baronet, who was a wine merchant at Málaga and had married François de Grévignée, daughter of a Walloon, also settled at Málaga. Kirkpatrick, who had been appointed Consul at Hamburg by the Grand Duke of Oldenburg, was in Paris in 1808 and was anxious to return to Málaga, but the French police suspected him of relations with England and had arrested his partner Turnbull. (William's) daughter, Maria Emanuele, born in 1796, was destined to be the mother of the Empress Eugénie, while her mother's sister, wife of Mathieu de Lesseps, was destined to be the mother of Ferdinand de Lesseps." [177]

But this affair is puzzling. The length of his detention is not clear. Nor are his exact relations with the Duke of Oldenburg. Consular Records in the Archives of the Duchy of Oldenburg confirm that William's brother, Thomas, was their Consul General in Málaga from 1807 to at least 1817. Correspondence in Oldenburg State Archives shows that William deputized for his brother as Oldenburg Consul in Málaga.

This arrangement gave William extra diplomatic or quasi-diplomatic protection. It would also have made a modest contribution to his consular revenues and may have had commercial advantages. It may also have been a way to reserve a prestigious post for his brother if it became necessary for him to move to Málaga. Perhaps it was a tactic to ensure the Kirkpatrick succession in their trading partnerships. Such a strategy, with triple objectives, would have warranted the risk of the journey to Paris with its menace of privateers, detention or worse en route. Doubtless there was business to be done in Hamburg and bills of exchange to be negotiated or collected. The acting role as Oldenburg Consul may also have been an insurance policy against the loss of his American post because he was a foreign national and not a naturalised United States citizen. In 1812 he was also an enemy national. He may have been aware of efforts by resident American citizens to remove him from his post on just these grounds.

William was in Paris with a banker, a business partner named Turnbull, when they were held by the police. Turnbull, as a British subject resident in Gibraltar, was arrested and detained. William was not arrested, but was held on suspicion of collaboration with the British. The French may have known that, despite his Consular position, he had retained his British nationality. But his Spanish domicile gave him an extra immunity.

"Englishmen domiciled, if not naturalised, abroad were not subject to detention, which indeed was prospective but was limited to persons then on French soil. The Berlin decree of 1807 ordered the capture of all British subjects - - found in territories occupied by French or allied troops; but this does not seem to have been enforced. Hence the Police registers show visits to Paris between 1806 and 1813 by Englishmen settled on the Continent".[178]

We know from his letters to the State Department that William was back in Málaga in January 1809. Writing on 18 April, he remarks that he was unable to send the Return of Arrivals, the shipping lists, from the previous July. But he did not explain that he had been in Paris and Hamburg for at least part of this period. Significantly in the circumstances he reports that the "Board of Control in Seville remains steady."

Political events in Spain were soon to bring mob violence to the streets of Málaga. Andalusia was nominally under the control of Spanish authorities in Seville while the French were confined north of the line of the Sierra Morena. They had invaded Catalonia and were pressing south of Barcelona to Tarragona as they tried to secure their occupation of the rest of country. But they faced growing opposition and increasing harassment from bands of guerrillas and more organised Spanish military formations.

As regional government weakened, so disorder grew. In the disturbed countryside agricultural production slumped leading to the collapse of urban trade and produce for export. Security in the remoter parts of the country was always fragile but the government's loss of control over large swathes of the rural hinterland allowed brigands to extract tolls of passage or worse from passing travellers.[179] Sometimes these bands acted under the cover of being Spanish patriots and anti-French guerrillas, but more often the motives were entirely materialistic.

Anti French sentiment in village communities, reinforced by local priests concerned at the godlessness of the French forces, was in sharp contrast to the pro-French attitudes found in the cities. The generally unruly state of the countryside, aggravated by a sense of insecurity and injustice, brought the countryside to the towns. The gulf between those in the countryside who owned no land, and the large landowners and town dwellers widened and relations polarised. Rural bands, whether driven by their priests or the thought of loot or plain resentment, acting in fits of "popular passion", burst into the main cities with vengeance or booty in mind.

This general disorder spilled over into violence and on two occasions during William's time in the city, rural insurgents invaded Málaga, out to wreak revenge on wealthy city dwellers and well-known *afrancesados*. His factories were burnt and his crops destroyed by the very people he had tried to lift out of rural poverty. The nation's desire for independence and to be masters in their own land, overcame the desire for civil order and economic opportunity which generally reflected the tolerant mood of the larger cities.

# 11. Life Under the Occupation, 1808 – 1812

Scots guile did not save William from the effects of the Occupation. The City's merchants had to endure the collapse of Spanish government in Madrid and re-adjust to the inept rule of the Supreme Junta in Seville and their failure to resist the French. But worse was to follow. By November 1809 the provisional authorities in Seville were discredited and were forced to flee to Cadiz. On 1 February 1810 King Joseph marched into Seville at the head of his French guards to be met with acclamation by many of the local population who hoped for a new period of effective governance and social reform.

During the two disturbed years before the city was occupied, Málaga was split between those who broadly supported the French and those who remained hostile to their illegitimate government. While there was some antagonism between these groups, there was also a degree of mutual tolerance. Much of the discussion and debate was limited to the Bourgeois, many of whom were of foreign origin, and it was concentrated in the new, more respectable cafés, which were springing up in the Alameda and the area to the east of the older streets.[180] The English historian Raymond Carr sets the context when he states that the supporters of the French "were often the progressives elements in Spanish society, liberal minded civil-servants who saw in Joseph's monarchy the hope of a reformed Spain"[181]

María José de la Torre Molina comments that the mood of the city was tense but calm and there were few outbreaks of public disorder. But the economic situation was dire and taxes were very high. During the actual Occupation the French executed some 98 people although most were not from the city. She also comments that although members of the economic elite held important positions in the Administration their "attitude was neither of submission nor of total collaboration".[182] She suggests two reasons for this apparent lack of conflict. There was the well-founded fear that the French knew how to impose on subjected communities which led six hundred notables to swear allegiance to the Bonaparte King. And there was also extensive pro-French propaganda in the form of a gazette published to reflect their rule in the best possible light.

But she also makes a significant point in relation to the political positions of the Kirkpatricks and de Grivegnées and the other foreign residents in the years before the Occupation. The French residents in Málaga were a well-established colony which was more than a small minority within the community. From 1798 pro-Revolutionary pamphlets and banned books circulated around the City. These were the ideas that stirred the *Amigos del País* at their meetings. Social gatherings had been organised by the *afrancesados* where Revolutionary ideas and doubtless the latest news, were discussed among a sympathetic audience. It seems that the French had prepared their ground and met a ready audience among a significant proportion of the residents.

But sentiment among the ordinary Spanish and the country folk was very different. As the French commander General Sabastiani, the new Duke of Dalmatia, set off to complete the conquest of Málaga and Granada, country people rose up against the inertia of the Andalusian authorities and their failure to resist the French. Before Joseph's forces could take control of Málaga, the City's Governor was murdered in the streets of Granada. In June, Málaga was raided by "Colonel" Avallo and his band of mountain men. Reports on the confused situation of the early period of the French occupation of Andalusia highlight the two sides of the Spanish reaction to the French presence; acquiescence or even jubilant welcome by the town folk, and fury from the peasants of the countryside.

The London journal *The Annual Register* had been founded by the conservative political commentator Edmund Burke. In a contemporary report of 1808 it stated:

> "The events of the first of these periods, which was but very short, or rather merely transient, were, as usual, in similar cases, for the most part, the effects of popular passion.
>
> The governor of Carthagena was murdered. General Truxillo, governor of Málaga, was murdered at Grenada. His body was dragged through the streets, cut in pieces, and afterwards burnt. The French consul at Málaga, Mornard, and some French merchants of that place, were secured on the 4th of June, from the fury of the people, in the Moorish castle of Gibralforo. A great quantity of arms and ammunition taken from an English privateer in 1800 had been lodged in a warehouse in the suburbs, to be sold. On the 20th of June a report prevailed that this magazine had been purchased by the French consul, for the use of the French army. The people of Málaga marched to the castle, and notwithstanding all the remonstrances of the deputy-governor, and resistance of the guard, burst into the castle, pierced their victim with a thousand daggers, and burned his

dead body in a bonfire made of the furniture and some wrecks of the consul's house. The depot was broken open, and all that it contained destroyed. All this was done in spite of every effort on the part of the municipal government of Málaga to prevent it."[183]

Málaga was only saved from further bloodshed by the presence of mind of the Dean and Chapter of the Cathedral who organised a holy procession to give thanks for their deliverance from the oppressors. The rioters joined the procession and calm was restored.[184] Sebastiani and the French occupying force soon arrived. Although they were welcomed with enthusiasm, their popularity rapidly declined. By the 5th February 1810 Málaga was in the hands of the French under the immediate command of Colonel Jean Baptiste Berton, who was made Governor in August 1811. The *Edinburgh Annual Review* commented that he resisted the Spanish guerrilla opposition with great energy and success.

"The Spaniards esteemed as much as they feared him and will do him the honour of declaring that he left Málaga poorer than when he entered it." [185]

A contemporary report illustrates the first reactions of some of Málaga's prominent French "collaborators". After the French arrived in 1810, a wealthy landowner in Málaga, organised a banquet for a number of enemy Generals, only to have his country estate attacked and his crops ruined soon afterwards. The landowner is not named in the report but it may refer to Henri de Grivegnée. He had an estate at Churriana and was a French supporter and his crops where ruined at an early stage of the occupation. Is it not clear if it was remnants of Aballo's forces who wrecked the cotton fields and spinning factories he had set up with William. Some reports say that it was their own workers who fired the crops and destroyed the factories. William later made use of some influence he had with the Duke of Dalmatia which may have stemmed from this banquet or from Sabastiani's and General Soult's reported attendance at his concerts. Many years later these violent events still prompt speculation as to whether this was "Anti-French phobia" or Guerrilla warfare or "social war" or just pure banditry.[186]

But it seems more probable that William was not in Málaga when the popular forces of "Colonel" Aballo took their revenge on *afrancesados* and the French forces occupied the City. A document found in the The National Archives of the UK at Kew, among a sooty bundle of miscellaneous letters simply labelled "Málaga" illustrates Kirkpatrick's difficulties after the French arrived and reveals his real nationality.

On 30th June 1810, the King's Privy Council sitting in the Council Chambers in Whitehall in London granted William Kirkpatrick, British Subject, an Order in Council permitting him to reside in Málaga for twelve months for commercial purposes. This is a significant document as it confirms that William remained a British Subject even while he acted as United States Consul. William's legal council in London, Messrs. Scott Butler and Co., justified William's return to Málaga on the grounds that he had large concerns in the City on the entry of the French and that he could not abandon them without "occasioning the total sacrifice of the same".[187]

As Kirkpatrick had to apply to the British Privy Council for permission to return to the city in 1810 it seems likely that he joined those who fled to the three British Warships in the harbour, when the French arrived in the City, and then found that the Royal Navy would not allow him to return. Despite the risks of long delay, he had to apply to the Privy Council in London rather than the Foreign Office or local British military commanders for permission to re-enter Málaga. The British naval blockade of Napoleonic Europe had been declared by an Order in Council and only that body could grant an exemption and allow a safe passage though the Royal Navy blockade.

By February 1811, with the City under occupation, Kirkpatrick appears to have changed his tactics. The French privateer *Sebastiani*, the Genovese crew still inflamed by the heat of their action, "still hot guns and the French Flag raised", brought five prizes into the harbour of Málaga. The captured vessels had sailed from the "free ports of Andalusia". There was the brig *Areñón*, the frigate *Palafox* and the English ship *Little Robert*, which had made sail for Havana. Their cargoes raised much excitement when they were auctioned at the French Consulate. Doña Rubio-Argüelles notes that 112 pipes of wine on board the *Little Robert* "belonged to the party of Guillermo Kikrcpatrik".[188]

This is a further indication of Kirkpatrick's activities at this difficult period. His reactions to passing events demonstrate that he was both pragmatic and enterprising. His attempts to circumvent French restrictions and the British blockade show Kirkpatrick was still trying to trade during this difficult period. As this consignment was shipped from one of the "Free Ports", it suggests that he was either no longer living in Málaga in 1811 or that he had found a way to maintain his trade by smuggling contraband shipments from the smaller ports along the coast, using his contacts in Adra and Motril. Like his brother John in

Ostende, his scruples did not prevent him from a little smuggling when the opportunity arose. We don't know if this is an isolated example or merely an occasion when he was discovered and lost his contraband. But it is an interesting reflection of William's personality and surely tells us that he had lost any respect he may have held for the French and was content to flout their draconian regulations. Financial necessity may well have driven him to try to run through their sanctions.

His British permit of June 1810 was still valid even if he had retuned to Málaga as soon as he had it to hand. We know from his Consular correspondence with Washington that he was writing from Málaga on 25 November 1809, but the next letter on the file is dated October 1812 and describes his arrest by the French authorities towards the end of the occupation. He must have obtained the British document as a precautionary measure to ensure that he was not stopped and prevented from returning to Málaga. But he had no shipping news to report and no secure means of getting his letters to Washington through the blockade.

His efforts to regain access to his warehouses in Málaga were an expression of his increasing desperation. His substantial international business was in ruins. The credit worthiness of his name was rapidly diminishing; his enterprises in Málaga during the occupation were the cause of envious and nationalistic outrage, and he was in serious trouble.

In an attempt to curb his brother's expenditure and authority, Napoleon had not allowed Joseph to sell English merchandise captured in the ports of Andalusia. William would have been only too well aware that his stock was in French controlled warehouses and at grave danger of total expropriation. Clearly he was anxious to return to the city and use what influence he retained to secure his working capital. He must have believed that if he returned to Málaga, his local standing, and pro French sympathies, would enable him to recover his belongings or obtain compensation if the authorities had already sold them off.

The date of his application to the Privy Council suggests that he feared that his property would be sold soon after the French arrival, anticipating that they would not scruple to capitalise on their conquest. And indeed in July 1811, Napoleon exasperated at the ineffectual rule of his brother, gave General Soult permission to sell off the expropriated goods on his own account.[189]

William was certainly in Málaga at the end of 1810. There is evidence in the City Archives of the extent of his collaboration with the Occupation authorities. In that year Kirkpatrick applied to Don Mariano

Luis de Urquijo, the Minister for the Secretary of State, for a license to manufacture acids and other chemical products, in partnership with Don Domingo Díaz. Doña Rubio-Argüelles comments that this was a "Machiavellian"[190] financial move; an opportunistic bid on Kirkpatrick's part to take advantage of funds his foreign status had protected, and also of the general state of war that was afflicting the country. Doña Rubio-Argüelles reaction is an interesting example of 1950 Spanish views of a foreigner's response to the Spanish War of Liberation. It may also reflect an understandable nationalistic approach to the Colonial nature of many of the foreigner's enterprises in early 19th Century Spain. This initiative, linked to William's soap manufacturing enterprise and extensive cotton schemes and lead mining and refining, justify his reputation as a leading Spanish industrial pioneer.

In the event King Joseph Bonaparte granted licenses to the two early industrialists, and exempted them from duties on the importation of tools and instruments. He also granted them use of Royal lands for the exploitation of the lead mines, an important element in their project. This appears to be Kirkpatrick's first foray into lead mining and processing.

In 1810 Francisco Bejarano notes that "Grevignee, Kilpatrik and Rersin" operated a factory for spinning and weaving of cotton.[191] William Maclure states that Kirkpatrick had substantial commercial contracts with the French occupation authorities in Málaga which were in addition to his employment of some 3,000 local people in cotton production and manufacture.[192] This is further evidence of their joint co-operation with the local authorities and is supported by Maclure's reports that the authorities in Paris became alarmed at the large quantity of cotton goods being produced in Málaga. Paris suspected that cotton was being illegally imported into Spain from Egypt, and then passed off as local produce. The French imposed restrictions on Spanish produced cotton which gravely affected their business. Kirkpatrick himself declares that he was ruined by the French invasion. But Maclure says he was their "partisan", so he prospered for a while during the Occupation until business collapsed under the French controls, and the complicated business transactions he had carried out on their behalf, unravelled.

Henri de Givegnée's position was less ambiguous. As a native of the semi-independent Walloon City of Liege his status was clear. Liege had been under French military occupation from 1789 and he would have been recognised as a strong *afrancesado*. For many years the Kirkpatrick family business enterprise had been largely directed towards France and the Pays Bas, with exports of Spanish produce to John Kirkpatrick and his predecessors in Ostende, which was the seaport for the rich agricultural areas connected by the Ostende-Burg-Ghent canal leading to the prosperous heart of Flanders. [193]

Records in the Provincial Archives in Málaga show that Henri became one of the principal suppliers to the Army of Occupation but was left with large debts on their departure. Many other leading citizens took the same route. Diego Quilty became chairman of the French controlled Ayuntamiento Constitutional, and others would have taken their lead from him.

At this point we need to confront William Kirkpatrick's support of the French regime of Joseph Bonaparte and try to explain the background to what seems to be a collaborative, unpatriotic, foolhardy or merely expedient course of action. Was he a genuine supporter of Napoleon's visions of a greater France; numerous great European nation states ruled by diverse members of the Bonaparte family? We know that there was discord within the French Army between those whose sympathies lay with the Republican cause, and the Bonapartist loyalists, and the opportunists like Soult. It seems unlikely that he was as romantic about revolution as some of the English lyrical poets like William Wordsworth, who greeted the French Revolution with the verse:

> Bliss was it in that dawn to be alive,
> But to be young was very heaven! — Oh! times, —

As Dr. Brian Jeffreys comments :

"After all the French were not mere foreign conquerors, but also to some extend representative of the ideals of the French revolution; in these ideals might perhaps lie the means of a reformed Spain. Many, looking at their inept and corrupt government, chose to accept the occupation. They became known as *afrancesados,* and because they put liberal ideals before blind patriotism and because in the event they proved to have chosen the losing side they were often attacked in later years. Fernando Sor was one of them. - - In general, however, justice is done today to their liberal and progressive ideas and it is recognized that they were not collaborators in the odious sense that the words has acquired since the Second World War but in fact patriots of a more sensible kind than the supporters of Fernando, whose government later turned out to be the worst fate that Spain could undergo."[194]

James Monroe, the United States Secretary of State, strongly supported the ideals of the French Revolution, although as US Minister to Paris between 1794 and 1796, he had to maintain George Washington's neutral stance to the French during their war with the British.

Liberal Spain's enthusiastic welcome to Joseph Bonaparte gives a further perspective to William's Francophile position. Málaga had a reputation as a liberal city although this political and social stance was stronger in the large foreign community than among the townsfolk themselves. The new "uninvited King" was a man of easygoing disposition who, in other circumstances might have succeeded as liberal constitutional monarch. That was certainly the part he tried to play. He saw himself as a welcome and even legitimate successor and an improvement on the discredited line of Bourbons who had ruled Spain for too long.

Progressives were inclined to see Joseph's rule as somewhat benign and those Spaniards he met found him amiable and well intentioned towards their country. But it was this amiability and his reluctance to exploit his position for the benefit of France which brought his downfall. In contrast the Supreme Junta in Seville had earned great unpopularity by pressing Andalusia for all the revenue it could extract to support Spanish resistance. But it was also seen as dishonest and militarily incompetent. While much of the rest of Spain rejected Joseph's attempts to earn a measure of popularity, Joseph's reception in progressive Andalusia was triumphal.

Joseph conceived the invasion of Andalusia as a grand gesture to show his brother that he too was a great general. Under the experienced Napoleonic soldier Marshall Soult, the invasion went well and the French troops, sometimes in conjunction with *afrancesados* Spanish forces, were welcomed with acclaim in many cities. Seville soon fell and at the end of January 1810 the remnants of the Supreme Junta fled to Cadiz leaving the city to the *juramentados* or those who willingly took the oath of allegiance to the "uninvited King", Joseph Bonaparte.

From Seville "his progress was extended to eastern Andalusia, and everywhere the story was the same. At every town and village the mayors and priests came forward to present their allegiance, girls spread flowers in front of his horse, and the people cried *"Viva el Rey!"* Of his entry into Málaga, Count Miot recorded that he was received "with a welcome far surpassing anything that could have been expected from a loyal and submissive populace. The streets were strewn with flowers, and hung with tapestries; at the windows elegantly dressed ladies waved their handkerchiefs; shouts of joy, cries of *"Viva el Rey"*, were to be heard on all sides. A ball and a bullfight were given in his honour. If ever Joseph Napoleon could have felt that he really was King of Spain, it was at this moment."[195]

In Granada his reception was also ecstatic. Michael Glover comments:

"There was no doubt that in both cities he was regarded as a saviour, but whereas in Seville and Cordoba he had been hailed as a deliverance from the excess of the Supreme Junta, in eastern Andalusia he was looked to as a bulwark against French oppression. Having found his advance obstructed by some half-armed bands of peasants, General Sebastiani had taken the opportunity to levy a contribution of five million reals on Granada and twelve million on Málaga. To supplement this, Sebastiani and his subordinate commanders embarked on a systematic pillage, for their own benefit. By confiscation and extortion, money and works of art were constantly looted and sent back to France by the wagonload."[196]

We can see how William Kirkpatrick, with his wife and daughters in Paris, and the French at the gates, was inclined to take their patronage and make what business he could. His City, its leading citizens, his father-in-law and their social and business associates, all compromised their allegiance to the concept of Spanish sovereignty. Sustained by what was left of their romantic views of republicanism they all became *afrancesados* to one degree or another.

But Napoleon was not about to allow his brother to enjoy his moment of glory. The French exchequer was desperate for funds and was not prepared to pay for Joseph's extravagances or indeed any more than two million francs a month for the bare pay of the army in Spain. Joseph was under continuing pressure to extract increasing bounty from the country he had been set to rule.

Napoleon believed that his brother was over anxious to placate Spanish opinion. He thus worked behind his brother's back to regain personal control of events in Madrid and beyond. He appointed his own Generals to rule a partitioned Spain with executive powers which exceeded those of the nominal King. His officers were ordered to implement a rigorous regime of extractions which further ruined the country.[197] The unscrupulous looting by these generals led to growing disillusionment among those elements who had initially supported the concept the French appeared to represent. Oaths of fidelity were forced from the populace by the imposition of severe financial and other penalties on those who refused.

Major General Lord Andrew Blayney had the misfortune to be captured by the French and taken through Málaga as a prisoner. He had been in command of a British expedition to liberate the City which had failed spectacularly. His description of Málaga paints a miserable picture of the French occupation.

> "Though [Málaga} still retains some external appearance of its former prosperity, it is but the insubstantial shadow of the departed reality. The total cessation of commerce and the losses consequent on the war have produced innumerable bankruptcies, and universal distress; the port ... has lost all appearance of commercial life, some fishing boats alone being seen in movement, while a few ... feluccas and other small vessels are laid up rotting. What a contrast with the former flourishing commerce of this city, whose annual exports were valued at half a million sterling. . . such have been the desolating effects of the unprovoked and unjustifiable invasion of the French."[198]

After a long march through the mountains from his refuge in Gibraltar, the Spanish General, Francisco López Ballesteros, raided occupied Málaga in the spring of 1812, taking the French garrison by surprise. The occupying forces retreated to the Castle of Gibralfaro. But with strong French forces hard on his heels, Ballesteros only stayed long enough to plunder the City of its remaining resources of recruits, specie and supplies before heading back to towards Gibraltar. General Ballesteros finally liberated Málaga in August 1812. It is calculated that by 1817, the French merchants of the city had lost some 40% of the wealth they had owned in 1765.[199]

Although de Grivegnée and Company prospered during the French occupation enjoying contracts for the provision of supplies to the French forces[200], their identification with the occupying authorities, and in particular with their Consul, led to their eventual downfall. It is clear that the French left without paying their dues although their Consul seems to have been able to transfer his own funds to Paris. Their difficulties are also confirmed by other comments about the plight of the Gallegos and de Lesseps families.

Even *afrancesados* who had aided them received harsh treatment from the departing Napoleonic legions. José Gallegos makes a particular point of describing the plight of the de Grivegnée y Gallegos family in Málaga. He had anticipated leaving the bulk of his very considerable fortune to his friends in Richmond, Virginia, but "the distressed situation in which my relations in Spain appear to have fallen of late" prevented him from being as generous to those around him as he would have liked. José also stipulated in his Will that his executors and heirs should ensure that the interest payments on the mortgages he owed to Henri should instead be paid to his sister Antonia and her family in Málaga and thus escape Henri's creditors.[201]

Given his Republican American connections and his friendship with the *liberale* Cipriano, Count de Teba, and what we can make of Henri de Grivegnée's position, it is likely that William genuinely favoured the French as promising an end to the *Ancien Régime* of old Europe and the best hope for a Republican outcome in Spain. But he too was in severe difficulties by the time the French left Málaga. On 23 June 1812 the United States Consul for Alicante wrote as follows from Gibraltar to Secretary of State James Monroe.

> "I have been distressed to learn that Mr Kirkpatrick Consul at Málaga had taken an active part on favour of the French ever since their occupation of that port and having accommodated them with all the effectives his house could command, they have brought in a very large account against him, and not having any more to give they have throw him and all his partners into Prison where they have remained on the last advices from Málaga, how the Consul of one nation can accept of any commission from another I very much doubt but if he has been so imprudent he has indeed paid very dear for it."

By the autumn of 1812 William's French sympathies must have turned bitter. On the 24 October he managed to get a dispatch to James Monroe, United States Secretary of State.

This letter tells of his arrest by General Marazin in the last days of the French occupation of Málaga, and his protest to Marshall Soult, the Duke of Dalmatia, French Commander in Chief in Seville, who ordered his release. He reported that he was arrested at the instigation of M. Proharam, the French Consul in Málaga, over a debt owed to him by Kirkpatrick's trading House.

William enclosed a letter, in French, which shows that this debt was paid off by Grivegnée & Company through a complicated financial swap of liabilities between the French consulate and Grivegnée &

Company, with funds eventually being drawn from the French Foreign Ministry in Paris to satisfy the Consul's personal dues from Kirkpatrick.

Grivegnée & Company had been supplying goods to the French authorities, but had not been paid.

Kirkpatrick paid the French claims against him by offsetting them with the balance owned to his father-in-law by the French Consulate. This reduced the amount the French owed to Henri and transferred the debt within the family. As the original debt had been to the personal account of Proharam, this sharp operator, surviving where his predecessor had met a dreadful fate, faced with the imminent collapse of French rule in Spain, had adroitly transferred his dues from a local Spanish creditor to the French State in Paris. Kirkpatrick's bill was settled and de Grivegnée transferred his credit with the departing French Consul to benefit of his son-in-law. This seems only to have settled a small part of the amount Henri was owed by the French, but the arrangement secured the release of William from the Gibralfaro, the grim fortress that overlooks the city.

This complex offset arrangement reveals something of the political situation in Málaga at this point and about the Kirkpatrick's trade during the Occupation. It also shows the way bills of exchange were settled by extensive swaps of credits and liabilities, involving numerous parties. This is also shown by some of the exchanges and offsets Kirkpatrick, William Laird and others discussed over quite small amounts involving modest trade in local produce. Bills of Exchange had to act as currency and the prevalence and complexity of these exchanges are evidence of the way they constituted working capital for trading concerns, in the absence of liquidity in Central Bank money supply and sophisticated banking arrangements. An example is an instruction to a ship's master or supercargo to ensure that, if he is able to sell his cargo in Gibraltar, he should ensure that he receives either cash or bills drawn on Málaga to enable him to load there with fruit and wine. Such bills drawn on Málaga would be discounted or cashed by Merchants in Málaga, thus making a transferable form of credit.

Meanwhile Doña Francisca Kirkpatrick and her daughters and nieces had been restricted by Napoleon's police and could not get permits to leave France.

> "Mrs Story and her four little children, also captured by a privateer, were liberated in December 1813, as likewise 'Madame Kirkpatrick' with her four children and two nieces, who had been residing in Paris."[202]

This reads as though Madame Kirkpatrick had been captured by a privateer but we know that she and the girls had been in Paris staying with her sister Catherine de Lesseps so the "likewise" refers to their liberation, not to the adventure with privateers, which seems to have been Mrs Story's fate. Madame Kirkpatrick eventually crossed the English Channel to London at the end of 1813 where they stayed until the spring of 1814. This would have been an occasion for the girls to perfect their English and meet their Kirkpatrick and Escott cousins and enjoy the relative freedom of London after the constraints of living as foreigners in Napoleon's Paris. Her expenses, and those of her daughters and nieces, are listed in the detailed accounts Juan De Lesseps presented to William Kirkpatrick some twenty years later. The Kirkpatricks and their cousins the Neumans seem to have been unable or unwilling to pay these long outstanding debts, due to a prominent member of their own extended family, suggesting that money remained scarce.

William was in Málaga in May 1814 where he was reporting on local events to James Monroe, the United States Secretary of State and was still there in October when he wrote to his cousins in Dublin, and sent them samples of local produce and asked for help in promoting his business.

We know that Kirkpatrick was considered an active partisan of the French during the Occupation but whether this was out of conviction, business pragmatism or his view of Washington's best interest is as yet unclear. He collaborated during this period to the extend of applying for manufacturing licences for chemicals and mining concessions and supplied goods to the Occupying Forces. He is accused of making the resources of his trading house available to the French. But his attempts to avoid French controls in Málaga by continuing his wine export trade through the "free ports" suggest that business came first. He must have been aware of his brother's smuggling activities in the Channel Islands and beyond, and was sufficiently disillusioned with the French to try to circumvent their restrictions. With their departure and the re-establishment of Spanish governance there was an awkward period of adjustment. His delicate political position may have been mitigated in the eyes of the Spanish by the rough treatment he had received from the French before they departed and he seems to have avoided the worst of the fall-out from the bankruptcy of Grivegnée et Cie. which ruined his father-in-law.

# 12. The Years of Tribulation

William Kirkpatrick must have looked to his last reserves to see him through the next few years. Relatives in Ostende were in similar straights and his London associates had been engaged in lawsuits. This would have been the point when he pawned what family silver had escaped the clutches of the French. Málaga was in a pitiable state after the ravages of the French occupation, General Ballesteros's earlier expropriations, and the predations of the guerrilla bands. The French had emptied the city coffers, cleared the churches of all their treasures and extracted all they could squeeze from the townsfolk. Food was in short supply as the countryside was denuded of men and the fields lay fallow. In the two years between 1812 and 1814 the Town Council was re-assembled with a new constitution which reflected more liberal views and set about managing the recovery of the City.

Institutions had to be renewed and social divisions reconciled. Part of that process was a careful listing of the citizens who had dealings with the French occupying forces. Doña Ángeles Rubio-Argüelles lists hundreds of Málaga residents who swore an oath of fidelity to Joseph Bonaparte. These range from senior officials in the city administration, clerics, and the local military and from generals to sergeants. William Kirkpatrick, as a foreign national and Consul is not among their number, nor is Henri de Grivegnée on this list, although he is shown as one of two "Consuls" in the employ of the French sponsored Royal Council on the 11 April 1811. The worthy Don Francisco Gallegos, Fanny's uncle and a cleric at Málaga Cathedral, is shown as one of those who had taken the oath of fidelity to Joseph and was now repenting.[203]

The Municipal Archives in Málaga hold a series of denunciations against those who sided with or aided the Occupying power. Although William is not mentioned, he seems to have been imprisoned by the Spanish officials of the "Regencia del Reino" over the end of November and into December 1812. The Málaga Municipal Archives holds two documents concerning his terms of confinement. He complained to Senor don Pedro Labrador of being troubled by the discomfort of his daily lodgings. But the governor countered by stating that the City had observed the conduct of the Consul of America during the occupation by the French and the way he had gone to the houses of the Senior French Officials with the contents of the vegetable garden on his country property.

The Spanish Mayor had little sympathy with William's objections to being lodged with soldiers, saying that it was not true that he is inconvenienced daily and, anyway, the whole city was suffering since the departure of the French. His were deemed unjust solicitations, particularly in the light of his behaviour to the Nation and his neighbours.

This sets the scene for the events that then unfolded and beset William and doubtless prompted his move to Motril. It may even be that the accidental death of his wife Fanny was not quite what it seemed. She must have been very distressed at the loss of their social standing and financial security and even more so at the disasters that befell her father, Henri de Grivegnée, and her sisters and nieces.

William's French sympathies had caused him many problems with the "patriots" despite his own diplomatic status and that of his brother Thomas. But María José de la Torre Molina takes the view that the investigation of the *afrancesados,* during a process of purification after the French evacuation, was not painful, and a positive attitude was taken of the political conduct of even those who had held important positions in their administration. This reading is echoed by Enrique del Pinto, who states that all were suffered to make plain their degree of complicity with the French occupiers, and no blood flowed in the river.

The attitude of the new Liberal Authorities to *los franceses* was that the collaborators had acted under duress and that in the main their policy was "benevolent". She notes that even those like William Kirkpatrick, who had maintained close relation with the French and their leaders, were not "admonished" during this initial period of liberal reconciliation.

But soon more revengeful hands were at work in Málaga. Henri de Grivegnée was to suffer a series of court actions that bankrupted his family and his company and also the Gallego family, and damaged Kirkpatrick's business too. As Kirkpatrick commented to his cousins in Dublin, the actions of the French had ruined his hopes of financial independence. His plan to establishing his own House and free himself from the association with his aging father-in-law had vanished, along with his ability to adapt his international business to the new trading conditions in a liberated Europe.

Political battles raged between the Liberals and those who supported the Conservative ideals of an absolute monarchy. Ferdinand VII, newly installed in Madrid, was totally unable to restore the relative ease of the years of Charles IV. The economy stagnated and the treasury emptied, all exacerbated by the loss of protected markets in the newly independent South American colonies. In April 1814 Ferdinand abrogated the Constitution of 1812 and a period of reaction and repression soon followed. Liberals were ill-treated and imprisoned and many fled abroad.

In this reactionary atmosphere it took Kirkpatrick some years to rebuild his business and his family remained in the safely of Paris where his daughters completed their education. His export trade would have been hampered by his loss of his personal credit and he may have had unpaid bills of exchange lurking unredeemable in many a European counting house. His brother Thomas had left Hanover, a city also made destitute by Napoleon's excesses and had taken up his post in Málaga as Consul for that great German city-state.

A typical example of the financial consequences of their system of interfamily investment is found in their relations with the Plunkett family. William Kirkpatrick, acting as Guardian, had invested 307,844 rsvs. in Grivegnée et Cie. on behalf of Donna Isabell Plunkett y Cortada, an amount she had inherited on the death of her father Guillermo Plunkett.

Donna Isabella demanded the return of this money, which the Company was unable to pay in cash, and on the 15 November 1815 she was compensated by being ceded the winery of La Tecia, in Jaboneros, a property Enrique had bought in 1792.

A series of legal cases in the files of the attorney, Juan de Sierra, reveals that Enrique de Grivegnée owned a large number of properties around the city and in Churriana. These were used as a form of security for the operation of their various joint businesses. During the years 1814 to 1816 these were either sold or seized by his liquidators to settle his debts.

While the earlier official policy was one of *rapprochement* with those who has sided with the French, we must also suspect that elements in the post Occupation government were not too concerned at the fall of prominent *afrancesados*. This was a period of Absolutist or Conservative rule and previous French supporters and those of known liberal views were in disfavour.

Manuel Muñoz Martín states that the house of Grivegnée et Cíe. was responsible for the provision of food to the French troops at the time of the French Invasion implying that they held the main French Army contract. This was clearly an important issue in the series of events which brought down Henri de Grivegnée. He became the target of the returned Conservative elements. The failure of the French to pay their bills had so weakened his capital position that he was extremely vulnerable to their court actions.

The following is a prime example. On the 14 August 1814, Don Gregorio Casadeball formally denounced Grivegnée & Cíe. to the new Málaga authorities. He alleged that he had bought 999.5 boxes of Havana sugar on instalment from the Company. These had arrived in Málaga in 1810 on the frigate *Rosary* and other ships. This consignments was initially stored in the company's warehouse, but was seized by the occupying forces who claimed that Grivegnée and Cíe. had not paid the colonial [import] taxes.[204]

Don Gregorio solicited in the Judgment that he should be paid for the value of the 999.5 Sugar Boxes from the funds and goods of the Grivegnée House and additionally for the damages that they had caused him and that a punishment should be imposed on the directors of the Grivegnée & Cíe. which would corresponded to the losses actually caused.

Grivegnée & Cíe. alleged in their defence that the boxes of sugar were confiscated by the Occupying Government as a formality and in a legal way  and that they had been returned to Grivegnée & Cíe. by the French, after their initial seizure, as part payment for the items the French had purchased during their time in Málaga as Occupation forces.

The Royal Junta for the Return of Goods Confiscated by the Intruder Government, which sat in Granada, decided on 9 December of 1815 that: "They Condemned Grivegnée and Cíe and its liquidator to refund to D. Gregorio Casadeball 340½ Boxes of Sugar or in its defect, its legitimate value at the time they were given by the Occupying Government to Grivegnée & Cíe. plus all the Costs incurred waiting for the Judgement to be made effective; and, that the House Grivegnée would additionally pay a fine of 100 Duchies. As a Consequence Grivegnée and Cíe. were declared bankrupt and liquidators were instructed to pay an indemnity of 321,465 Reales of Vellón to Don Gregorio Casadeball.

In an attempt to pay off the larger debts, the liquidators of the Society of Gallegos, Enrique Grivegnée, William Kirkpatrick and a don Diego Gazatambide Rivera commenced a law suit again the Convent Hospital of San Juan de Dios for the restitution of the Mother House which had belonged to de Grivegnée before the French troops had seized it and given it to the Convent Hospital. This case was abandoned on the 13 March 1816 at William Kirkpatrick's urgings to avoid the "expenses and misfortunes that a lawsuit brings". The Mother House of the Convent must have been very close to the Kirkpatricks' home in this old street and may even have been the Kirkpatrick y Grivegnée's "stately house".

On the 10th August 1816 the Kirkpatrick brothers went into partnership with William Parkinson. Their joint venture, a Sociedad de Negocios, was named Kirkpatrick, Parkinson et Cíe., and was commissioned to conduct both internal and external trade. Although Parkinson is described as being of Málaga, he would have been a son or nephew of their London clerk and business partner Jeremiah Parkinson. Jeremiah's daughter, Eliza Anne Parkinson, married William Escott Kirkpatrick of Brussels, the son of John Kirkpatrick of Ostende. Robert Stothert Kirkpatrick and his wife Caroline Van Baerle of Brussels named a son William Parkinson Kirkpatrick, illustrating continuing family links with the Parkinsons.

From the timing we must assume that this was Kirkpatrick's way of sidelining the difficulties which had overtaken the house of Grivegnée et Cie., and was a mechanism to continue trading, using their own name and that of their London partners and relations.

In that post Waterloo era, their aim must have been to take advantage of what promised to be a renewed age of European prosperity, and also to re-establish links to the City of London, and their relations and trading partners of the pre-war days. The Articles of Association prohibited the members from participating in other companies or speculation without the knowledge of the other partners and were clearly designed to protect their venture against the disasters overtaking Henri de Grivegnée, and in part William Kirkpatrick, whose varied and lingering debts were proving difficult to clear. Kirkpatrick, Parkinson et Cíe was wound up on 30 October 1819.[205]

In 1813 Doña Francisca and her family returned from London to Paris where they again lodged with her sister, Catherine de Lesseps. It was at this point that Don Cipriano Palafox y Portocarrero, known simply as Colonel Portocarrero, makes his entrance. After the French evacuation of Seville, Cipriano had been ordered to leave his post as commander of the Arsenal and retreat to France with the French forces. The circumstances which compelled him to take this action remain ambiguous. It is probable that he was following the orders and example of his superior Spanish Officers in the Royal Corp of Spanish Artillery, and that in the political confusion of the moment there was no clear alternative legitimate military authority.

Cipriano was in Paris as a Spanish officer serving with French forces and then as a semi prisoner of war. He became a frequent visitor at the de Lesseps' house. It was here that he first met María Manuela Kirkpatrick y Grivegnée and her mother Doña Francisca.[206]

Paula de Demerson has found a letter dated as early as 1813 from Doña Francisca to Eugenio, Count de Montijo, that shows that she tried to intervene to effect a reconciliation between the brothers. This letter implies that the friendship between Cipriano and the older Kirkpatricks had been formed some three years before they met again in Málaga. This says much about William Kirkpatrick's political outlook. Cipriano was a notorious Liberal and probably held the anticlerical views which went with their advanced political theories.[207] In 1813, Cipriano's prospects were very uncertain. Unable to return to Spain, denied his income from his estates and his titles renounced, he was merely another penniless Spanish officer with few prospects other than existing on half pay while the political situation played itself out. Yet the Kirkpatricks' offered him friendship and help in a foreign land when their own situation was also uncertain.

The amity between the Kirkpatricks and the idealistic Spanish Colonel, far from home, wounded and disfigured, must have developed during this time. The Colonel appears to have been in a fragile state, as his allegiance to the liberating ideas of Napoleon's new order were now in sharp conflict with his loyalties to Spain. He was also at odds with his brother Eugenio, the Count de Montijo, who refused to send him his dues from the Teba estates. To the young María Manuela and her sisters he would have been a romantic figure. If we can go by his portrait, he was a handsome man, lithe and military in aspect, but with his good looks tempered by a black eye patch and damaged limbs.

Don Cipriano became a frequent visitor to the Kirkpatrick's houses in Málaga after his return from France. Letters in the d'Alba Archives show that Colonel Portocarrero was staying in Churriana in April 1816. He was in great disfavour with Madrid, well known as a *libérale* and *afrancesado* who had fought for Napoleon. He was on special licence from the King who had given him permission to visit Spain to arrange his affairs with his brother, the Count de Montijo. He was in ill health and suffered from his old wounds and he was in danger of overstaying his permit. That Kirkpatrick entertained such a Liberal outcast with strong Napoleonic views in their own home in Málaga is a strong indicator of Kirkpatrick's own sympathies.[208] The two men must have sought some companionship from their joint troubles and enjoyed their common political views. William Kirkpatrick spent most of his life in Continental Europe and had clearly acquired the wider intellectual outlook of a "modern" man of Europe. The man of 1817 had come a long way from Dumfries and the parochialism of his boyhood in the Scottish borders.

A short personal letter from William to Cipriano survives in the d'Alba Archives. Dated 30 March 1816 it reveals much about their friendship. The subject matter concerns mundane affairs of business, quarantine restrictions, and delayed post from Bernard Henry, the American Consul in Gibraltar. But the tone is interesting. They are clearly on very familiar terms. William uses abbreviations which must be well know to them both. Tellingly he also calls him his "abulo fr y amigo".[209]

María Manuela married the dashing colonel in Málaga on 15 December 1817. In the days when marriage alliances tended to be both socially aspirational and sound financial planning, this marriage was much more than a love match. It was not only a statement that the Kirkpatrick's financial position was still sound in this post-Waterloo period but also signalled his place in society and his political outlook. But the "penniless" colonel was not William Kirkpatrick's first choice as husband of his oldest surviving daughter. William resisted the match and he did not attend the marriage. It was to be a fateful allegiance which changed the fame and fortune of the whole Kirkpatrick clan.

From the beginning of 1818 William was troubled with a different, but more immediate change to his life. During the negotiations with the Montijos over his daughter's marriage settlement, William learnt that he was to be replaced as U.S. Consul. This unwelcome news may have come from friends in Washington or possibly from U.S. citizens in Málaga, as he accused an American in Málaga of plotting to use the bankruptcy of the House of Grivegnée as a way of removing him from the Consularship.

This was to be a testing period for Kirkpatrick. His actions and his dispatches at this time reveal much of the character of the man. He marshalled his lawyer, Juan de Sierra, and all his Spanish friends and Diplomatic colleagues to his defence, and wrote to his U.S. Navy contacts for support as well.

The official reason for his dismissal remains obscure. The newly appointed Secretary of State, John Quincy Adams, removed him from post and appointed George G. Barrell in his place. This Adams was the second son of the former President John Adams who had been instrumental in William's initial appointment.

Adams admits that Barrell's lobbying or persistent importuning for the post irritated him and that he had scolded Barrell. But Barrel had come to the State Department with the recommendation of John Adams, and the younger man seems to have been reluctant to gainsay his father the former President. But James Monroe, the newly elected President, who had taken office on 4 March 1817, also wanted Barrell appointed. This was the President who later was to give his name to the Monroe Doctrine, and secured the Purchase of Florida from the Spanish Crown.

When Monroe was Secretary of State he had numerous dealings with William. These may have influenced his attitude and his final decision. But his papers contain at least one letter supporting Williams's retention in the post. Oliver M. Perry wrote to Monroe on the 5 September, "recommending that Mr Kirkpatrick be continued as consul at Málaga".[211] But it seems that Robert Montgomery's report of 1812 complaining of William's poor judgement and partisanship towards the French finally had an effect.

Writing to his father on the 21 December 1817, John Quincy Adams's comments give a special poignancy to the events around William's removal. This was the point when William's laboriously constructed world seemed to be crashing down. Barrell's appointment appears almost causal, the removal of a confounded nuisance.[212]

> "Your letters of 25 and 26 November, and of the 8th instant, have been received. Of Mr. Mason, the bearer of the first, I have seen much less than I could have wished; and of Mr. Barrell, who brought the second, a little more; for coming not only with your recommendation but with a volume of others all highly respectable, he pushed his importunity to such an excess that I lost my temper with him, for which he was really more to blame than I was. He will get the place that he is soliciting, although there are at least three other candidates as respectable, and two of them nearly as importunate as himself. I remember laughing heartily at the description in

one of Quincy's speeches, of the sturdy beggars for office here at Washington, and I am sometimes strongly tempted to have it reprinted in the form of a sheet almanack, and hang over the mantlepiece of my chamber at the Department, for the amusement of those gentlemen, while I "sit with sad civility and read" the quires of vouchers and testimonials and pathetic narratives with which they support their claims to office, which they have no sooner got than it becomes in itself a new machine for complaint and lamentation and crying claims for more. Of the whole tribe of those door-bursters of public confidence with whom I have yet had to deal, Mr. Barrell was I think the most intrepid and pertinacious, until I found myself in mere self-defence compelled to give him a downright scolding.

Upon which he affected to apologize to me, as being unacquainted with the *etiquette*, and began to bedaub me with flattery, which brought me quite to the end of my patience. I believe he has been as unsparing of etiquette with the President as with me, for when I mentioned his name and showed his papers, the President smiled and directed me to have the nomination of him *immediately* made out, that he might hear no more about it. As this is a piece of secret history, I must ask you to receive it as confidential; for not withstanding all this, I dare say Mr. Barrell was fully deserving of your recommendation and will be a very good officer."

Perhaps James Monroe felt that the time had come for a fresh face or younger man. New American administrations make sweeping changes to officials across a very wide range of posts. Perhaps in American eyes William had become too close to the British, or to the Spanish political hierarchy, although this would seem a useful asset for a port Consul. Their concern could have been that the fallout of the failures of the House of Grivegnée had so tarnished his reputation, that it would affect the dignity of the Consulate and the Reputation of the Republic. But some of the local American community had turned against him or just saw the opportunity to take over a prestigious and profitable post which they thought should be held by an American national.

The tone of the testimonials Kirkpatrick and Juan de Sierra obtained in his defence suggests that William certainly thought that this could best be countered by highly flattering comments about his character. However, the Americans are very practical in these matters and the State Department in Washington may have feared that William was facing, or was likely to face large unpaid bills, and could no longer fund the Consulate and the demands of the U.S. Navy. This view is supported by a letter William wrote to his old friend Commodore Bainbridge, requesting his help, and assuring him that his friends would always find the funds he needed for the Consular post and financial support for the purchase of Naval supplies.

The local U.S. Consul was required to provision the ships of the U.S. Navy or at least provide the necessary credit for the purchase of supplies. He would normally do this by cashing or countersigning promissory notes from the Captains of the ships. If William Kirkpatrick's credit was ruined by the failure of his trading concerns, then his counter signature was worthless, and his value as a Consul diminished. Thus, he made a point of stating that his credit worthy friends would come to his aid, and countersign his Bills issued on behalf of the American Navy or cash them for the funds needed to re-supply the fleet.

The record includes an extract from this letter to Commodore Bainbridge, United States Navy.

> "I have now a favour to ask you, it is briefly this, I have been assured that the misfortunes of my house are meant to be made a handle of the endeavour to get me removed from office, applications have or are intended to be made for the Consulate by an American here, and though I have every confidence that government is too just to think of superseding an old servant who has always supported his Post with dignity and has not been wanting to the Duties attached to his office because his Circumstances are reduced, yet I will infinitely obliged by your enquiring on the Subject, and use your influence to prevent any change being thought of. The Navy has always been promptly and well served, the same will happen hence forward, as I have friends who will come forward with any sums that may be required for their supplies." [212]

On the 25th March 1818 William wrote to John Quincy Adams:

> "The enclosed is duplicate of my last dispatch to your department I have since been honoured with your dispatch of the 12 January in which you are pleased to mention that [it] had been approved that of Mr G. G. Barrell having been appointed to the consulate at Málaga. This however is the first official information that has reached me, I therefore very anxiously wait for your --- advices on the Subject, as I will no doubt learn from the Consul, of my removal from an office I have now held for eighteen years,

during which I have used every possible exertion in favour of the citizens of the United States, on every occasion Supported my Post with dignity, never have been wanting to my duty, as you sir may be confirmed by reference to my Correspondence with your predecessors in the department of State or to the different commanders of the navy who have visited this Port. Should the change have been effected by the means of false representations of designing men, I confide in that Justice so characteristic in the American government, that an opportunity will be afforded me of clearing my character, & making the Detractors appear in a proper light. Mr Barrell had not yet arrived here - -."

William made the most strenuous efforts to avoid this loss of status and income. He certainly had plenty of energy and the will for a fight back and his most prestigious contacts were rallied in support. With his notary, Juan de Sierra, he obtained a long series of commendations and references from the leading figures in Málaga. These included both Civil and Military leaders and other Consuls. In William's own words, obviously translated from the Spanish for the Secretary of State, he sought to

"identity in legal form and previous citations of the Attorney General, the degree of estimation I enjoy in the Place, my conduct, deportment & demeanours. As such I request your Excellency, may cause as Witnesses, to be examined, who can make a deposition on the subject, and be pleased on the degree of approval by way of information to expose what you think fit on the proposed object, delivering to me the original dispatch which I demand in justice and reason."

signed Willm. Kirkpatrick.

William Laird also certifies that Juan de Sierra is a King's Notary of the number allotted to the City and the Military Tribunal and has produced this document "judicially".

The American State Department files contain letters of support from William's brother Thomas as Consul and commercial Agent for the German Duchies of Holstein and Lunenburg, and also from his friend, William Laird, the British Consul, and also the French, Austrian, Prussian Consuls, and Emil Schotte the Danish Consul, Guillermo Rein the Consul General for the Hanseatic States, and the Consul of the Kingdom of Sicily.

These testimonials show the extent to which William had rehabilitated himself after the disasters of the French Occupation and its aftermath. Don Rafael Truxilla de Molina, Knight of the Grand Cross of the Royal and Military Order of San Hermenegildo, [an ancient Visigoth], Major General of the Royal Armies, Military and Civil Governor of Málaga and also Indentent Sub Delegate of the Customs House, and Judge Protector, was careful to qualify his signature by stating that he signed on the advice of the Auditor of the War (Tribunal), his assessor.

Later in the documents he comments:

> " Having seen this dispatch, His Excellency before me said, that he ought to approve and did approve in conformity to Justice the forgoing justification in regard to the Conduct of Willm. Kirkpatrick in the direction of the Consulate of the United States of America, which he had and continues to have in his charge, for leaving apart the unfortunate Occurrences of the failure of the House of Trade in which he was concerned the cognisance of which belongs to the Commercial Tribunal. On the subject of his Character as Consul he has conducted himself with correctness, attention, and friendly Intercourse with the Spanish Authorities in so much that no complaint has even been made or appears against him in the Tribunal of Foreigners or has His Excellency ever noted the smallest defect in his Deportment for which this dispatch is delivered to him in Original and for the Purposes he may require & that he may be furnished on its exhibition with the copies or Testimonies he may solicit."

Other local dignitaries included: Don Fernando Chacón Manrique de Lara, Count of Molina and of Toribio and Brigade General of the Royal Armies who certified that:

> "from times past by friendly Intercourse and communications, William Kirkpatrick - - who is a person of a decent conduct, good life and Customs, exact in the discharge of his obligations and adorned with the best qualifications, on account of which he merits a distinguished Estimation in this city, which in honour of the truth is what I am acquainted with & can Expose and that it may produce the proper effect I sign this in Málaga."

Other signatories were: Don Joseph Argumosa, Colonel of the Royal Armies and King's Lieutenant in this place, Dr Don Joseph Fermin de Tautequi, the Attorney General of the Tribunal of War, and Don Carlos Engracia Carrasco, also a Colonel and Town Major for Málaga.

Don Joseph Mariano de Llanos, Independent director and first founder of the Royal Maritime Company stated:

> "with his right hand placed on the clasp he wears on his breast offering to say the truth on what he might know & might

135

be asked and being on the terms of the Petition on which this dispatch takes its origin, answered that he knows Wm. Kirkpatrick, Consul of the United States of America in the Kingdom of Granada residing in this Place which employment he publikly attends to with the greatest exactness without it being possible for any fault to be found on which account & being a Person of Probity and well founded Credit in his operations of a regular life, good customs, superior deportment & just administration, he merits the best opinion in this City associating with person of the first Rank & enjoying with them all the consideration which his good conduct entitled him to which is all what he knows and can say on the subject."

All swore on oath and variously described him as a man of the utmost propriety and dignity fulfilling his post with honour.

These letters of vindication were sent to Washington to be laid before the Secretary of State. But it was too late, minds were resolved, and his illustrious testimonials did him no good. Barrell sailed from Boston in mid April 1818 to takeover the Consulate.

On his arrival in Málaga on the 3rd of June, George Barrell delivered his letter of appointment to William, assuming that he had already heard of his dismissal from the Secretary of State. It is clear that William, while well aware of Barrells' imminent arrival, had received no official explanation, nor did he ever appear to receive one. William stated that he would have the Consul's accounts ready in a few days. While William had fought hard to retain the post, both he and Barrel seem to have behaved with dignity. William also requested a few more days in which to clear up outstanding affairs in particular that of a Mr Richardson.

On 10 June 1818, Barrell wrote to John Quincy Adams, to say that he has delayed the handover of the consular business for a few days because William Kirkpatrick wants to:

"finish an affair then on his hands, respecting the Estado of a Mr Richardson, who had committed suicide, and was an American citizen. As the final close to this Business would take place in a few days, and would in all probability give Mr K a commission of about five hundred Dollars, I most cheerfully acquiesced and I desire he would take his own time."

As the Estado was expected to yield $500 commission it must have been relatively substantial for the time, say $5,000 to $10,000.

On the 1 July 1818 William wrote to the Secretary of State in aggrieved tones.

"-- On Mr Barrels arrival here three weeks ago I was honoured with your Letter of the 24$^{th}$ past which I observe with regret, does not contain the smallest reference to the motives that has induced the present [percipient] removal of me from office as I had fancied myself I has some claim to I consequently take the Liberty of again requesting your Kind Attention to what I wrote to you on this Subject on the 26 March last on this subject, an answer to which I shall with confidence expect."

"On the 26 Ult. I delivered over to Mr Barrell in conformity to your desire, the Seals of Office, Arms of the United States, Books of Protests, and others connected to the Consulate, with papers regarding the New Navigation duty, the only unfinished consular Business, that [resides?] under my direction."

"You will find inclosed a note of Disbursement by me on Account of government since the beginning of 1818 amounting to $18.95 cents, from whence is to be [?] $11 for one months advance wages from Hubbert in October last on the discharge from his Brig Zephyr of Charles Colbuson, the other two months I paid as [?] recent at the time of sending him on board the U. S. ship Constellation on which he was admitted as passenger by commodore Shaw, for the small Balance that remains due to me of $7.95 Cents I have taken the Liberty to draw on you at sight, to the order of Wm. Wilson and request that you may honour it. I also beg leave to wait on your wish, the Semi Annual Returns of Arrivals here from the 1 January last but yesterday week which my functions as Consul ceases Consequently any further Correspondence with you Department.

I have the Honour to be, with much respect - your most obedient servant."

A final footnote on the loss of his consular post lies in the records in the Archives in Washington.

"KIRKPATRICK, WILLIAM. July 18, 1818. Málaga; charges against George G. Barrell, United States consulat; circular respecting and offering the services of Kirkpatrick & Co. to transact such business as the Government may require in that place."[213]

While William may have believed that he lost the Consulate because of the Bankruptcy of his father-in-law's business and the scheming of local Americans, it seems that it was merely Barrell's persistence which won the day.

Whether the loss of the Consulate and the social status which came with it hastened William's departure from Málaga is unclear but he retained his old friends and contacts as is shown by his correspondence with William Laird to whom he sent wine and hams. His knowledge of the government would have aided his battles with Spanish officialdom over his lead enterprises. The authorities in Granada exhibited a degree of understandable protectionism that hampered his efforts to export the lead ore from the mines in the mountains behind Adra and Motril.

So at the end of 1817 and in early 1818 we have a contradictory situation. On the one hand William is to lose the Consulate because of the financial implications of his connection to the failure of de Grivegnée. On the other hand are reports of his affluence. He was widely reported to have been a very wealthy father-in-law at the time of his daughter's marriage in late 1817 to Cipriano who, in contrast, is usually called impoverished, although this condition was relieved by the revenues from the Teba estates reluctantly trickled to him by his brother.

In 1816 the partnership of Kirkpatrick, Grivegnée & Co. had been re-constituted and strengthened with new members. From the evidence to hand we must assume that William was able to re-establish his business by combining with his brother Thomas and William Parkinson and others, and that his previous reputation carried them for some years.

A United States Circuit Court report of 1819 reveals that the young Henri de Grivegnée took the place of his father, and that George G. Barrell also joined the business in 1816. The American schemer who fought and won the Consulate came from within William's own circle and had been a trusted associate. This must have been a particularly hard blow for William, and surely hastened his departure from Málaga.

The period to 1820, while fraught with political and business difficulties, appears prosperous enough. But it is illuminating that he started to shift his interests from commerce in Málaga to extracting natural resources in the hinterland. That his mining enterprise was eventually a success says much for his shrewd Scottish foresight. He had felt the wind on his back and decided it was time to move on.

# 13. Last Days In Málaga

William Kirkpatrick's descendent, Don Enrique Kirkpatrick Mendaro, comments that the "patriots" imprisoned William at some point after the French departed and that this was probably the underlying reason for the collapse of his plantations in 1821. It seems that these cotton enterprises were the mainstay of his relative prosperity during the period between 1812 and 1821. His trading name had been compromised by the lingering debts left by the French some eight years earlier and his financial status never fully recovered.

The backlash against Liberalism and King Ferdinand's repressions of the period between 1814 and 1820 caused an outburst of popular anger which led to the Colonel Riegos's uprising in Cadiz in 1820. This wave of suppression was felt in Málaga too and is probably the underlying reason for Kirkpatrick's departure to Motril and the change of his business to mining although the decision was clearly based on the effects of a compounding series of events.

An anonymous diplomat writing on Napoleon III in 1865 comments:

> "But so great had been the respectably of his (William Kirkpatrick's) names, so considerable, that the reputation of his private house long survived the downfall of the firm. Kirkpatrick's salon, enlivened by the three daughters maintained its glory and power of attraction to be  introduced to it was considered – as of yore - an enviable distinction".

> "Kirkpatrick however, in the course of time, became unfortunate in his business, which, the more extensive it grew, was the more heavily affected by the cosmopolitan convulsions, which shook commercial relations for a long time after the restoration of the old system in Europe."

> He closed or sold his warehouses in Málaga and "never opened them again. - - When again he went into business, he crossed to America, where he made some money by working lead mines and where he died." [214]

This is surely a simple transliteration error with Almería, the province to the east of Málaga, where he moved to when he left Málaga in about 1821. But it has led to statements that William died in America.

The bankruptcy of the House of Grivegnée & Cíe., in the period after the French evacuated Málaga, unleashed a cascade of financial disasters on the Grivegnée, Gallegos and Kirkpatrick families. Manuel Muñoz Martín has catalogued a long series of testamentary documents relating to this incident and the events which followed.[215] These undermined William Kirkpatrick's own finances and led the whole family to take legal measures to protect their assets.

Paula de Demerson, drawing on Cipriano's letters, records that María Manuela was extremely distressed at the sudden death of her mother and that her Will left assets amounting to 51,243 rsvs. 17 marevedis to her eldest daughter to be held in trust by Cipriano until his own death. Cipriano is so concerned at his wife's loss of weight that he is taking her to Granada as a distraction. He comments that if he does not do something soon, she will wilt away. While this may be part of Cipriano's continual battle with his brother Eugenio for his dues from his estates, it shows that the Cipriano was in Málaga at this period and had the freedom to move about Andalusia. These letters also show that both he and his wife had access to Churriana and his property in Ardales.

William's sister Harriet Kirkpatrick was not immune from these troubles. A legal document of the 29 August 1816[216] reveals that in 1808, doubtless during his visit to France, she had given her brother William the very substantial sum of £1,700 pounds Sterling. Muñoz Martín calculates that this is the equivalent of 148,923 rsvs. of which £500 was her own property, the balance belonging to her sister Ana and brother-in-law Jacob in Dumfries.

In a testamentary document drawn up on the 29 August 1816 she states that when the House of Grivegnée was declared bankrupt the Court of the Consulate seized all the assets and she received nothing. She stipulated that once this sum was received, half of it would go to her nieces, William's three daughters, and the other half to her godson Carlos Chiquero who was in France.

The death of his wife in 1822 and the consequent fallout from the dispersal of her assets triggered William's final withdrawal from Málaga. This was precipitated by the practice of using the dowries of wives and daughters to capitalize business enterprises. Maiden sisters, aunts and associates deposited their surplus capital in family concerns rather than government treasury funds or city bonds. The result was that a combination of business adversity and death in the family could bring disaster.

The consequent de-capitalisation of his trading enterprises seems to have been the largest contributor to his business demise. It is clear that the Kirkpatrick daughters were anxious to secure their legacy from their mother, not by perusing actions against their father, but by safeguarding their inheritance from their father's creditors. This obliged William to cash or liquate his assets in such a way that they could be shown to be the legitimate property of his wife and thus pass directly to his daughters. But there are strong indications that Kirkpatrick had secured other assets far from the eyes of the Málaga officials. He had started his mining ventures in Motril some years previously. They had the advantage of being well away from prying officials in Málaga Municipality, and perhaps more importantly, they were far removed from the view of envious creditors. But also they were independent of the whims of foreign governments and foreign trade credit. They could operate on local capital which could be found within Spain. His daughter Henrietta was married to a Cabarrús who must still have had banking contacts in Madrid and the Reins and Lorings would have had spare capital to invest.

A study of these testimony documents shows that, while William retained custody of his wife's dowry for eventual dispersal to their daughters, he had also used these funds to buy properties and capitalize his various business ventures.

In addition he had undertaken a large number of inter-family obligations in the form of guarantees and trusteeships for dowries and other securities which he invested in the Company of Henry de Grivegnée et Cíe and into further trading partnerships and arrangements.

When Dona Francisca died suddenly and tragically on the 14 February 1822 her affairs were dealt with under the arrangements which had been drawn up in March 1808 to protect her dowry and safeguard her daughters' inheritance during the troubled times which were closing in on Málaga. Her executors were her father, don Enrique Gallegos, her uncle Francisco, and her brother Enrique, and her brother-in-law Michael Narciso Power, and also her brother-in-law Thomas Kirkpatrick. She left all her assets to her three daughters.

While this arrangement may have served well enough during the French occupation and its aftermath, fulfilling its conditions greatly contributed to the downfall of the house of Kirkpatrick. The need to find substantial sums to pay to his daughters and to liquate assets like the house in Churriana and other inherited properties drew capital from the business and brought calamities. From a testimonial document of 1822 it appears that William too had begun to suffer ill health.[217]

In this document written on 28 June 1822 William himself blamed the past war with France and other incidents for the "great losses in my way of commerce" which have reduced his fortune to the minimum stating that the "goods he has today are totally the property of my deceased wife that have to be divided between my daughters". Kirkpatrick had ceded his finca, El Veedor in Churriana, to his daughters who, on the 17 May 1823 sold it to Francisco Javier Abadía. [218]

William was unable to see to these arrangements personally and delegated the task to William Rein, which he fulfilled on the 20 July 1822. These goods were registered with the Court in Veedor near Churriana and comprised the clothes of his late wife, jewels, household glassware and a team of oxen. As Manuel Muñoz Martín comments, "It was not much".

This time William was unable to seek help from his father-in-law The de Grivegnée family were virtually destitute by 1818. A series of legal actions forcing Henri's bankruptcy had stripped his assets and left his house so bare of furniture that he had abandoned it. The family were only rescued by a gift of 17,000 rsvs. and later another of 20,000 rsvs. which arrived by letter from José Gallegos in Virginia and were declared as additional dowry payments to prevent them also being seized by the Court. These troubles greatly affected his health and he suffered from pleurisy which kept him from attending to his business, Henri died in February 1822, his funeral cost his relatives 3,902 rsvs.[219] William had his independence, but in circumstances so distressing no one could have foretold them even a decade previously.

# 14. 1820 – 1823. The Liberal Triennium and Its Aftermath

The principal Square in Málaga in the XIX Century.

In the years after his marriage Cipriano started to play a prominent role in Málaga society. He may have been encouraged by his ambitious wife who would have been only too aware of the social opportunities which were beginning to open up for her as the Countess, or Contessa de Teba and a member of the family which held the Dukedom of Granada. Although their income was modest, their rank within Andalusian society, rather than Málaga's foreign community, was well above that of her father and mother and their circle of friends. But Cipriano's infamous parsimony must have tried María Manuela and blunted her ambitions.

Dramatic events around the unlikely figure of Cipriano highlight the situation in Málaga at the close of this short period of Liberal control. This family drama must have contributed to William's reasons for leaving the city.

Attempts to re-establish a Constitutionalist or Liberal regime in Madrid during the years after 1814 failed, and Spanish Liberals had to endure an increasingly incompetent and reactionary regime in Madrid. But in early 1820 all that changed dramatically.

In January Colonel Rafael del Riego y Núñez led a military rebellion in Cadiz and prepared to march to Madrid to re-instate the Liberal constitution of 1812.[220]

> "Swayed probably, moreover, by his own bold and adventurous spirit, (Colonel Riego) determined to march upon Málaga, and

endeavour to excite a rising in that city. The column proceeded to Málaga by difficult roads, between the mountains and the sea, its rear being continually harassed by the cavalry under O'Donnell. - - It, however, shook off the pursuing column, and advanced upon Málaga. The governor had collected a few troops, and taken a position in front of the city; but, on the first fire, he retreated, and fell back upon Velez Málaga. The troops of Riego entered Málaga, which exhibited a singular and equivocal aspect. The city was illuminated, and acclamations were heard from the windows; but every door was shut, and no one chose to commit himself in a cause of which such unfavourable omens were already formed. About twelve next day, the columns of O'Donnell were seen approaching. The attack was soon commenced, and an obstinate conflict took place in the streets of the city. The constitutionalists succeeded in repulsing O'Donnell, who took up his quarters for the night about half a league from Málaga. Notwithstanding this success, Riego, in looking round him, could see no hope of maintaining himself in his present position. No movement whatever was made by the inhabitants; and his numbers were quite insufficient to enable him to make head against the repeated assaults of a superior enemy."[221]

Although Riego withdrew from the City and the initial revolt withered out in the Sierra Morena, the spark of revolution had flared to flame throughout the country and numerous insurrections broke out. A military force which was raised to suppress the supporters of the 1812 Constitution, defected to the rebels. The news excited progressive elements in Madrid who rose in support. After violent scenes Ferdinand VII was forced to submit to the Liberal Constitution of 1812 which he had agreed to restore on his accession in 1814 but had reneged on.

Cipriano rushed to support Riego and the Liberal resurgence. In April 1820 Liberals in the City established the Patriotic Confederation of Málaga with the Count de Teba as its president. This must have been regarded as a great coup for the Confederation as by this date Cipriano had become the heir apparent to his brother's Dukedom of Granada, and as such had become a leading local grandee in his own right.

The vice president of the Confederation was the arcipreste del Sagrario of the Cathedral, Francisco López.[222] This presence of a prominent cleric within the Liberal cause was not unusual and other clergymen defied their more conservative and protectionist colleagues by supporting progressive elements. The Kirkpatricks in Málaga appear close to Fanny's uncle Francisco Gallegos at the Cathedral who often officiated at their religious rites of passage. It would be significant, but not surprising, if he too were of the more enlightened wing of the clergy and an indicator of the family's wider political views.

The new governments in Madrid and the provincial capitals moved to re-instate the reforms of 1812-1813 period but Ferdinand refused to act as a constitutional monarch or help build a new system of government. Reaction set in again, anti Liberal revolts broke out, and a French force under the Duke of Angoulême invaded from the north to re assert Bourbon authority. Harsh measures were once again taken against Liberals. Rafael Riego was captured at Jaén near Granada and executed in Madrid on 7 November 1823.

These events were close to home for the Kirkpatricks and they must have feared for Cipriano who was only saved by the vigorous intervention of María Manuela, who pleaded for his life in the face of an angry mob. He was fortunate to escape with his life.[223] Supporters of the Absolutist cause killed many of his associates in a brutal orgy of revenge. The King had Cipriano arrested and taken to the grim headquarters of the Inquisition in Santiago de Compostela. He was later permitted to live under house arrest in Granada where María Manuela had already taken residence.

The "reaction of 1823 far exceeded the scale and ferocity that of 1814. During the next two years thousands of liberals were driven into exile, considerable property confiscated, many hundreds arrested, and scores of executions carried out."[224]

William was 54 in 1820 and may have been tiring of the hustle and bustle of Málaga and the political dangers, intrigues and squabbles among the Consuls. His father-in-law was bankrupted and in ill health. His daughters were married, and the struggle of keeping his finances in order was taking its toll. The earlier somewhat liberal regime had enabled him to recover something of his old position. But the days of his renewed prosperity and quiet recovery in Málaga had come to an end. In 1818 William had been removed from his United States Consular post. He would have lost what was left of his social and political standing in Málaga and his diplomatic immunities as well. He had long since relinquished his acting roles as Hanover Consul General and Oldenburg Consul to his brother Thomas, who was established at No 2 Almería, in the heart of Málaga. His partnership with William Parkinson also came to an end at about this time.

The further outbreak of yellow fever in 1821, surely hastened his departure. The Count de Teba's narrow escape would have illustrated his exposed political position in Málaga and confirmed how wise he had been to move to the quieter political waters of the smaller town of Motril.

Enrique del Pinto states that the following two decades were terrible for Spain and that the Conservative Absolutists again took their revenge on those who had benefited from the French regime and who had shown Liberal tendencies. Kirkpatrick continued his trade in wine and local produce from premises in Adra and developed his interest in the lead mines of the Sierras. But he and his family found that they remained very close to the political troubles that beset Spain over the years which followed.

We can only imagine Williams Kirkpatrick's views of the meteoric rise of his oldest daughter, the brilliant and dynamic María Manuela. For some years after their marriage the couple lived in Málaga and the Count de Teba clearly enjoyed the few years of Liberal administration. Cipriano must have been arrested shortly after the fearful events surrounding the collapse of the government of the 1812 Constitution. The Cabarrús family too were not immune. Their family fortune were successively confiscated and restored as regimes changed and their political fortunes waxed and waned. Amid these alarming events William would have found pleasure at the safer marriage of Carlotta to his nephew Thomas, and the increasing numbers of those grandchildren who were close at hand.

Some reports say that María Manuela was with Cipriano when he was in Santiago di Compostella; others hint that she was in Biarritz, perhaps part of a Spanish refugee set. It was said that she revelled in the freedom that the absence of her puritanical and antisocial husband gave her to enjoy the more sophisticated society of Granada. María Manuela certainly moved to her husband's house at 12, calle de Gracia in Granada and enjoyed the prestige of her position as Countess de Teba and the wider cultural scene of the provincial capital.

María Manuela had entered a very different world from that of the foreign commercial colony in Málaga. She had an excellent French education and had been exposed to a wider political and social world while living with her Aunt Catherine de Lesseps in Paris. Now she was part of the political and Court circle of the Montijos and the wider Portocarrero Palafox and Guzman family. She was to play an increasingly prominent role in a very different setting.

The Montijo House on Calle de Gracia, Granada.

Cipriano's older brother Eugenio, Count of Montijo, had been an infamous womaniser. He was married, but had no heirs. Exasperated by his excesses, his wife Ignacia had obtained a form of legal separation which had scandalised Spain. To her chagrin she was then confined to a convent where she died protesting her lot.

> "on 16 February 1800, Eulalio de Guzmán Palafox, Count de Teba, [Montijo] and his legitimate wife, Maria Ignacia Idiáquez y Carvajal, decided to extend in writing their decision to separate and live each in the house and town they liked, with full personal independence ... convinced that their union could

not continue, because they could not agree on anything, and because they could not expect of this marriage anything but displeasure, discord and resentment.

Family and government alike became alarmed, and to obviate the break between the parties concerned—in spite of their mutual agreement—brought pressure to bear so urgently and efficiently that in the following month they had succeeded in enclosing Maria Ignacia in a Málaga convent. In a letter of March 29, she complained bitterly of having given freedom to her husband "who had the right to demand quite a different solution" while she had to suffer the grievous punishment of seeing her youth fade away in the austerity and desolation of a convent, insufferable to some temperaments, and which will put an end to my life with anguish and despair".[225]

Some of Eugenio's brothers-in-law, the husbands of his numerous sisters realized that her death allowed Eugenio the opportunity to re-marry. This would give them hope of an apparently legitimate successor who would deprive Cipriano and María Manuela of the Montijo inheritance. In this way they planned to gain control of the Montijo estates during the infancy of this newfound "heir". This second marriage astonished those who knew him. He was old and incapable, subject to terrible rages and exhibiting classic signs of a serious breakdown in health and sanity. Subsequent events strongly suggest that his brothers-in-law were manipulating him. They were desperate to see the Montijo fortune kept within the family and away from Cipriano and his "foreign" wife.

The Duke of Parcent, who was married to Eugenio's older sister Maria Ramosa Montijo, set up his (or perhaps his father's) mistress, as the new wife, and some sort of marriage took place. Some say she was a distant cousin, others that she was a cigarillo or even a woman of the streets. If these descriptions are correct, it is extremely unlikely that this alliance would have obtained the Royal approval, thus putting into doubt its validity and certainly complicating questions of inheritance. What astonished everyone even more was the announcement that the new countess de Montijo was with child, and that the birth was imminent.

Cipriano and his wife were entitled in law to attend the birth and thus validate it. But under the terms of Cipriano's house arrest, they were not permitted to visit Madrid. María Manuela obtained permission to visit Valladolid near where the Montijo had estates and property and where the King was in residence. She obtained an invitation to attend a royal ball and as a Grandee was invited to dance in the same quadrille as the King.

This gave her the opportunity she needed to ask for and obtain Royal permission to attend the birth in Madrid. María Manuela's arrival at the splendid Montijo mansion unannounced caused pandemonium. The unpregnant "mother" rushed screaming to her room and there attempted to stage the birth scene with the aid of an orphan boy who had been procured especially for the role.[226] María Manuela made short work of the whole fiction. She was soon in command of the house, the "wife" was pensioned off and the foundling was taken into the family and cared for and well educated. He eventually became a colonel of Engineers in the Spanish Army.

Eugenio died on 16 July 1834 and Cipriano inherited the titles, honours and estates and palaces of the Montijo. Manuela or Mariquita, as she was known in the family, embraced the new life where there was money for everything, fine houses, travel and invitations to Court. As Eugénie later said, they had moved from living on 5,000 francs to living on 500,000.

Perhaps William Kirkpatrick's pragmatic and entrepreneurial spirit was stirred by his daughter's dynamic steps to safeguard her husband's inheritance, further her own prospects and spread her wings on much wider stage. But he would also have recalled past conflicts with his self-willed daughter. Quite how his more puritanical Scots sisters viewed these goings on is quite another matter.

Cipriano took up his seat in the Senate representing his ancestral origins in Badajoz in the Province of Extremadura. Now he was one of the richest men in Spain. But he had learnt parsimony during the hard times in Paris and later in Granada where he had kept his family on a strict budget, and he rejected calls for carriages and ribbons, Paris frocks and society entertainments, preferring the quiet pleasures of home life and like-minded friends. Many writers report that the couple grew apart during these changed times.

We have no indications as to what William Kirkpatrick made of his daughter's new status although his lawyer is careful to call her Excelencia or as we would say in English "Lady" María Manuela. We can image that his Scots upbringing and the relatively modest social circles composed of the families of local Dumfries lairds and country gentry tempered with his own rather Jacobin as opposed to Jacobite views might have caused him to view their status with some distain tinged with private pride at her success. His own semi ironic request for double epaulettes for his

Hanover Consul's post and his lavish musical entertainments show that he was not immune to a little luxury. Doubtless he knew perfectly well that there was no holding back his daughter who is described by one recent English writer as "dynamite"[227].

But he was never to see his daughter and her children again. A mutiny in Madrid forced further changes. Eugénie was witness to an appalling incident in front of the Montijo town house where a Friar was stabbed and she saw the blood leap from the very wound. María Manuela gathered up three of her children and set off for Paris on the 18 July 1834. María Manuela was in Paris for next five years. Their third child, a son named Paco, died in France.[228] William's daughter Carlotta, his sister Henrietta, and many other siblings all died before him.

# 15. The Pioneer Industrialist

On a business and financial level it is clear that William Kirkpatrick's claim to a place in history comes more from his pioneering industrialization in Granada than from his straightforward trading activities in Málaga. Aside from the prominence of María Manuela and fame of Eugenia, his real legacy is in the synthesis of capital and enterprise in developing industrial processes in southern Spain.

When he left Málaga, he first moved up the coast to Motril in the Province of Granada. Here he was near the main deposits of lead and other minerals in the high country behind the town. These mountains are part of the uplands which lie inland along the southern Spanish coast from the heights of Gibraltar to the peninsular of Cartagena. With its extensions, they form the series we know as the Sierra Nevada. These Alpine type peaks are frequently cut by deep river valleys making for separate ranges which have local names. The Sierra de Gador which rises to 2179m behind Motril is such a subordinate range. These mountains of mica-schist and shale are often overlaid by thick limestone caps on which there are large deposits of lead and other ores, in veins or bedding layers between the limestone strata.

Miners found difficulties working these remote areas. There were few if any cart tracks and unprocessed ore had to be brought to the coast by pack mule. The winters were severe and shortened the working year by some months. The rock itself was hard, and progress very slow, making development expensive and time consuming, and the tunnels needed propping and shoring with boards. Water from snow melts penetrated deep fissures in the rocks and needed constant draining.

There are indications of William's early interest in mining long preceding his departure from Málaga. Motril and Adra were to become centres for lead processing and the Kirkpatricks, as pioneer Spanish industrialists, played a vital role in their early development. A year or so later he moved up the coast from Motril to Adra where he was closer to the mining activities in the Sierra Gádor, some 20 kilometres inland. Smelting took place all the way up the coast from Adra to Cartegena and included Motril, Garrucha, Mazarron, and Almería. British commentators remarked that by 1868 the Spanish had made more progress in metallurgy as far as the smelting of lead and silver-bearing ores was concerned, than they had in mining techniques, although the ores had been relatively un-contaminated by other trace elements like antimony or arsenic.

William Laird, The British Consul in Málaga, replying to a letter from his old friend and namesake, wrote on the 17 February 1821:

"My dear Tocayo – I am glad to find by your kind letter of this 5th [February 1821] inst. that you had returned safe to Motril after a pleasant (& I hope) a profitable journey to Granada, may your expectations respecting the lead branch be verified to your utmost wish" –

Again on the 28 February he wrote:

"My Dear Tocayo. I am sorry to see your letter of the 4th with the trouble and vexation you have had about the lead ore, and I repeat my best wishes that success may crown your endeavours towards re opening the Mines."

Cleary William Kirkpatrick had been engaged with his lead mining projects from the previous year at least and his visit to Granada in January 1821 was to discuss them with the Provincial authorities. Laird's reference to the "Lead Branch" suggests that this was to be a separate enterprise from his commercial activities. Whether William was re-opening old mines or mines which already belonged to him but had been closed is unclear. He was back in Motril "that horrid place" according to Laird, in early February. While William was away investigating the mining prospects, Fanny was minding the business in Málaga. In another letter Laird confirmed that he had paid Mrs Kirkpatrick for the hams sent from Motril.

In this series of letters from William Laird, there are references to Kirkpatrick's difficulties with the Spanish authorities over export licences for the lead ore. (See Appendix Two) Their restrictions must have prompted William, and later his nephews, to expand into refining the ore and producing lead products for export. His entrepreneurial talents were still strong, and he pioneered methods of adding value to the raw produce of the small mines of the interior. This was a typically practical solution to the Government's reasonable efforts to obtain maximum tax revenue from the export of unprocessed ore.

William Kirkpatrick's early difficulties with the Spanish authorities probably came from the lack of appropriate legislation and ordinances governing the development and exploitation of the nation's mineral resources. This was overcome by The Royal Ordinance of Ferdinand

VII of 4$^{th}$ July 1825, The Mining Act.[229] Whether Kirkpatrick had a hand in getting this through the Cortes in Madrid is unknown. But in the decade which followed he was able to expand his mining interests and start local processing.

A report in 1844 notes that lead mining on private account in southern Spain was, "for many years nearly confined to the Sierra de Gador, the produce of which from 1821 to 1830, according to Domingo Perez amounted to 380 million of reales, but afterwards declined in consequence of the difficulties of finding a market".[230]

The size of this industry is shown by the demand for coal, which rose to 200,000 quintales in 1845 for lead smelting in Adra and iron working in Málaga, requiring special measures from the government. Coal was also required for bunkering the steam ships which had started to appear at the ports.

William lived long enough to see the transformation of shipping by these small vessels. Steamers had started to appear in the Mediterranean in the late 1820s and he may have travelled on them between the ports of Andalusia. *The Times* of London carried a report of the Steamer *Transit* leaving Málaga on the 2$^{nd}$ June 1836 and arriving at Falmouth in England a few days later. They were soon to play a vital role in transporting copper and other ores to Swansea in Wales for processing and returning with coal for the local smelting processes.

An English visitor to the region gives us a picture of the industrial and mining enterprise William Kirkpatrick pioneered during this period of his life.

Professor D.T. Ansted, M.A., F.R.S., a Geologist and Mining Engineer, toured Spain making geological and economic notes on his travels. Writing in 1854, on his return to London, he commented that:

> "Adra owes all its importance to the smelting-houses for lead, which have directed hither a large part of the lead ore not only from the sierra immediately adjacent, but from various places along the coast, as far as Carthagena. A considerable shipping business is thus produced, as the smelting requires fuel, which is obtained from England chiefly, and the lead, when produced has to be exported. The principal smelting-house includes a manufactory of sheet-lead, lead pipes, shot, red lead, white lead, and even pigments, and was established originally by the late consul, Mr Kirkpatrick, but it is now chiefly in Spanish hands."[231]

While Professor Ansted may be referring to Thomas James Kirkpatrick who was for some years Honorary British Vice-Consul in Adra, the letters from William Laird, British Consul in Málaga, given in Appendix Two, show that William was instrumental in opening up the lead mining and processing trade from the area. Both John Kirkpatrick and his son Thomas James Kirkpatrick, and later his son Alejandro Kirkpatrick, continued the operation of William's mines after his death as is shown in the documents concerning the administration of William's Will.

But the enterprising William Kirkpatrick's mercantile operations spanned a range of activities. This was a busy period in his life when he was very much the entrepreneur, raising capital and buying and selling mines and quarries rather than operating them directly himself. The death of his wife and the loss of his Málaga interests seem to have prompted a renewed burst of activity. He was also dealing in land and starting lead processing works and chemical plants and then selling them on. It is remarkable that Kirkpatrick became the true capitalist once he was freed from the constraints of working with the merchant Henri de Grivegnée and the trading environment of Málaga.

A sample from the surviving legal documentations illustrates his later years.[232] In September of 1829 he was active in Almería, dealing with a Don Miguel Chacon, where he won an Court action over a *letter of import* valued at 2000 rsvs. In March of the following year he was involved with a mine in the Cañada del la Higuera in the Sierra de Gador and in July he had a solicitor handling affairs at a stone quarry at Montefrio in Adra. Later in the same year he granted a Power of Attorney to Juan Kirkpatrick and then another to Don Francisco Cueto. He sold his interest in the Santa Rita mine in the Barranco del Termino de Albondon to Don José Lambek for 5,920 rsvs.

On the 24 December 1830 he asked the Ayuntamiento de Velez de Benaudalla, a few kilometres inland from Motril, on the main route to Granada, for a licence to construct a factory to smelt lead ore. After a dispute over the land William sold the building for 10,000 rsvs.

Other deals followed. In 1831 he received 10,336 rsvs. from a Donna Rosalia Villega and gave a Power of Attorney to Don Yebra Garcia to act for him in matters to do with the well of San Guillermo in the Sierra de Gador, and in August he sold his interest in the San Pedro mine in the same area.

He was still closely involved with the Rein family who also were neighbours in Adra. A vintage advertising poster for *Rein & Co, Málaga* shows them as exporters of raisins, almonds, olive oil, wines and lead, the curious combination of products which they were still offering in the 1890s. Lead in the form of lead acetate was for many years a notorious additive to wine and contributed to many a gouty old age and early death from lead poisoning. The 19th Century popularity of spa treatments, like that later available at the Count de Teba's property at Carratraca near Ardales, on the road from Málaga to Teba, was because they were often successful at expressing surplus lead from body tissue by immersion in hot water for prolonged periods. This relieved the symptoms and prolonged life.[233]

Clearly the Reins of Málaga also saw the potential of the lead industry up the coast from Málaga and encouraged its development with capital investments. The Reins were closely associated with the Loring family. On the 5 August 1831 William committed himself to paying 32,000 rsvs. to Sociedad Rein, which he guaranteed against the mine del Molinero in the Sierra de Gador and the mine del Templo in the Sierra Nevada. Later results suggest that the Sierra Nevada mines were his most productive operation. Further powers of attorney were granted and in January 1833 he bought a white alcohol factory for 9,806 rsvs. from Don Fernando Reyes Perz.

It is probable that William Kirkpatrick became involved in the manufacture of the white or methyl alcohol because he was dealing in fortified wine. White spirit or Methyl alcohol was added to wine and liquors to strengthen the alcohol content. His earlier foray into acid production in Málaga during the French occupation were for the wine industry, as excessively dry or bitter wines were sweetened with a syrup of sugar of lead or lead acetate.

When Eugenio, Count de Montijo, died in 1834, Cipriano set about ensuring the recovery of the family's finances after his brother's disastrous tenure. When Cipriano died in 1839, his careful management of the his estates and properties ensured that he left María Manuela in possession of a great fortune. The French writer and member of the extended Bonaparte family, Comte Primoli, in the *Revue de Deux Mondes* of 15 October 1923 put the Montijo income at 500.000 francs or £20,000 a year. This was a very substantial income in 1840.

Whether his daughter's capital helped William finance the development of his mining enterprises is unclear. But in the period between 1834 and William's death, the Lorings and Reins, and others, must have been only too aware that William's oldest daughter was very likely to have the means to support her father if he defaulted on a loan. Those administering his probate certainly thought that María Manuela was the best source of funds for their development. They may not have appreciated the depth of the coolness between father and daughter.

Miniature of the Empress Eugénie

This is emphasized by William's absence at his granddaughter Eugénie's christening at the Church of the Madeleine in Granada in May 1826. Events may have forced his absence, but it was noted by the Marquise de Campoverde, who stood on William's behalf. His letter to his aunt María Manuela, translated from the French, records the occasion. The Marquise was a Brigadier in the Royal Engineers, and married to Ramona Palafox, the daughter of Eugenio's sister Ramona Palafox y Portocarrero, who had married the 6th Count de Parcent.

Madrid, 9 février 1853

"My dear Maria, I received with great pleasure your letter of January 26, the announcing the coming marriage of our cousin Eugénie with the Emperor of the French. I have announced the news to Ramona and my sisters and we all want this union to bring happiness to Eugénie, which I hope you will have the goodness to say to her on our part. Who would have said to me that, by holding this little girl in my arms to become a Christian at the baptismal font of the Church of the Magdalesia, representing her grandfather, I would mount on the throne of France for a day. God is great!

Be reserved for you as many years as you want. Nephew and friend. "Pepe." [234]

Financial accounts in his testamentary papers reveal that in 1836 and 1837 William was operating at least six mines. These were the San Guillermo, Ohanes, Mano, Flamenco, Consuelo and Animas mines. Juan Kirkpatrick opened or put into production further mines after his uncle's death. These were Enriquita, Carlota, Amelia, Angeles, Loma Alta, and San Sebastian. They were still in production in 1855.

Later there were more mines, Contessa, Rojo, Rosalie and Augustina. Enriquita seems to have been the most productive mine after Nevado and received the largest development expenditure.

From December 1837 to December 1838 the balance of Juan Kirkpatrick's account with the estate totalled 44,627.32 rsvs. and required a subsidy of 15,000 rsvs. from the House of Juan Kirkpatrick to balance the books. In 1838 the production of the mines was worth 6,936 rsvs. with a balance of 23,696 rsvs. coming from the Nevado and No. 1 Enriquita.

These and later investments appear to have been made on a fairly long-term basis. After William's death, Juan Kirkpatrick noted that some of his mines would have to be closed and others developed, but that it would take some time for them to be profitable.

The whole family, including Henriette, María Manuela and Juana del Plink, was eventually involved in the enterprise either as investors or recipients of payments from these enterprises. Although the accounts are clearly presented, the system on which they are based does not give a clear picture of annual profits or losses, as these are probate accounts rather than trading figures. The individual annual production figures for each mine are modest with an average of about 1,156 rsvs. each. Animus mine was the most productive in this period.

Some idea of the scale of operations can be gathered from the accounts of Juan Kirkpatrick who spent some 37,000 rsvs. between 1837 and 1844. The estate of William Kirkpatrick had a cumulative debt of 104,747 rsvs. from 1839 to Dec 1856 when the estate accounts seem to have been wound up. Juan Kirkpatrick also had a balance of 33,490 rsvs. bringing the total debits to 138.237 rsvs. For most years the estate accounts with Juan Kirkpatrick show a large amount to his credit. Whether he really subsidised the operation of the mines by 15,000 to 30,000 rsvs. per year or whether this is a running total of cash held to the credit of the estate is unclear. It seems unlikely that he would continue to subsidise the other beneficiaries for twenty years after the death of his uncle.

Alexander Thomas Kirkpatrick's account with Juan Kirkpatrick ended in Dec 1856 but again the balance is unclear and includes a substantial sum in favour of Juan who may have been acting in his capacity as a banker.

The fact that the family retained their involvement for at least twenty years after William's death suggests that they eventually made money from William's early decision to shift his business focus to mining.

William spent the last sixteen years of his life in Adra where he also involved himself in a Casa de Comercio in the town and small scale agricultural projects and land dealings while continuing to exploit, and buy and sell, his mining concessions. In November 1826 he and a neighbour, Bonifacio Amoraga, petitioned the commandant of the Merchant Navy of the Naval Province of Almería to arrange for the demarcation of two small parcels of gritty useless sandy land, some 60 to 80 yards long and 20 wide adjoining both the beach and the Royal Highway, about which there was a dispute. Quite why this land was of sufficient value to warrant a formal "census" is unclear, although it may have been because it was in front of William's own house. This lay between the house of José Rein and the Scholl Brothers y Grunt y Norte. William would have wanted to secure the rights to the property on the beach between his own house and the sea. Disputes about sea views have a long history in Spain.

His testamentary papers suggest that his house was on the seashore, near the port. His sister Harriet, who had moved to Spain from Honfleur in France, joined him in Adra. She died at his house in 1824. Some years previously she had moved to Málaga where she too had owned a property at Churriana. His second daughter Carlota, who had married her cousin Thomas Kirkpatrick Stothert of Ostende in 1818, died in Adra on 10 of February of 1831. Her youngest child Alejandro stayed on with his grandfather when his father Thomas took the rest of his family back to Ostende.

In later life, William continued his cordial relations with the British Consul at Málaga who sought his help on delicate matters of business. The Laird's letters show a very warm regard for his old friend whom he affectionately calls "Billy", and complains that he was unhappy at his absence from Málaga. The correspondence also shows that Kirkpatrick kept a close eye on consular matters in Motril and Adra, and gave both Laird and his superior Lord Castlereigh in London, confidential information on the performance of John Roman, the local British Honorary Consul. Whatever his official position with regard to the invading French army and its Spanish partisans, William's personal situation was well understood by the British, who did not harbour grudges against him once Napoleon was safely on the far away island of St Helena.

Their relationship is further revealed in another letter; a fine example of Scots ironic humour!

> "the wine you sent me was very <u>Bad</u>. That its all gone, and I must return the barrel to get a fresh supply; in the beginning I thought it too sweet and luscious but others liked it so well that they have been uncommonly active in assisting to consume it, and they have almost persuaded me that it is excellent."

William was still busy with legal affairs in 1836. In March he bought a plot of land in part of the Pago de la Boca del Rio, from Antonio Moreno García, for 500 rsvs. A neighbour was a Ramona Rein.

In August 1836 William Kirkpatrick was still very much in control of his assets although he was making arrangements for them to be managed on his behalf. The detailed arrangements of these contacts give us an insight to Kirkpatrick's world as he approached the last year of his life. He entered into a form of tenancy partnership agreement with Miguel Gutiérrez, a neighbour of Roquetas, to take charge of the factory of Guijarral, and its surrounding lands, for a period of four years. The intention was that Sr.

Gutiérrez would work the land to Williams's instructions, plant it with seed which William provided, and share the grain produced. William had bought this property in February 1826. It comprised five fanegas (about 7.5 acres, at 1.5 acres to the Málagan fanega).

The land in the pastures was to be planted with fig trees, and the more arid sections with prickly pears. Sr. Guitérrez was to take particular care of the produce of the land against theft. The fruit of the land was to be exclusively William's property, and he was to determine the time of harvest.

The mill associated with the property was to house Sr. Guitérrez and his family who were to pay for repairs. He also had to observe "good farmer's law and customs of the region", allow fields to lie fallow as necessary, and sow seed in good time. One stipulation gives an insight into the detailed economics of small scale farming in the period. William was to provide the seed. When the grain was threshed, the tenant was to separate and return the quantity William had provided, the remainder was then to be divided between them. Complicated arrangements were also spelt out about two oxen which were to be used to work the land. These involved also the stipulation that the straw was to go to the oxen. All this was agreed, signed, and witnessed by Francico Carmona, William's agent and manager who also ran his the Casa de Comercio in Adra.[235]

In December 1836 William granted a power of attorney to Francisco Carmona to deal for him in the matter of building on this land and another plot. William stated that he planned to be "absent for some time". The phrase is redolent with foreboding. He must have known that he was unlikely to return to Adra. This was just before he moved back to his daughter's house in Málaga from whence he never returned.

Washington Irving, the American diplomat and famous man of letters, wrote of his visit to William in Adra during his time as United States Minister to Spain. Irving served at the Embassy in Madrid from 1826 to 1829, and was later Envoy Extraordinary and Minister Plenipotentiary to the court of Queen Isabella II from 1842 to 1845.

In a letter dated 15 February 1843 concerning a vice-consular appointment in Adra, he writes:[236]

"I knew the grandfather of the Empress, old Mr Kirkpatrick, who had been American Consul at Málaga. I passed an evening at his house in 1827, near Adra, on the coast of the Mediterranean." [237]

# 16. Final Days

William Kirkpatrick made a Will on the 14 May 1836 at a time when he was gravely ill with a malady which had troubled him for some years.[238] This lingering illness rather suggests that he too suffered from an excess of lead in his system although it does not seem to have affected his mental processes. Lead poisoning is hardly surprising for anyone involved in early lead processing and mining quite apart from what might have been in the wines he doubtless enjoyed, or the utensils used for drinking them from, and the heavy lead content of the glass of that period.

His Will is with the records of his Attorney, Juan de Sierra, in the Provincial Archives in Málaga. He made his daughters and their children his heirs, and he appointed his nephew, Don Juan Kirkpatrick and his agent, manager and man of business, Don Francisco Camora, as his executors. Camora's role was supervised for the family by Matías Huelín who did not seem to hold Camora in great favour. Matías Huelín, an elder of the Brotherhood of Vintners died in Granada. His son, Guillermo Enrique Huelín y Neumann was later heavily involved in the lead mining and processing business in Garrucha, Almería.[239]

This testament reveals details of the William's domestic arrangements and the fate of his daughters. Carlota married to her cousin Thomas Jaime Kirkpatrick of Ostende, had died in Adra on 10th February 1831 leaving five children, Thomas, Maria, Guillermo, Juan and Alejandro all carrying the surname Kirkpatrick y Kirkpatrick. The surprise is that the youngest child Alejandro, who was born in 1829, was living with his grandfather while all the others were with their father in France. William's other daughter Enriqueta had already lost her husband, Don Domingo Cabarrús.

Documents relating to his Will suggest that the Villa in Adra, with its contents, was a comfortable home. The total value of the smaller household items was 3,640 Reales. The d'Alba Archives hold a 1936 typescript which is a transcription of the private section of his Will. This gives instructions on the dispersal of his personal possessions. These pages give a further perspective into his character in the last days of his life.

Listing his bequeaths in order of precedence he states that the Count de Montijo admits that he has a sufficient "mountain of gold", but William gives him his sword, and pistols made by Sinares of Málaga.

To María Manuela he gave his portrait and also a portrait of his mother and the engravings she gave him which were in his rooms. To Enriqueta he also gave a portrait and a dozen silver spoons.

To his son-in-law, Thomas Kirkpatrick, he bequeathed the gold ring which had been given to him by Robert Kirkpatrick of Málaga and Woodford who had died in 1781. William also gave Thomas his tortoise shell snuffbox.

His nephew Juan Kirkpatrick was given his gold repeater pocket watch while his sister Juana of Dumfries was to receive £10 and then £5 then a year for life. These legacies for his Scottish siblings show that the family maintained contact despite years of separation. Harriet Kirkpatrick's presence in Málaga and Adra would have strengthened these links to their brothers and sisters back "home". His library of books went to his grandchildren, the children of his daughter Carlota.

William Kirkpatrick was precise and decided. His clothes were to be donated to the poor men of Adra by Juan Kirkpatrick, but only after Juan had selected any he wanted for himself. Doubtless the odd few sets of Consul's full dress uniforms complete with their gold braided epaulettes would come in useful to an aspirant Honorary Consul.

Then there is a curious bequest. He states that the Communion plate necessary for celebrating the sacraments of Mass, which were with Collman Lambert y Cie. in London, were his property, and that he yields them to these Messieurs or their successors. Coleman Lambert were merchant bankers in the City of London, and heavily involved in large scale trade financing with the United States during this period.[240] This statement suggests that he had deposited the Communion plate with them as security and that he was willing to forfeit them, presumably against unpaid debts or overdue bills of exchange.

This poses a number of questions. The French forces made off with the gold and silver from the churches of Spain, and Málaga Cathedral was stripped of its treasures. Did they pass some of it to William in the dark days of the Occupation as payment for goods and services? Was it shipped secretly to London to secure debts? There is no sign of Coleman Lambert's records surviving in any British Archives, so we will probably never know. He also instructs his executors that, if he dies in Adra, he should be buried in the "Chapel".[241]

The detailed inventory included with his testimony papers lists paintings along with household utensils. As we would expect of a United States Consul, George Washington features but so too does

General Lord Wellington and Frederick the Great. There is also a battle scene – perhaps Waterloo. A man's paintings, especially when they are portraits and are found in his house at the end of his life, say much about his politics and outlook. Napoleon is absent, but Wellington sits with Washington. Perhaps the Paris police were right in 1808 when they believed that he was communicating with the English?

The inclusion of Frederick the Great in his portrait gallery is significant as it surely highlights William's Enlightenment sympathies. Frederick II, Elector of Brandenburg was a moderniser who scorned the pretensions of the old European monarchies and reformed Prussian government and military. A believer in enlightened abolitionism he also supported religious tolerance and rejected the divine right of kings. This all point to an ideal to which William Kirkpatrick may well have aspired and helps explain his probable support for the earlier reformist ideals of the French Revolutionaries.

While obligations and debts may have out-weighted his liquid or easily realizable assets, his daughters inherited the mines which provided substantial revenues in later years.[242] This all indicates that he was able to salvage something from the disasters of 1822 or that he had cannily hidden away assets, as any good Scot would, to ensure their security. Perhaps his enterprise with the mines, and trade from his premises in Adra, and with his friend William Laird, ensured that he lived a comfortable enough old age, although weighed down by the illness which eventually killed him when he was in his 73rd year.

The records relating to the later Administration of his Will are in the National Archives in Madrid. These contain documents signed by William in Adra in December 1836, and show that William only moved into his daughter's house in Málaga later that year or very early in 1837. He died in the morning of the 20th January 1837.[243]

Some reports state that William died destitute. But he was still dealing in land and property within days of his death although some of the arrangements were designed to protect his assets during his absence. He held stocks of wine in Málaga with his brother Thomas, cargoes on a felucca and other business concerns. His wealth may have been considerably reduced, but he was still active and engaged in affairs, and owned valuable assets. Letters to and from his daughters and their husbands and their advisors in the period following his death, and later concerning the administration of the estate, show that his affairs were in difficulties, but that he was by no means destitute. The balance sheet was sound enough on the worth of the mines although the trading accounts may have been in deficit.

The letter from Matías Huelín to the Count de Montijo of the 18 April 1837 gives the current value of his estate as 478,933.31 reales. This included the Villa in Adra, fincas, various plots of land, some with complications of tenure, a stock of iron and wine, other stock in production, furniture and the value of an expedition of the felucca, or lateen rigged trading vessel, the *San José*. These realizable assets amounted to some 80,000 reales leaving a balance of some 16,564 reales to be found in cash, if the main assets, the fincas, and the lead mines were to be preserved for the benefit of the three heirs. Thus William's net estate of some 400,000 reales was valued at something like 300 man-years work of a town based labourer or using Manuel Muñoz Martín's rate of 87.60 rsvs. to the pound sterling about £4,566, a large sum by early 19th Century standards. [244]

These letters reveal also the extent of the Count de Teba's involvement with the resolution of William's estate. We know that María Manuela was a powerful woman who would not have meekly allowed her husband to manage her inheritance. She must have viewed her husband's involvement in her families as both useful and appropriate and a confirmation of his long-standing friendship with the Kirkpatricks who befriended him all those years ago in Paris. Reports of her poor relations with her father suggest that she was content for her husband to deal with his friend on these matters.

We can imagine William Kirkpatrick in the last months of 1836 realising that his end was approaching. His wife, his sister and his favourite daughter were long dead; there was no female family member in Adra to nurse his dying days. Did he board his felucca for the last time to take the short trip by sea to Málaga? Perhaps there was a Post Office Cutter or packet boat or passenger steamer with more comfortable accommodation. Was he carried on board the small craft on a litter or was he able to walk? It seems unlikely that he took the rough post over the hills and valleys to find the comfort of his daughter's final care. We must hope that the Mediterranean sparkled for him one last time and his trip was a reminder of happier days. Did the dockworkers in Málaga recognise the old Consul or had he been away too long. Did they raise a cheer or a jeer or just wave a friendly greeting to the sick old man? We will never know, but it seems fitting that he should end his days where his career began; where he made his name and fortune.

One report said that William died in the United States, another Barcelona, but he died in the cold of a January morning, in Málaga, in the house of his daughter, Henrietta the widowed countess de Cabarrús. Although he retained his British nationality, his real political allegiances remain obscure. His Jacobite ancestry and "liberal education" linked to his wide experience of world events, and his progressive inclinations would have predisposed him to sympathise with the reforms promised under a Napoleonic French regime. His support of the French forces when they entered Málaga may have been ambiguous, but he prospered for a time under their administration, supported by the produce of his cotton plantation at Churriana and the share in the soap manufacturing and other business. But it is a cruel paradox that it was the French who ruined his business.

# 17. Summing Up

Did William Kirkpatrick die a good Roman Catholic? His Will shows that he certainly died a Catholic and asked for Masses to be said. But he did not specify how many nor did he leave special funds for this purpose. However he left modest amounts to the Church. His sister Henriette Kirkpatrick converted to Roman Catholicism as is revealed by her Will. In the previous generation both Robert and Juan Kirkpatrick are shown by their Spanish Wills to have remained Protestants.

Jane Stoddart[245] comments that William Kirkpatrick and all his descendants were Roman Catholic and that a Protestant would never have been admitted, as he was, to the best Andalusian society. But the records of the Presbyterian St Michael's Church, Dumfries shows the marriage of William Kirkpatrick of Conheath to Mary Wilson of Kelton on 22 December 1755 and records their 19 children.

Thus the parents of William of Málaga were married by the Established Church of Scotland, the Presbyterian Church not the Episcopalian or Anglican Church and certainly not the Roman Catholic Church. He must have been brought up as a Protestant and converted to Roman Catholicism later in life, probably at the time of his marriage to Francesca de Grivegnée.

On the question of religion it is notable that when his daughter Carlota married her cousin Thomas Jaime Kirkpatrick, on the 12 January 1818 they had to obtain a Papal Bull or permission and licenses of their holiness because they were cousins and they had to give the commitment that "the children whom they have to be baptized in the Catholic Church". This implies that Carlotta was a Roman Catholic but that Thomas James and thus the Ostende Kirkpatricks remained Protestants.

It is significant that William's parents conformed to the Presbyterian Church rather than the more Establishment Episcopalian Church, unlike their relation, the well-known antiquarian Charles Kirkpatrick Sharpe of Hoddam. Sir Walter Scott recorded that "though residing in the land of the Presbytery, (he) is an Episcopalian and a Tory, or rather an old cavalier, with much of the respect for high family, contempt of the Covenanters, and dislike of democratic principles, proper to that designation."[246] But the Kirkpatricks were shrewd survivors; they "deftly supported the Crown while sending sons to support to the Stuart cause at Killikrankie in 1689".[247]

William used all his family's overseas contacts to obtain the US Consular post at Málaga.

While this appointment had numerous advantages, he must have been partly motivated and perhaps inspired by the revolutionary ideals and anti-English sentiments of the New Republic. This interpretation is supported by his long-standing friendship with Cipriano Portocarrero y Palafox, who had fought to Napoleon's last gasp on the Heights of Chaumont, at the gates of Paris in 1814. These views, the Jacobin ideals of the French Revolutionaries, with their anti-clerical overtones, would seem strongly in conflict with the *Ancient Regime* Scottish Jacobitism of the followers of the "Bonny Prince" Charles Edward Stuart and their longing for a Catholic Stuart restoration.

While William and Cipriano may have had early Jacobin sympathies, their support of the invading French Army suggests that they repudiated the extremes of the Revolution, after the excesses of the Terror, in favour of Napoleon's progressive ideas. By 1823 when Cipriano faced the anti Liberal mob he was still very much a Liberal, but as his daughter Eugénie reveals, her father never lost his enthusiasm for the ideals of Bonapartism.

William left no engraving of Napoleon in the list of his possessions. The paintings in his house at his death are not those of a man of the old order. He celebrated the more enlightened among his great contemporaries. He had the image great Duke of Wellington in his personal gallery, and surely retained his fidelity to the British Crown while remaining a true Scotsman at heart.

He was an enlightened, worldly man of affairs, an innovator, entrepreneur, and a man with an eye for business and profit, numbers and detail; who was passionate about music and enjoyed the company of men of a similar outlook. He had maintained warm relations with two of his daughters and left the turbulent María Manuela his portrait; even though he returned to her the engravings she had given him. Clearly he had a special affection for Alejando, his grandson.

Hippolyte Taine[248] sums up the troubled years William Kirkpatrick lived through: "When we see a man . . . . apparently sound and peaceful habits, drinks eagerly of a new liquor, then, suddenly fall to the ground foaming at the mouth . . . . we have no hesitation in supposing that in the pleasant draught there was some dangerous ingredient". As Cobban says the man was France, the liquor was the Enlightenment and the fit was the French Revolution, but the metaphor equally applies to those of a progressive mind in 18<sup>th</sup> and early 19<sup>th</sup> Century Spain.

Thoughtful men like William and Cipriano and Henri de Grivegnée, and many others throughout Europe and America, were caught up with the ideals of the new age, but many were ruined or imprisoned or worse, and must have been disillusioned by its frightful outcome and its aftermath, the reaction of the repressed and beaten peoples who demanded that they too had their day in the sun.

# Appendices

# Appendix 1

## Comparative Currency Valuations:

In the 18th Century a common labourer in the Royal Mint in Madrid was paid about 3½ reales de Vellón (rsvs.) per day, while those in a more confidential post, such as a watchman, might have earned 6 rsvs. per day. Although the value had depreciated by the turn of the century, by 1810 members of the more organised *partida* or guerrilla bands were paid one reales a day with generous rations.[249]

At this time the rsvs. was a coin minted of an alloy of copper and silver although it was later a copper coin. It was worth half the value of the pure silver *reales de Plata*. The *Reales de planta fuerte* was introduced after 1737 which was then worth 85 *Maravedíes*. The gold *Escudo* (esc.) was worth 16 *reales de plata fuerte*. Málaga seems to have continued to use rsvs., which were valued at 2½ rsvs. to one *reales de plata fuerte*.

Reales de Vellón later became a widely used unit of standard value rather separated from the coinage that had become very diverse. By 1811 after a very poor harvest the price of wheat in Burgos rose from 80 reales a *fanega* (1 to 2 Bushels) in June, to 244 reales by the end of the year.[250] Thus William's net estate of some 400,000 reales was valued at something like 300 man-years work of a town-based labourer or using Manuel Muñoz Martín's rate of 87.60 rsvs. to the pound sterling equal to about £4,566, still a substantial sum by early 19th Century standards.

# Appendix 2

## Letters in the British Consular Service files at Kew

These give some sense of William Kirkpatrick's life after he moved up the coast to Motril and Adra. These are British Foreign Office copies of letters from the British Consul in Málaga, "W. L." (William Laird) to William, his good friend, his "Tocayo.

A letter from Laird, dated 16th February 1821, mentions Mr. Barrill who succeeded William as United States Consul at Málaga in December 1817.[251] William Laird's Consulate accounts were audited by Barrill who countersigned them; a fine example of early Anglo American co-operation that shows that Laird held few grudges against his friend's replacement.

A Consular letter of late September 1816 lists bills of exchange drawn on both Kirkpatrick Parkinson Co. and Kirkpatrick Grivegnée Co., showing that both concerns were active in trade at this time. Difficulties with bills of exchange often appear in these letters. They were then a form of cheque and were the principal means of payment for both private individuals and business concerns.

An 1816 example of these complexities is found in William Laird's letter to London.

He has to make up the sum of £622-16-5d. which he did by sending seven bills drawn on London:

£500 Drawn by Kirkpatrick Parkinson Co. on Messrs James Dikin & Co. of Liverpool payable in London @ 1 ½ % Usance.

£25 by X Webb @ 14% on Alefsrs. Stanger & Liathis

£24-16-3d. By Lieut. J. Ball @ 10% on the Navy Board

£18-8-9d. by Lewis David @10% on ditto.

£16-16sh. My own bill @ 30 % on ditto.

£30-2sh. My ditto @ditto on the (Navy) Vitualling board

£7-13-5d. Drawn by Kirkpatrick Grivegnée & Co @ sight on Wm. Higgins of London.

£622-16-5d. which exactly balances this account.

He comments. "I am sorry to say that not a bill on London could be procured the day on which the money was paid nor on the 25th (the subsequent post) excepting the £500 to prevent further detention.

I have been obliged to trouble you with the other small bills, which although troublesome, have the advantage of being drawn at short. I can't express to you the difficulties I have met with to bring this Business to a conclusion & although you have been deprived of the use of your money for twelve months, you are not only allowed interest, but are the only creditors of Schiave, that will receive not one sixpenny piece. I therefore hope that this settlement will give you satisfaction, & if I can in any shape be useful in future, I hope etc. etc."

The City of London was the clearing centre for huge volumes of such bills that were sent around the world ensuring payment for goods dispatched and service rendered, ships provisioned and Customs and port duties paid out on behalf of ship owners and governments.

Their reliance on this method of cash transfer emphasises the lack of developed Banking facilities in the Málaga at a time when letters of credit were already a well-established form of international payment. This confirms the impression that the insecurity of maritime trade routes and underdeveloped road connections severely restricted the growth of more normal credit and financing facilities in Southern Spain at this time. Thus foreigners with established connections on the Atlantic coast of America, and in Europe, were in a better position to trade, than local Spanish producers and agriculturalists.

This effect on a more domestic level is shown by the remarkable correspondence found at the beginning of William Kirkpatrick's testimony documents; see also the end of Appendix Three. Here Juan de Lesseps, the son of Catherine de Grivegnée and Matthias de Lesseps and a banker in Paris, is lamenting the fact that Bills or IOUs issued in London in 1812 by William's wife, Fanny Kirkpatrick, and endorsed by Juan Lesseps, remain unpaid in 1837. Such instruments of international credit had their domestic uses too.

The 1821 letters from William Laird show that William was engaged in both a wholesale trade in wine by the barrel and in hams - although this may have been a favour for his friend. He was also engaged in trying to export lead ore from mines in Granada. The Consul wrote to William at Motril, (Granada Province) where he first moved when he left Málaga

1. WM KIRKPATRICK ESQ. 17TH FEBRUARY 1821 MOTRIL
    "My dear Tocayo, I am glad to find by your kind letter of this
    5th inst. that you had returned safe to Motrill after a pleasant (&
    I hope) a profitable journey to Granada, may your expectations

respecting the lead branch be verified to your utmost wish.

The wine you sent me I by no means dislike, and although very good of its kind it is luscious to drink by itself for which reason, my next, shall be common sweet wine, not Muscatel. The Hams must come here and I must avail myself of a proper opportunity to forward them by, as the Guardia Costa are taking and Countermanding every vessel belonging to Gibraltar without the smallest opposition being made in our part "enqui venoran a parar estas misus" (sic). God help you my dear Tranyo & believe me to be always yours W.L."

2. WILLIAM KIRKPATRICK ESQ. 28TH FEBRUARY 1821 MOTRIL

"My Dear Tocayo, By yesterday's post I had the pleasure to receive your letter of the 22 inst. Enclosing one for Lord Castlereagh which I forwarded to his Lordship this day.

I believe that you know what I have already suffered by having the Port of Almeria under my charge and you also know the generous principles upon which I have acted by giving up to the Vice-consul the whole of my emolument there, to prevent their doing mean or dirty things, but I have by no means gained my purpose. If Roman has acted wrong, I think he can make no apology, as I directed him in all cases of Doubt to apply to Mr Gorman, whose respectability and integrity are well known, and by following his advice, no error could be committed, he has followed the opinions of others, he must stand to the consequences, but I can give no decided opinion until I see Capt. Jay as Roman writes me, that he had paid the full produce of the wreck – Although it is not my wish to enter in Cabals, nor become a party in intrigue I notwithstanding, consider it my duty to take care, that the orders of Lord Castlereagh, are carried into immediate execution and if there are any just grounds for complaint, against Roman I have no doubt of his being removed: in the mean time Lord Castlereagh's answer will convince Mr. D. Spencer that his name was first on the list sent, and I shall be well pleased that his own letter may produce the desired effect.

I am heartily tired my dear Tocayo of Almeria, and determined hence forward to have as little intercourse with its Vice-consul as possible; exclusive of giving up my fees, I have paid many hundreds of reales of Postages, about disputes, which I could never understand, and its now time (as your brother said) to turn over a new leaf. Before I take the active part in bring matters to a conclusion, I wish to see Capt. Jay, that I may be fully acquainted with the nature of his dispute, and if I can render him any service, you may believe I will most readily do it, observing that I answered the letter he wrote to me, on the same day it was received, directed to the care of Mr Gorman."

### 3. WM. KIRKPATRICK ESQ. 4TH APRIL 1821 MOTRIL

"Captn. Jay having given me some reason to think that you would come this way soon, I delayed replying to your kind letter of the 18th Feb. in hopes of being enabled to discuss the Captain's case verbally, but your obstinacy in remaining so long in that horrid place obliges me to take up the pen. Capt. Jay's complaint seems to be so well founded that it has given me a deal of uneasiness every thing in my power has however been done, to procure him redress, and as Mr Gorman had kindly undertaken the settlement of accounts with Mr Roman, I am in hopes matters will finally be settled to the Captain's satisfaction. The wine you sent me was very <u>Bad</u>. That its all gone, and I must return the barrel to get a fresh supply; in the beginning I thought it too sweet and luscious but others liked it so well that they have been uncommonly active in assisting to consume it, and they have almost persuaded me that it is excellent. With your leisure, I shall be expecting my hams and I hope they are small. As well as that you have recovered my small libranza on our friend Hburol."

### 4. WM. KIRKPATRICK 18TH APRIL 1821 MOTRIL

"My dear Tocayo, I should have delayed replying to your favour of the 9th inst. Until an opportunity had offered of returning the small barrel, had I not observed that our friend Mr Mala Vilasco had only paid you 158 R. On the 2nd February 1820 I paid that Gentleman order to Divereux 248, 24; I have had no transaction with him since and it seems rather strange, that at the expiration of 14 or 15 months, he should only repay one half without assigning a reason, especially as my libranza was for the first sum; pray endeavour to clear up this matter, for although the sum is small, I am determined not to lose it.
I am assured by the Captn. of the Port, that a vessel will sail for Motril in a few days, and by her, I propose returning the Barrel to be replenished; if what you send is as good as the last, I shall be well satisfied, and I think it would be better (should she return) to send the hams by her, as carriage by land, will I suspect add considerably to the price.

If business retains you in Motril it must be attended to, but I sadly mistrust you Billy, and believe me always yours most truly."

### 5. WILLIAM KIRKPATRICK 12TH MAY 1821 MOTRIL

"I write you a few lines purely to acknowledge the receipt of your letter of the 25th Ult. and to inform you of the trouble and vexation I have had with the hams.

As they brought no Gina, and were not on the Register, they could not be admitted to entry, and it therefore became necessary to get them brought on shore clandestinely, which has been at such an expense, as I shall be ashamed to charge: things are not now as they were formally and much precautions are taken to prevent fraud, as would surprise you – I have paid Mrs Kirkpatrick Reals 509 being the amount of Hams, and charges in Motril Let me know the cost of my Wine and pray recover of Mr Melases the 90 R 21 mrs. Believing me always yours most truly."

### 6. WM. KIRKPATRICK ESQ. 2 JUNE 1821 MOTRIL

"My Dear Tocayo, I mentioned to you when here, that I owe no balance to Mr Malta Vilaves of Hbunol, and I grounded my opinion upon the supposition that I had always paid the amount of hams, when I receive them, consequently drew in your favour for the cost of same from hoops (?) paid to Divereaux by his order. I now send annexed a statement of every transaction I have had with Mr Vilaves since the commencement of our correspondence, and you will find that he owes me 40, instead of my owing him 90 l. as stated by him to you. This balance is corroborated by his own letters and libranzas, so that I hope he will make no difficulty about paying it. But if he should (which I have no reason to suppose) means will be found to get the money. I have got a small barrel prepared and when a vessel offers it shall be sent up."

### 7. WILLIAM KIRKPATRICK ESQ. 25TH JULY 1821 MOTRIL

"My Dear Tocayo, I have to acknowledge the receipt of your favour of the 15th inst. And to inform you that Capt. Williams demand from Birmutu (?) 91 l. overpaid in his own tonnage & 37 ½ l. by order of Capt. Ron. for so much over charged: that the 107 l. will be recovered as soon as any English vessel is dispatched, the hams are of no sort of consequence and if no opportunity offers soon, Don't send them, I am very sorry to hear, that the Spanish government has put a stop to the exportation of lead ore. I hope they will soon be sensible of the error and amend it, in which case I shall trouble you with the reimbursement for Aranzini, but I am afraid he wont be allowed to act unless the appointment is approved of by the King. Surely every man has a right to name an agent, where he pleases and it is but reasonable to suppose, that by having a proper Power he might be permitted to act for me without the King's interference especially as his fees wont afford the expenses in Madrid. Pray favour me with your sentiments on this point, the barrel will be sent by first vessel which offers for Motril, but at present there are none."

8. WILLIAM KIRKPATRICK ESQ. 1ST SEPTEMBER 1821 MOTRIL
"My Dear Tocayo. I am sorry to see your letter of the 4th with the trouble and vexation you have had about the lead ore, and I repeat my best wishes that success may crown your endeavours towards re opening the Mines.

Your grievances are however confined to a few, but here we are studious in our endeavours to annoy mankind, and unfortunately we succeed but too well.

You must have heard of a most infamous report (raised no doubt for most particular purposes) of an infectious distemper having introduced itself among us, and in consequence, of all vessels being forced to quit the Mole and remain in the Bay, until further notice. As there is not a sick man amongst the vessels and fewer on Shore, than ever happened at this season of the year, instead of taking in to consideration the effect, we are now deliberating about the cause of the order given, surely this conduct cannot last. God knows when an opportunity may offer of sending my Barrel and I regret it the more as I want the wine, luckily the hams have not been sent. We are told that the reports will be ready on the 8th so that I hope an opportunity may offer for Almeria about that time."

All signed Wm. Laird.

# Appendix 3

## Testament of Guillermo Kirkpatrick Wilson
### *in translation from the Spanish.*

In the name of Our Lord Almighty God. Amen. Note and make manifest all that this public writing of my last will and testament will be seen, as I, William Kirkpatrick, native of the city of Dumfries in Scotland, legitimate child of the legitimate marriage of William Kirkpatrick and Maria Wilson, his legitimate spouse, my parents who are already deceased, may God rest their souls, both were from the city of Dumfries.

I, inhabitant of the village of Adra and, by chance, today resident in this city (Málaga), taken ill and in my sickbed of some graveness, but of sound mind, memory and natural understanding, that Our Lord God has served to grant me, believing as firmly and truly in the articles and mysteries of faith that Our Holy Mother and Catholic Church of Rome has, believes and confesses, under whose Divine faith and belief I have lived and remain so, and stay until my end, a true faithful Catholic and faithful Christian that I am, and fearful of a natural death, just like any other person alive, as true as its doubtful, ignoring the moment of my death, I want to be ready with the proceedings as such a Christian I must practice; and remain one of their servants as a living testament, with the Divine assistance that of course I implore, grant, and command the form and manner of my testament as follows:

Firstly, I entrust my soul to Almighty God who created me from nothing and redeemed as man with the infinite price of his precious blood, life, passion and death, begging to His Divine majesty deigns to forgive my sins and errors so that I can rest in his Holy Kingdom, in which my soul was raised, and the body returned to the land from whence it came in remembrance of its misery.

And when His Supreme will has served to take me from this present life to the Eternal, my body will be offered to the ecclesiastical sepulchre and sacred place, destined by the Government, with the manner of funeral that my executors, have well considered, according to which I have communicated them, to whose address is entrusted, from my last and deliberate will.

I commend by my soul, intention and charges of conscience and pray masses to be willingly undertaken by my executors, who also entrusted this matter, also with the distribution of the alms that may be given by each one, and the deduction of a the fourth part that is held "Colecturía", and of what remains of the celebrated masses, to the priests, at their discretion and freely available to them.

I give alms of eight reales of vellón for the pious works of the bishopric once and for all, and of established favour to the widows and orphans of the military personnel who died in the War of Independence (against Napoleon), the twelve reales forewarned by the Royal Order.

I declare that, on November 2 in the year of 1791, I celebrated my marriage in this city in its parish church of San Juan Dios to Francisca Grivegnée y Gallego, in which marriage we procreated our legitimate children: María Manuela, Carlota Catalina and Enriqueta Kirkpatrick y Grivegnée, of which the first, married to his Excellency Count of Montijo of Teba; the second, who married Tomás Jaime Kirkpatrick, died leaving their legitimate children: Tomás, María, Guillermo, Juan and Alejandro Kirkpatrick y Kirkpatrick, of which the latter I have by my side, giving him assistance and education; his other brothers and sister live in France in the house of Thomas, his father; and the third daughter married to Domingo Cabarrus who was of the neighbourhood and councillor of this Illustrious Town Hall, is today in the state of widowhood and domiciled in this city.

I declare that the aforementioned Francisca Grivegnée y Gallego, my beloved wife, died in this city on February 4 1822, under the last will and testament that together and in accordance with me was held before the notary Juan Feliz Carrion, that was dated 4 March 1808, according to which he made division and partition of their property and estates of the deceased, conventionally and amicably, among the nominees, my three daughters and respective sons-in-law, by public deed and on behalf of Guillermo Rein, of this Trade, my Special Representative, with date in this city July 20 of the year 1822, by which were all these my daughters fully reintegrated as of much belonged to them through maternal and legitimate inheritance.

I declare, I have my domicile, room and dwelling in the said villa of Adra, where I have the house and a plot of land in front of it that I occupy, several parts of the mine and the trade agency that I have established there, aware of everything, my goods and my papers, correspondence and books that as of today is in the charge of my nephew Juan Kirkpatrick and Francisco Carmona, my internship and dependant, both neighbours of that village; the first one is there now and the second, is resident at the moment in this city, (in the event of my death) will give the news and will say everything with the regularity, honesty and good faith that it is characteristic, and deserving of them both, worthy therefore of my trust and good affection.

I declare, I have assisted my daughter Enriqueta Kirkpatrick y Grivegnée, in assisting to their expenses with 500 "reales" monthly, and to my grandchildren, sons of Carlota Catalina Kirkpatrick, my other daughter already deceased, to help with their education, 2,000 francs per annum to be delivered by the hand of Tomás Jaime Kirkpatrick, their father, whose quantities, it is my will, should not to be changed in any way by my death, of the same monthly and annual, payment as specified, leaving them to continually provide, by their own means as I have done, until the general Liquidation, Division and Partition of all my property and estates, but if any of my heirs opposes this my provision, which I hope not, through the filial love that they profess me and fraternal love that unites them, it should be estimated as such relief or Aid that is given in life as "legados" [legacies], "mejoras" [improvements] or other form that more of it place in law, because it comes from my last deliberate will.

The use of the prerogatives and powers as the inheritors, accountants and liquidators of my property and wealth: my brother Tomás Kirkpatrick, Consul of Hanover in this city; my son-in-law his Excellency Count of Montijo and of Teba; to my friends, Matías Huelín and Francisco Carmona; and Juan Kirkpatrick, my nephew, who together and individually, I confer and give more authority, special and full rights as required, for that, verified upon my death, to proceed extra judicially, conventionally and in an amiable way to the completion of a timely inventory of my property and wealth, to its valuation for experts to choose to their satisfaction, to the adjustment and liquidation of my appropriations assets and liabilities; to the partial and general of the one named by my trade agency according to the customs, qualities and circumstances under issue and it is formed, to the perception billing and collection of respect by the result of all I appropriate, and should have where this receipts and guards that are appropriate, covering and also paying whatever it is from his office and responsibility, all to come to stop the state of the final division and partition of the amount of my monies between my heirs: my daughters and grandchildren, to whom I say that the controls are and will be my legal representatives to make and practice in carrying out my desire.

Requesting particularly and specially that the nominees Thomas Kirkpatrick, my brother, and Matías Huelín take appropriate legal care to ensure that capital of my inheritance corresponds with the needs of my grandchildren, in order to always keep and fulfil and complete the desires that suits them best, for which purpose and (taking account of other individuals who may express, their occurrences, anxieties and convexities) I confer this broad authority without any limitation, with free, frank and general administration, power and authority to prosecute, as being necessary: To swear, challenge, test, delete, pay appeal, plead and replace with regard to lawsuits and with relief of expenditure; prohibiting absolutely with respect to my probate, liquidations partial indicated, the general account and partition of my property and wealth, all figures of sound judgment and judicial intervention, since it is to be allocated in a conventional and friendly, way I leave, as coming from my last deliberate wish.

Taking charge of this matter, the nominees, my legal representatives will use in the execution of this, my will, not just at the end of the year that the law grants, but also to give them more time if they have need of it to evaluate with the thoroughness and accuracy that is required of them; and I call for the common benefit of all involved in this matter: my children and heirs.

Appointed by my executors to the same Thomas Kirkpatrick Wilson, His Excellency Count of Montijo, Matías Huelín, Francisco Carmona and Juan Kirkpatrick, to those who themselves, together and individually I confer the necessary power for that, upon my verified death, they (my heirs) have permission to enter into my property and take what they see fit and sufficient; and selling them in public or private auction, with the funds, pay for this, my testament and religious cause, as soon as possible.

In the remaining remnant of all my property, titles, rights, actions and future inheritances, I institute, chose and name appointed by my unique and universal heirs: To Her Excellency María Manuela Kirkpatrick y Grivegnée, Countess of Montijo and of Teba, to Enriqueta Kirkpatrick and Grivegnée, my legitimate daughters, in my marriage to the Francisca Grivegnée and Gallego, my deceased wife; and to Thomas, Maria, Guillermo, Juan and Alejandro Kirkpatricky Kirkpatrick, my grandchildren, head and representation of my other daughter the Carlota Catalina Kirkpatrick and Grivegnée, their deceased mother, born of the contracted marriage to Tomás Jaime Kirkpatrick, so that everything we have, to carry, enjoy and inherit by third parties equal, with the blessing of Our Lord God, who they praise and they entrust; because that is my last deliberate wish.

And thus: I revoke, annul as of no value, or effect all any other documents, codicils, proposals, legacies and powers for the same effect of wills which have been previously made or granted in writing, in word and in another manner and, with subject, to the mentioned testament, which was made together with my deceased wife Francisca Grivegnée, before the notary Juan Feliz Carrion, on March 4 1808, and the recent 'secret testament' (testamento cerrado), which was made in the village of Adra, before the Notary Fernando Ayllon, now deceased, exist there and still remains in my desk so that none are to act, nor make judicial neither extra judicial faith, except that now I want and command is taken, secured, and meets and execute by such my last will, and testament.

In whose testimony I so say, and attach to the undersigned notary and witnesses who are resident in the city of Málaga to 14th May 1836 and I affirm, being present in the form of witnesses: Bro[?] Sarlabos[?], Joaquin Calzado and Joaquin Galindo, a neighbour of this city.

Within the presence of those here to which I add: that the payments to be made to Enriqueta Kirkpatrick, my daughter, during the liquidation and partition of my assets should be 600 monthly instead of the 500 previously stated; and on my death this is my provision approved and signed by my pulse and hand. It is by its presence herein an integral part of this my testament, kept and fulfilled as in the same way and stipulated, as coming from my last and final will.

And I am the undersigned honorary secretary of His Majesty, Public Notary of this number, that with the same witnesses to everything I have been present, I give faith and I know the testator.

Signature: William Kirkpatrick and Juan de Sierra.

NOTES TO THE MARGIN
I give faith [Spanish, to give verification]: that the ballot or memory that the testator (William) Guillermo Kirkpatrick was reserved do for this disposition has been, in effect, formalized by

the same, placing and protocol today of the date in the public register of scriptures my numeral writing; and at the end of this will be included in the consequent effects that I note in Málaga, January 2 1837.
Signed: Sierra.

ANOTHER:
I give 'Hijuelas' of this disposition at the request of executor Tomás Kirkpatrick that heralds the death of the testator in the morning, in Málaga, January 20 1837. Signed: Sierra.
I gave the original of this disposition to the executor don Tomás Kirkpatrick in two dossiers (papers) of the third seal and four of the fourth in its intermediate. Málaga, January 21 1837. Signed: Sierra.

ANOTHER:
I give a copy of this disposition to the part of her Excellency María Manuela Kirkpatrick, Countess of Montijo and of Teba, in two dossiers of the third seal and four of the fourth in its intermediate. Málaga, November 26 1839. Signed: Sierra.

William Kirkpatrick's Testamentary documents constitute a large file in the National Archives in Madrid. The series starts with Antecedentes or authorisation documents, drawn up at his Villa in Adra on the first of March 1836. These include a letter dated 31 April 1836 from M. Lesseps addressed to Monsieur Guillaume Kirkpatrick. This is a very detailed account of sums of money advanced to Fanny Kirkpatrick y Grivegnée and her daughters, María Manuela, Carlotta and Henrietta, in October 1813 through to 1814. Elisabeth is also listed and a Mathilde, as are M. & Mme. Kirkpatrick and another Mme. Kirkpatrick in Honfleur. These notarised accounts are set out in a professional style and in a clerical hand. The signature of the Paris banker Juan (Jean-Baptiste Charles) Lesseps is shaky and perhaps that of an old man. They express the hurt and indignation that a banker might feel when an old and trusted client lets him down. But they may have been prompted by larger events.

John Goldsworth Alger in his book, *Napoleon's British Visitors and Captives* notes that many British prisoners, some of whom had been detained or even imprisoned in France from 1802, left the country after Napoleon's abdication in March 1814. Although they took their French mistresses and children with them, many left their debts behind.

After Napoleon's 100-day return and eventual defeat at Waterloo, the French were obliged to pay the sixty million francs compensation for confiscations of British assets. When these funds were properly allocated, a balance of nine millions remained. The disgruntled creditors of the vanished prisoners believed that it was only right that a portion of the unused balance should be used to pay off their bills which amounted to some £140,000. Eventually negotiations were held from 1837 through to October 1839 but nothing came of their attempts or of a French delegation to London.[252] Juan Lesseps may have had some knowledge of these events in 1836 and have been reminded of his own debts for he set about recovering them from his relations in Málaga.

# Appendix 4

## The Will of Robert Kirkpatrick of Woodford in Essex and previously of Málaga.

**This is the last Will** and testament of me Robert Kirkpatrick of Woodford in the County of Essex, Esquire first I give and bequeath unto my grand niece Mary Craig Wife of Caldwell Craig of the island of Tobago, Esq. a Sum of Two thousand five hundred pounds also to my grand niece Charlotte Aiskill and to my grand nephew Ffauris Aiskill Junior I give the sum of two thousand (five hundred) pounds apiece and likewise give unto my grand nephew Abraham Kirkpatrick (Olinsen?) and John Kirkpatrick Escott the like sum of two thousand five hundred pounds each when they shall have attained the age of twenty one years but if either of them shall happen to die before they attain that age; then my last will is that the said Sum already mentioned to be given to any person so dying Shall be equally distributed between the said Mary Craig, Charlotte Aiskill, Ffauris Aiskill Junior and the survivors of them, the said Abraham Kirkpatrick Sutton? And aforesaid John Kirkpatrick Escott but so not withstanding that any of such survivors in case he should happen to die under the age of twenty-one years as aforesaid shall also equally be divided amongst the said Mary Craig, Charlotte Aiskill and Ffauris Aiskill junior.

I give unto my clerk Jeh. Parkinson for his attention and fidelity in my concerns five hundred pounds and also I give unto my friend Betty Whiteboy now residing with Charles Kirkpatrick, the son of William Kirkpatrick of Dumfries, James Kirkpatrick of Bristol and Sarah Sayne Bovet[?] wife of John Sayne Bovet of Taunton the sum of five hundred pounds a piece and I further give to my friends Ann Allen of [unreadable] Ann Whiteboy, the wife of William Whiteboy of Thinnick? Sarah Shrapnell of Wilvelscombe Mary Escott of Bristol, Ffauris Aiskill son of the aforesaid Caldwell Craig and Robert Simpson[?] apothecary the sum of fifty pounds each and in so give to my friend Richard Workelesly and Sarah Worklesly his sister. The sum of twenty five pounds apiece.

To my devout James Quidley[?] I give Twenty pounds and to Ian Scolly I give ten pounds. They having served me with reliability for many years. And my Will further is that every legacy herein by me given which exceeds the sum of fifty pounds shall be paid in manner following that is to say one fourth part thereof within six months and the remaining within two years after my decease.

Having thus disposed of part of my property amongst my friends and infant relations with respect to the rest and residue of my estate and effects of what nature or kind so ever and where so ever situated I give and bequeath the same to my dear sister Ann Kirkpatrick and my great nephew John Kirkpatrick Escott equally to be divided between them.

Lastly I so revoke all former wills whereto for made and I do hereby restitute and appoint my said nephew John Kirkpatrick Escott and the aforesaid James Kirkpatrick of Bristol to be executors of this my last will and testament In Witness of which I affix my seal this sixteen day of November in the year of our Lord One thousand Seven Hundred and Eighty One.

Robert Kirkpatrick

Signed and Sealed and initialled by the above named Robert Kirkpatrick the testator as his last Will and Testament after the initialisation of these words which the sum of fifty pounds in the presence of us who at his request in his presence and in the presence of both of us have here to for subscribed our names as Witnesses: Sarah Reed, James Reed, Ann? [253]

### Notes on the Will of Robert Kirkpatrick of Woodford in the County of Essex dated 1781 who died on the 4 April of that year

Beneficiaries include:

Grandniece Mary Craig, wife of Clanwell Craig of the Island of Tobago

Grandniece Charlotte Aiskill

Grandnephew Ffauris Aiskill junior.

Grandnephew Abraham Kirkpatrick Sleston or Olsenston or Hewston.

Grandnephew John Kirkpatrick Escott

Jeh. Parkinson "my clerk". This appears to be Jeremiah Parkinson who was thought to be Robert Kirkpatrick's partner rather than clerk as mentioned in the US Consular document. A Parkinson also appears in the name of Robert Kirkpatrick's firm.[254]

"My friend" Betty Whiteboy now residing with Charles Kirkpatrick, the son of William Kirkpatrick of Dumfries, is a beneficiary.

James Kirkpatrick of Bristol is named as an executor of the Will.

A Mary Escott of Bristol is a beneficiary.

His "Dear sister Ann Kirkpatrick" is a residual beneficiary and clearly Robert expected her to benefit by more than £2,500.

Similarly his "dear nephew John Kirkpatrick Escott" presumably the father of his grand nephew of the same name.

The witnesses are Sarah and James Reed who may be the same James Reed who is mentioned in the US Consular documents as a sponsor of William Kirkpatrick of Málaga.

The Craigs appear to have Charleston connections as a Margaret Craig married a Thomas Kirkpatrick in York Co. S.C. in 1778. [255]

Robert was described in his death notice in *The Gentleman's Magazine* of 1781 as a "very confidential merchant in The Spanish trade". *Burke's Peerage and Baronetage* states that Robert Kirkpatrick was the son of Sir Thomas Kirkpatrick, 2nd Baronet, and Isabel, eldest daughter of Sir William Lockhart, Bt. of Carstairs. He was born in 1717 and died in 1781, leaving no descendants. He is shown as "a merchant in Spain". [256] While this may link Robert of Málaga more closely to the main Closeburn line of Kirkpatricks, the evidence from the Wills suggest that Burke's Peerage is wrong. The bequeaths listed in Robert Kirkpatrick's Will and the naming of his sister Anne confirms, that he was the son of the James Kirkpatrick who lived in Cullompton, the grandson of Thomas of Knock, the kinsman of the Baronet of the same name.

# Appendix 5

## Journal of the executive proceedings of the Senate of the United States of America: 1789-1805, entry for Wednesday, January 1, 1800.

The Senate proceeded to consider the message of the President of the United States, of the 31st ultimo, nominating Timothy Pickering, and others, to office. Resolved, That they do advise and consent to the appointments, agreeable to the nominations respectively.

Ordered, That the Secretary lay this resolution before the President of the United States.

The Senate proceeded to consider the message of the President of the United States, of the 20th of December last, nominating Copeland Parker, to office. Resolved, That they do advise and consent to the appointment, agreeable to the nomination. Ordered, That the Secretary lay this resolution before the President of the United States. The following written message was received from the President of the United States, by T. B. Adams, Esq. Page 332

Gentlemen of the Senate:

I nominate William Kirkpatrick, of Málaga, in Spain, to be Consul of the United States at that port, in the place of Michael Murphy, Esq. deceased. JOHN ADAMS.

United States, January 1st, 1800. The message was read.

Ordered, That it lie for consideration.

# Appendix 6

## Letter to Alexander Kirkpatrick, Esq. Dublin
## from William Kirkpatrick.

My Dear Sir,                      Málaga 26 October 1814

I have learnt with infinite satisfaction from my nephew, who had the pleasure of seeing you, in Dublin, a short time ago, that you continue to enjoy good health, and had the goodness to introduce him to several of your merchants in the wine and fruit trade, from which I have great hopes much benefit will result to my new establishment and for which I beg you may admit my best thanks.

Since I had last the pleasure of seeing you in Dublin, I have experienced many ups and downs in the world. I have seen myself completely independent but the French invasion ruined me.

However, thank God, I have again, thro' the assistance of my friends, got upon my legs in a pretty extensive line of business, with every expectation of doing well, which I am convinced you will be glad to learn. When an opportunity occurs of recommending my house, I beg you will not fail to do so to any of your friends in the habit of speculating in this quarter, a word from you may have good effect. I take the liberty of enclosing you Capt. William Fox's Bill of Lading for A.K.

2 Boxes Muscatel Raisons, 1 box of Almonds and two boxes of grapes. Shipment. To your address, on board the brig "Mary" which have the goodness to retain and admit for the use of your own table.

Capt. Foxe will deliver you this on his arrival.

I sincerely wish you every happiness, and with true regards,

My dear Sir

Your most affect. C.G. [i.e. cousin germane showing the relationship with the Irish Kirkpatricks.]

William Kirkpatrick

Kirkpatrick & Grivegnée

*From* Chronicles of the Kirkpatrick Family *by Alexander de LaPere Kirkpatrick.*

# Appendix 7

*A typical bill of exchange from the period. Cited in The Proceedings of the Old Bailey Ref: t17591024-18*

317. (L.) Thomas Usher, otherwise Clark, was indicted for falsely forging an acceptance to a bill of exchange, with the name Anthony Merry thereunto, for the payment of 250 l. and for publishing the same, knowing it to be forged, with intent to defraud Sir Charles Asgill and Co. May 30. 1758. +

The Bill of Exchange: reads:
Laos Deo, Málaga, 5 Feb. 1758.
Exa. per 250 Sterling.
At Usance and half, pay this our first, per Exchange, to Mr Domingo Gneico, or Order, 250. Sterling, value received of the same. Which place to account, as per advice from
Thomas Quilty and Co.
To Mr Anthony Merry, Merchant in London.
Accepted Payable at Sir Charles Asgill's and Co.
Anthony Merry.   [A British Consul in Málaga]

# Appendix 8

## Jean Forbes Kirkpatrick

William's uncle, yet another John Kirkpatrick, settled in the Isle of Man where he married a Jean Forbes. Whether he is the Juan Kirkpatrick of Málaga of the 1730s is unlikely. They had one son, also named John, who was at school in Dumfries. This nephew later helped his uncles, John of Ostende, and William of Málaga, by contributing his portion of the inherited family lands, being two fifths of Nether Glenkiln,[257] towards the final settlement of the debts of their father, William of Conheath. On a tomb, enclosed with iron railings, in the Churchyard of Kirk Christ, Lezayre, 6 miles from Ramsey, Isle of Man, is the following inscription:

"JEAN KIRKPATRICK, WIFE OF JOHN KIRKPATRICK, MERCHANT IN RAMSAY, [Isle of Man] WHO DIED OCT. 26, 1766, AGED 24, TO WHOSE MEMORY THIS STONE, AS A PROOF OF THE SINCEREST REGARD, AND A SACRED TRIBUTE TO WORTH AND INNOCENCE, IS ERECTED BY HER DISCONSOLATE HUSBAND."

QUAM VENIENTE DIE, QUAM DECEDENTS REQUIRO
ET MEAM MORIENS REMINISCES UXOREM." [258]

# Appendix 9

## John Kirkpatrick's Mercantile connections

*from Jan Parmentier, pages 247 - 248, as translated by Gijs Speltincx*
are listed thus:

National:

| | |
|---|---|
| Brussels: | Alexander Ivens for Spanish wine and Jean Sterckx for grain. |
| Tournai: | C. Venture and the Company Williamiez for wine and brandy. |
| Louven: | Company Impense and Jean Marshall, wine and hides. |
| Furnes: | Arsène Joseph Decae for horse beans. |

International, Mainly Anglo Saxon mercantile houses.

| | |
|---|---|
| London: | Gavin Young & Cie, hides. |
| | The Company of Kirkpatrick, Escott and Reed for Banking. |
| | John Parkinson and William Hamilton, East Indies Trade and Madeira wine. |
| Cork: | John Anderson & William Dickson, beef and barley. |
| Ayr: | Peter Lockhart, ship owner and smuggling. |
| Larne: | Matthew Quinn, ship owner. |
| Forres: | James Mackie, Alexander Fraser and James Sunter, all ship owners |
| Swansea: | William Jones, ship owner. |
| Torshavn: | |
| (Faerøes) | Rosenmayer, Flore & Cie, tobacco, wine and brandy |
| Lisbon: | John Cockburn and John Hamilton, wine and hides. |
| Madeira: | Charles Alder, Madeira wine. |
| Barcelona: | Edmund Connelly, brandy |
| St Petersburg: | William Porter & Cie and Hill, Cazillet & Cie, fruit and wine. |
| Salem: | Zacharias Stone, Shipping |
| Charleston: | Adam & William Tunno and Thomas Mulloy, wine and brandy |
| Genoa: | Nicolo Allegretti, East Indies Trade. |

# Appendix 10

## On Board the United States Frigate *Philadelphia*, East of Málaga about ten miles. Monday, August 29, 1803. 259

To James Simpson, Esq.

DEAR SIR, I wrote you from Gibraltar on the 24th instant, mentioning that we should sail the next morning for Malta.

Hearing at the Rock, that two Tripolitains were off Cape de Gatt, made me proceed with all expedition to examine that part of the Spanish coast. On the 26th it blowing very fresh, at 8 p.m. being nearly up with Cape de Gatt fell in with a ship carrying only her foresail, which had a brig in company, under the same sail. It being night, and her guns housed, prevented an immediate discovery of her being a cruiser. After hailing for some time found that she was a vessel of war from Barbary; on which information I caused her boat to be sent on board the frigate Philadelphia with her passports, from which I discovered that she was a cruiser belonging to the emperor of Morocco called Mirboha, commanded by Ibraham Lubarcg, mounting twenty-two guns, and manned with one hundred men. By not making ourselves known to the officer who came on board, he confessed that the brig in company was an American, and had been with them three or four days, was bound to some port in Spain, had been boarded by them but not been detained. The low sail the brig was under induced me to suspect they had captured her, notwithstanding their having your passport, which it must appear from the sequel, was only obtained to protect them from American ships of war. I sent my first lieutenant on board to examine if they had any American prisoners; on his attempting to execute my orders, he was prevented by the captain of the cruiser. This increased my suspicion, and I sent a boat with armed men to enforce my instructions; after they were on board they found captain Richard Bowen, of the American brig Celia, owned by Mr. Amasa Thayer of Boston, and several of his crew, who was taken on the 17th instant, from Barcelona, bound to Málaga, within two or three leagues of the Spanish shore, and about twenty-five miles to the eastward of Málaga. The captain and the crew they had confined below deck, which they always did when speaking a vessel. After making this discovery I immediately ordered all the Moorish on board the frigate, for I made no hesitation in capturing her, after such proceedings on their part, and violation of the faith of passports which ought to be sacred. Owing to the high wind and sea, it took me the greater part of the night to get the prisoners on board and man the prize, which detention occasioned losing sight of the brig. The following morning discovering many divers directions, the day was spent by the frigate and prize in chasing to find the captured brig : about 4 P. M. made her coming round Cape de Gatt from the eastward, standing close in shore for Almeria bay.

Owing to the wind not being very fresh, we were going slow in approaching her ; the greatest exertions were made by lieutenant Coxe, in towing and rowing the prize. Fortunately the wind increased in the evening, and we re-captured her at twelve o'clock at night. The Moors confessed that they came a cruising for the sole purpose of capturing Americans to be sent to Tangier.

I have received a paper from them written in Moorish, which they say is their authority from the governor of Tangier for so doing. I enclose this to John Gavino, Esq. with a particular request to have it safely conveyed to you, that you may be informed of the circumstance and act accordingly. I believe the governor of Tangier is much disposed for hostilities with the United States; the Moorish prisoners accuse him as the sole cause of their present situation. I sincerely hope that the capture may be productive of good effects to the United States with the emperor, who may be assured that if he goes to war unjustly with the United States, he will lose every large cruiser he has, and God grant that it may not in the least prove a disadvantage to you. My officers and self have made it a marked point to treat the prisoners not only with the lenity that is due from humanity, but with particular attention and civility, to impress on their minds a favourable opinion of the American character. That you may receive this information as early as possible, I despatch my boat on shore at Málaga, to request William Kirkpatrick Esq. consul, to send it by express to Gibraltar. I shall be extremely anxious to hear from you, as also for the arrival of Commodore Preble, to receive his instructions relative to the captured ships. I am bound to Gibraltar bay with the prize, but am fearful we shall be detained for want of an eastwardly wind. I am, &c.

WILLIAM BAINBRIDGE Cmdr. U.S.N.

From *Naval Documents Related to the United States Wars with the Barbary Powers. Vol. 1.*

# Family Trees

# Kirkpatricks of Conheath

**Thomas KIRKPATRICK of Knock**
I

I
**Robert KIRKPATRICK** = Henrietta Gillespie
of Glenkiln                        of Craigshield
b. 1678 Garrell [Kirkmichael]
executed in Edinburgh 1746 as a Jacobite

| I | I | I |
|---|---|---|
| **Thomas** = Janet Craig | **Robert** | **William** = Mary Wilson |
| of Craigshields unmarried | **of Conheath** | m.22 Dec 1755 |
| b. March 1737 | b 1739 | b. 1737 |
| | | d. 1787 |

I

I
Mary b. 5 June 1758 m. Thomas Wilson of Edinburgh,
John b. 1 Aug. 1760 d. Honfleur 28 Sept 1828 Merchant at Ostende,
        m. Jane Stothert of Arkland who died in Havre on 22 Feb 1846
William of Málaga b. 24 May 1764 d. 20 Jan.1837 in Málaga
        m. 2 Nov 1791 Francesca (Fanny) Maria de Grivegnée y Gallegos
Thomas b. 25 July 1766 died Málaga on 9 April 1837, no issue (Málaga)
        m.        (1) Dorothea Kilbi
                    (2) m. Juana Plinck y Nagel in Málaga who died on 1 Oct 1809
Jane Forbes b. 18 Sept 1767 d. 21 Dec. 1854, Dumfries
Rose b. 12 April 1770 d. April 1833
Harriet b. 3 June 1772 d. Spain 9 March 1824
Robert b. 24 Nov 1774 d. London. This is not the Robert of Málaga.
Alexander b. 1780 d. 11 Aug. 1814 at Wilmington, South Carolina
        or New York no issue *ref.* J. Campbell Gracie

Of the 19 children born of this couple 10 were stillborn or died very young.

# and the Málaga Connection

I

**James KIRKPATRICK** = Elizabeth Capper
b. 1686 Scotland                Honiton, Devon
Settled in England              Lived in Cullompton
see English Kirkpatricks.       m. 10 Oct. 1692.
Their descendants, Robert, Abraham, John, Anne and Elizabeth
were all connected to Málaga and James to Bristol.

| I | I |
|---|---|
| **John** = Jean Forbes | **Henrietta** = William Kirkpatrick |
| of the Isle of Man | Ballie of Dumfries |
| d. 1787 | d.29 June 1785 |

Sources: Enrique Kirkpatrick Mendaro, Marquis de Placetas,
unpublished family history, *William Kirkpatrick y Wilson*, Anexo V.
J. Campbell Gracie, *Ibid,* from information from Miss Jane Forbes Kirkpatrick.

Note: Some sources show that George Kirkpatrick, who founded the Irish
Kirkpatrick lines associated with Coolmine, was a brother of Robert Kirkpatrick
of Glenkiln and Garrell and of the James who settled in Devon. This James
appears to be separate from the James Kirkpatrick who also settled in the south
of England and founded the Isle of Wight family. Both the Coolmine and
Isle of Wight Kirkpatricks kept in touch with their Málaga cousins, and some
intermarriage took place in later generations.

# Descendants of William Kirkpatrick y Wilson

**William KIRKPATRICK y Wilson**　　　　　　　　=
Born Dumfries, Scotland 24 May 1764
Married 2 Nov 1791 Málaga
Died 20 Jan 1837 Málaga

                        **I**

I            I

**Antonia**　　　　　**María Manuela** =　Cipriano Portocarrero
b. Málaga 1792　　　b. 24 Feb 1794　　　y Palafox Count de Teba
died young.　　　　　m.15 Dec 1817　　　7th Count de Montijo
　　　　　　　　　　　d. 22 Nov 1879　　　d. 15 March 1839
　　　　　　　　　　　in Madrid

                  I

I            I            I

**Francisca** = Duque d' Alba　　**Eugénia Inacia** = Louis　　**Guillermo**
**Paca or Paquita**　　　　　　　**Augustina**　　　Napoleon III　died young
b. 9 Jan 1825　　　　　　　　　　b. 5 May 1826
Numerous descendants　　　　　Empress of France

                  I

I
**Louis Bonaparte y Guzman**
b. 16 March 1856
d. 1 June 1879, Zululand, South Africa.

# and Fanny de Grivegnée y Gallegos of Málaga

**Françoise Maria de Grivegnée y Gallegos** (Fanny)
Born 1769

Died 4 Feb 1822, Málaga

---

| I | I | I |
|---|---|---|
| **Carlota Cantalona** = Thomas James | **Heniquita** = Domingo Cabarrús | **Guillermo** |
| b. 18 Jan 1796     Kirkpatrick | b. 1797     y Quilty, Count | **Enrique** |
| m. 1818 Gibraltar   y Stothert of | d. 27 Oct 1872 de Cabarrús | b. 11 March 1797 |
| d. 10 Feb 1831     of Ostend | Descendants | died young |
| Descendants     b. 1792 Ostende | | |
|      d. 1841 Ostende | | |

Sources:
Don Enrique Kirkpatrick Mendaro, Marqués de Placetas.
Memoir *Respecting the Family of Kirkpatrick of Closeburn in Nithsdale*
Imbert de Saint-Amand   *Louis Napoleon and Mademoiselle de Montijo*,
Hutchinson, London, 1900.
Málaga Cathedral Archives, Sacristy Parochial Baptisms including special small folder Leg 491, No 3. 1822 – 1823 – (Cabarrús.)
Archivo Histórico Provincial de Málaga, Notary Files.
Major General Charles Kirkpatrick, *Records of the Closeburn Kirkpatricks,* The Grimsay Press, Glasgow, 2003

# Guzman, Palafox y Portocarrero

## Descent of the Condes de Teba and de Montijo

Don Christobal Gregorio Portocarrero    =   Maria Fernandez de Cordoba
b. 2 June 1693                                y Portocarrero
Funes de Vilalpando 5th Compte de Montijo.
Ambassador to the Court of St. James, London, Oct 1732
Minister in the Spanish Court
Ambassador Extraordinary to the Elector of Hungary 29 Nov 1741
d, 15 June 1763.

                     I

I
Christobal Pedro PORTOCARRERO    =    Maria Lopez de Zuniga
b. 1728                                    Daughter of Comte de Miranda,
m. 2 April 1747                         Duke of Penaranda
d. 1757                                  born 28 April 1733

                  I

I
Maria Francisca de Sales y Portocarrero   =   Felipe Antonio Palafox y Croy De Havre
6th Comtesse de Montijo                 7th Marquis de Ariza
Born 10 June 1754                      Born 1739, San Sebastian
Died in 1808                          Died 1790, Madrid
A noted Liberal Intellectual

                                                          I

| I | I | I |
|---|---|---|
| Maria Ramona | Maria Tomasa | Maria Gabriela |
| m. José Antonio | m. Fran. Alvarez | m. Luis Palafox |
| de la Cerda, | de Toledo | y Meizi |
| Conde de | Duque de | le Marquis |
| Parcent | Medina Sidonia | de Lazan |
| issue | issue | issue |

Notes: Conde de Parcent associated with the Conde de Teba in supporting Joseph Napoleon in court circles in Madrid.

Ref. *José Bonaparte Rey de Espana 1808 - 1813*, C.S.I.C., There are letters from Eunénie to the Compte and Comptess de Parcent in *Lettres Familières de L'Empératice Euénie,*

Llanos y Torriglia. Madrid 1983. The Marquis de Lazan was a *frère aîné* to don Joseph Palafox-y-Melzi, Capitaine General and defender of Saragossa in 1808. Born in 1780, died 1847. There are references to Don Christobal Gregorio Portocarreo in the *Gentleman's Magazine* for the relevant dates.

| I | I | I |
|---|---|---|
| Maria Benita | Eugenio Portocarrero y Palafox | Cipriano Palafox |
| b.1782 | 7th Conde de Montijo | y Portocarrero |
| m. 1799 | Duque de Granada, etc | Artillery Colonel |
| Antonio Bellvis | b. 12 Feb. 1770 | b. 1784 |
| de Moncarda | d. 16 July 1834 | 8th Conde de Montijo |
| m. le Marquis | Commandant General, Infantry | m. 1817 **María** |
| de Belgida | m. Ignacia Idiaquez y Carvajal | **Manuela** |
| issue | 2<sup>nd</sup> "marriage" unconfirmed | **Kirkpatrick y** |
| d. 1864 | | **Grivegnée** |
| | | daughters, |
| | | Paco and Eugénie |
| | | d. 16 July 1839 |

# The English Kirkpatricks

*(**Not** of New Cross, Isle of Wight)*

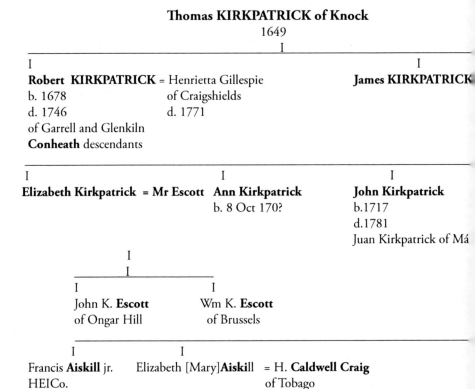

**Thomas KIRKPATRICK of Knock**
1649

**Robert KIRKPATRICK** = Henrietta Gillespie
b. 1678                 of Craigshields
d. 1746                 d. 1771
of Garrell and Glenkiln
**Conheath** descendants

**James KIRKPATRICK**

Elizabeth Kirkpatrick = Mr Escott   **Ann Kirkpatrick**
                                   b. 8 Oct 170?

**John Kirkpatrick**
b.1717
d.1781
Juan Kirkpatrick of Má

John K. **Escott**       Wm K. **Escott**
of Ongar Hill        of Brussels

Francis **Aiskill** jr.    Elizabeth [Mary]**Aiskill**  = H. **Caldwell Craig**
HEICo.                                        of Tobago

The attribution of James Kirkpatrick of Bristol to the family of James Kirkpatrick of Cullompton remains controversial. Some sources suggest that this James was the founder of the "Indian" Kirkpatricks of Hollydale, near Bromley, Kent. But the Wills of Robert and Abraham Kirkpatrick, and of John Escott Kirkpatrick, suggest that James of Bristol was their brother and "head of the family". Others descendants are mentioned in Robert Kirkpatrick's Will: Charles Kirkpatrick, the son of William Kirkpatrick of Dumfries, James Kirkpatrick of Bristol, and Mary Escott of Bristol The reference to "my dear sister Ann Kirkpatrick" as residual legatee with "my dear nephew John Kirkpatrick Escott" confirms the identity of Robert Kirkpatrick of Málaga.

|  | I |
| --- | --- |
| Elizabeth **Capper** | George **KIRKPATRICK** |
| of Cullompton, Devon | b. 1671 |
| m. 30 Oct. 1692, Honiton, | Founded Irish line of |
| Devon | Coolmine and Drumcondra |
|  | d. 1738 Garrell, Dumfries. |

| I | I | I |
| --- | --- | --- |
| **Abraham Kirkpatrick** | **Robert Kirkpatrick** | **James KIRKPATRICK** |
|  | Unmarried | of Bristol |
|  | of Málaga and | Barrister at Law |
|  | Woodford, Essex |  |

| I |  |  | I |
| --- | --- | --- | --- |
| Charlotte **Kirkpatrick** = Francis **Aiskill** |  |  | Daughter  =  **Dr Sherston** |
|  | British Consul in Málaga |  |  |

| I |  | I |
| --- | --- | --- |
| Charlotte **Aiskill**  =  James **Reed** |  | Abraham K. **Sherston** |
|  | Director of Bank of England |  |

| I | I |
| --- | --- |
| Son **Reed** | Daughter = Mr **Elvington**, |
|  | Deputy Gov. Tower of London |

# The de Grivegnée, Gallegos, de Lesseps

Antonio **Gallegos** = [Flora Esturla?]
of Alhaurin el Grande
Málaga

Antonia **Gallegos** = Baron Henri de **Grivegnée**
b. 1751           b. 1744 Liege
d. 1833           Merchant of Málaga
               m. 1766 in Málaga
               d. 1823

Françoise **Grivegnée** = William **Kirkpatrick**    Catherine **Grivegnée** = Mathieu **de Lesseps**
b. 1769          b. 1764 Dumfries,   b. 1774           French Diplomat,
(Fanny)         U.S. Consul        resident of Paris    Count of the Empire
m. 1791        Málaga, d. 1837    d. 1853           b. 1774, d. 1832, Tunis
d. 1821

Theodore **de Lesseps**      Adéle **de Lesseps** = Dr. Jules Tallien **Cabarrús**
Director of Consulates                        cousin of
Senator under 2nd Empire                 Henrietta Kirkpatrick
                                    and the son of Thérèse née Cabarúss,
                                    later Madame Tallien and
                                    then Princesse de Chimay

Referenced and drawn from various sources: (Indicative only)
*Louis Napoleon and Mademoiselle de Montijo*, Imbert de Saint-Amand, Hutchinson,
         London 1900.
Málaga Cathedral Archives, Parochial records.
Will of Joseph Gallego of Richmond, Virginia.

# and Cabarrús Connection

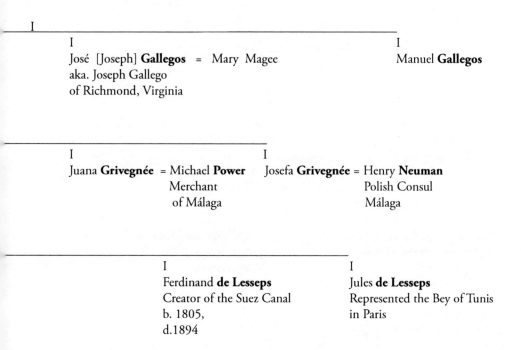

| José [Joseph] **Gallegos** = Mary Magee | Manuel **Gallegos** |
| aka. Joseph Gallego | |
| of Richmond, Virginia | |

| Juana **Grivegnée** = Michael **Power** | Josefa **Grivegnée** = Henry **Neuman** |
| Merchant | Polish Consul |
| of Málaga | Málaga |

| Ferdinand **de Lesseps** | Jules **de Lesseps** |
| Creator of the Suez Canal | Represented the Bey of Tunis |
| b. 1805, | in Paris |
| d.1894 | |

# The Descendants of

**William KIRKPATRICK y Wilson**     =
Born Dumfries, Scotland 24 May 1764
Married 2 Nov 1791 Málaga
Died 24 Jan 1837 Málaga

I

| I | I | |
|---|---|---|
| **Antonia Maria Ann** | **Maria Mañuela** = | Cipriano Portocarrero |
| b. Málaga 1792 | b. 24 Feb 1794 | y Palafox, Count de Teba |
| d.y. | m.15 Dec 1817 | 9th Count de Montijo |
| | d 22 Nov 1879 | d. 15 March 1839 |

| I | I | I |
|---|---|---|
| **Thomas Kirkpatrick** | **Guillermo Kirkpatrick** | **Juan Kirkpatrick** |
| Provincial Governor | b. 6 December 1824 Málaga | b. 12 Nov. 1826, Motril |
| In the Philippines | m. 1868, Ma. Antonia | d. 22 Apl. 1846 |
| | O'Farrill Montalvo | at Segovia Military Academy |
| | d. Havana 26 Feb 1877 | |

I

| I | I |
|---|---|
| **Guillermo Kirkpatrick O'Farrill** | **Concepción Kirkpatrick O'Farrill** |
| b. Havana 8 April 1870 | = Alfredo Escobar |
| General of Artillery | Marques de |
| = Ma. Victoria O'Donnell y Vargas | Valdeiglesias |
| Marquesa de Altamira in Madrid | in Madrid |
| 30 May 1900. | |
| d. 7 January 1952 Madrid | |

**From whom descends**
**Don Luis Kirkpatrick O'Donnell, Baron of Closeburn,** b. 19 August 1910 Madrid;
m. Blanca Mendaro 2 February 1933
**Don Enrique Kirkpatrick Mendaro, Marques de Placetas,** b. 17 May 1943
m. 11 October 1969, Granada.

Sources:
Don Enrique Kirkpatrick Mendaro, Marques de Placetas.
Málaga Cathedral Archives, Sacristy Parochial Baptisms including special small folder Leg 491,
No 3. 1822 – 1823 – (Cabarrús.)
Archivo Histórico Provincial de Málaga, Notary Files.
Major General Charles Kirkpatrick, *Records of the Closeburn Kirkpatricks,* The Grimsay Press,
Glasgow, 2003
David R. Ringrose, *Spain, Europe and the "Spanish Miracle, 1700-1900".*

# Carlota Catalina Kirkpatrick y Grivegnée

**Françoise Maria de Grivegnée y Gallegos**
Born 1769

Died 4 Feb 1822, Málaga

| | | |
|---|---|---|
| I | I | I |
| **Carlota Cantalona** = Thomas James | **Henrietta** = Domingo Cabarrús | **Guillermo** |
| b. 18 Jan 1796 Kirkpatrick | b. 1797 y Quilty, Count | **Enrique** |
| m. 1818 Gibraltar y Stothert | d. 27 Oct 1872 de Cabarrús | b. 11 March |
| d. 10 Feb 1831 of Ostende | Descendants | 1797 |
| Descendants b.1792 Ostende | | |
| d. 1841 Ostende | | |

I

| | |
|---|---|
| I | I |
| **Alexander Kirkpatrick** = Maria Gimenez | **Carlota Kirkpatrick** = Conde Guitaud |
| b. 26 Jan 1829, Adra | |
| British Vice Consul, Vera | |

I
I
I
I

**Tomas Kirkpatrick Gimenez**
**Alejandro Kirkpatrick Gimenez**
**Guillermo Kirkpatrick Gimenez**     **with descendents**
**Encarnación Kirkpatrick Gimenez**
**Carmen Kirkpatrick Gimenez**
**Carlota Kirkpatrick Gimenez**

# The Descendants of

**William KIRKPATRICK y Wilson**
born Dumfries, Scotland 24 May 1764
married 2 Nov 1791 Málaga
died 24 Jan 1837 Málaga

| I | I | | I | |
|---|---|---|---|---|
| **Antonia** | **María Manuela** = | Cipriano Portocarrero | **Carlota Cantalona** = | Thomas James |
| b. Málaga 1792 | b. 24 Feb 1794 | y Palafox Count de Teba | b. 18 Jan 1796 | Kirkpatrick |
| died young | m.15 Dec 1817 | 7th Count de Montijo | d. 10 Feb 1831 | y Stothert |
| | d. 22 Nov 1879 | d. 15 March 1839 | Descendants | of Ostende |
| | in Madrid | | | |

I

**Enriquetta Cabarrús Kirkpatrick**
= Felix Maria de Vejarano in 1857
Count de Tajo
I

| I | I | I |
|---|---|---|
| **Felix Vejarano Cabarrús** | **Maria Vejarano Cabarrús** | **Antonia Vejarano Cabarrús** |
| = Maria Bernaldo de Quiros | = Francisco Ansaldo Otalora | = 1.Rodríguez-Casanova |
| | | 2. Attanville |
| | | 3. Conde de Bacciochi |

**From whom descends Carlos Trías Verjarano of Marbella.**

Sources:
Don Enrique Kirkpatrick Mendaro, Marques de Placetas.
Málaga Cathedral Archives, Sacristy Parochial Baptisms including special small folder Leg 491, No 3. 1822 – 1823 – (Cabarrús.)
Archivo Histórico Provincial de Málaga, Notary Files.
Major General Charles Kirkpatrick, *Records of the Closeburn Kirkpatricks*, The Grimsay Press, Glasgow, 2003

# Henrietta Kirkpatrick y Grivegnée

**Françoise Maria de Grivegnée y Gallegos** (Fanny)
born 1769

died 4 Feb 1822, Málaga

|  |  |
|---|---|
| I | I |
| **Henrietta** = Domingo Cabarrús | **Guillermo Enrique** |
| b. 1797  y Quilty, Count | b. 11 March 1797, |
| d. 27 Oct 1872 de Cabarrús | d.y. |
| Descendants | |

**Paulina Cabarrús Kirkpatrick** Condesa de Cabarrús
= Emilio Faer Angulo y Pons

|  |  |
|---|---|
| I | I |
| **Cipriano Faer Cabarrús** | **Maria Del Carmen Angulo** |
| = Clotilde de Semprún | **Cabarrús** |

# The Line of

**William KIRKPATRICK of Conheath**     =
b. March 1737
d. 1787

I

| I | I |
|---|---|
| **John KIRKPATRICK** = Jane Stothert | **William KIRKPATRICK** = Françoise |
| of Ostende      of Arkland | of Málaga      Grivegnée y |
| b. 1 Aug 1760 | b. 24 May 1764      Gallegos |
| | three daughters |

I
I

| I | I |
|---|---|
| **William Escott Kirkpatrick** | **Thomas James Kirkpatrick**. = **Carlota Catalina** |
| = Eliza Ann Parkinson | of Motril, Spain      **Kirkpatrick y** |
| dau. of Jeremiah | **Grivegnée** |
| Parkinson of London | Issue in Belgium |
| Issue in Belgium | |

I
I
I

**William Henry Kirkpatrick** = Emma van Baerle
b. 8 Jan 1828
Le Havre

I
I

| I | I | I |
|---|---|---|
| **Henry Kirkpatrick** | **John Kirkpatrick** | **Edward Kirkpatrick** |
| Unmarried | = Margurite Braule | Unmarried |
| | d. of Count Braule. | |
| | Issue | |

Sources: *Records of the Closeburn Kirkpatricks* by Major General C. Kirkpatrick,
Don Enrique Kirkpatrick Mendaro, Marques de Placetas, and Claudia Castro in Honduras.

# John Kirkpatrick of Ostende

Mary Wilson
b. 1739 d. of John Watson of Kelton
d. 29 June 1785 at Conheath

---

| I | I |
|---|---|
| **Thomas KIRKPATRICK** | **Alexander KIRKPATRICK** |
| of Málaga, | of Wilmington |
| b. 25 July 1766 | b.1780 |
| Married twice | no known issue |
| 1. Dorotea Kilbi | |
| 2. Juana Plink 1 Oct 1809 | |
| No issue | |
| d. 9 April 1837 | |

---

| I | I | I |
|---|---|---|
| **John Kirkpatrick** | **Robert Kirkpatrick** | **Maria Isabella Kirkpatrick** |
| worked with his | | = Joseph **Kirkpatrick** |
| Uncle William | | of St. Cross of |
| Kirkpatrick | | the Isle of Wight |
| in Málaga | | Issue |

---

| I | I |
|---|---|
| **Robert Stothert Kirkpatrick** | **Edward Kirkpatrick** |
| = Caroline van Baerle | = Victoria Berlioz |
| | British Consul, Honduras |
| | Issue in Honduras |

---

| I | I |
|---|---|
| **Mary Kirkpatrick** | **Lucy Kirkpatrick** |
| = Theodore Plunker | |
| Their son Henry W. Plunker | |
| married Daisy Richardson | |

# Bibliography

*Website references change over time, and full verification, including page numbers and editions dates are best sought in the original publication.*

## Primary Sources:

### Archivo Histórico Nacional, Madrid, (AHN)

Estados-Carlos 111, EXP. 877, Item 12, 1795. Enrique de Grivegnée.
Leg. 52, B No. 6 (a – h) Testamentaria de Guillermo Kirkpatrick Wilson.
  Sección de Diversos, Serie General. Papers of the Cabarrús Family, legatos 1-54.
Deed of Aparcería, 29th August 1836, Testamentary documents, Leg, 52 – b – 6.
State Document 3.158/8. 1800. Eulalio de Guzmán Palafox, Count de Teba
Expedientes de la Junta de Dependencia de Extranjeros.
ESTADO, 625, Exp.21, 1801-03-12
ESTADO, 637, Exp.8,   1807-03-07
ESTADO, 625, Exp.19, 1801-01-15

### Archivo Histórico Provincial de Málaga (AHPM)

Holds numerous references in the notarial records of Juan de Sierra and other attorneys. Note variants: Kirpatrick, Kilpatrick, Kirkpatrick etc. also Scott for Escott.
See references in the sequences:----

| Signatura | | Folio | |
|---|---|---|---|
| 2,620 | 1758 | f. 1018 | Roberto Kirkpatrick and Anna |
| 2,628 | | f. 582 | The document reads Juan Kirkpatric Scott. |
| 2,260 | 1758 | f. 399 | Juan de Kirkpatrick. |
| 2,622 | 1780 | f. 610 | Roberto Kirkpatrick. |
| 3,551 | 1800 | f. 735 | Guillermo Kirkpatrick. |
| 3,631 | 1820 | f. 312. | Enrique Grivegnée (death). |
| 3,837 | 1818 | f. 20 | Tomás Jaime Kirkpatrick. |
| 3,837 | 1818 | f. 20 | Carlota Kirkpatrick. |
| 3,873 | 1808 | f. 13 | Grivegnée et Cie. |
| 3,874 | 1811 | f. 48 | Isabel Plunkett and William Plunkett. |
| 3,943 | 1816 | f. 171 | Legal action against the convent of San Juan de Dios. |
| 3,943 | 1816 | f. 407 | Kirkpatrick, Parkinson et Cíe. |
| 3,944 | 1817 | f. 370 | María Manuela Kirkpatrick and Cipriano Palafox y Portocarrero. |

| 3,944 | 1816 | f. 415 | Enriqueta (Harriet) Kirkpatrick y Wilson |
| 3,944 | 1817 | f. 521 | Marriage of María Manuela Kirkpatrick. |
| 3,945 | 1818 | f. 20 | Thomas James Kirkpatrick marriage to Carlota Kirkpatrick y Grivegnée |
| 3,946 | 1819 | f. 705 | Tomás Kirkpatrick and Juana Plink. |
| 3,946 | 1819 | f. 771 | Kirkpatrick, Parkinson et Cíe. |
| 3,949 | 1822 | f. 730 | Francisca (Fanny) Kirkpatrick |
| 3,949 | 1822 | f. 819 | Action by Gregorio Casadevall |
| 3,950 | 1823 | f. 308 | Tomás Kirkpatrick and Juana Plink. |
| 3.950 | 1823 | f. 209 | Carlota and Henriette Kirkpatrick |
| 3,950 | 1823 | f. 39 | Tomás Kirkpatrick and Juana Plink. |
| 3.963 | 1836 | f. 97 | Guillermo Kirkpatrick y Wilson. |
| 3,963 | 1837 | f. 54 | Tomás Kirkpatrick and Juana Plink. |

## Archivo Municipal de Málaga, (AMM)

Legato   143 f.5 Juan Kirkpatrick 1730 – 1732, famine relief.
Legato   106. f.10.213 Catastro de Ensenada.
Signatura C-45 bis. Applications for qualification as Hidalgo.
Legato   176 f.49 Censo.1818, Thomas Kirkpatrick.
Legato   99 f.194 – 195 Grevigne, Henrique, commerciate.
Agustina Aquilar Simòn, *Inventario de Documentos de la sección de propios, rentas, censos, arbitrios positos, contribuciones y repartos de Archivo Municipal de Málaga.* 84- 9655 – 32 –9.

## Archivo Histórico Provincial de Almería.

Actividades Mercantiles de William Kirkpatrick y Wilson en Adra in an undetermined Notaries File.

## The National Archives of the UK, Public Record Office, Kew, London (TNA of the UK)

C 13/107/35    Kirkpatrick v. Kirkpatrick Escott.
C12/2133-1    John Kirkpatrick Escott.
C 213/460    Petition of the English Factory at Málaga
PROB 11/1027    Will of Abraham Kirkpatrick, 1777.
PROB11/1077,    Will of Robert Kirkpatrick, 1781.
PC 1/3918    Bundle of documents. Order in Council of 30 June 1810.
FO 927/17    Málaga (Consul's) Correspondence, March -April 1821.
     Entry book of general correspondence, 16 Feb 1821.
FO 185/90,    Consular papers.
*Proceedings of the Court of Appeal*, London, (1789) Kirkpatrick cases.

British Parliamentary Papers, Reports of the Committees, Session 19 Feb.-10
Sept. 1835 Vol. VI.

## United States National Archives II, College Park, MD.

Department of State List of Communications copied in "Foreign Letters", United
States Ministers, Instructions. Volumes 1-5. Málaga, Kirkpatrick
William, Consul (24 Jan 1800 – 21 May 1801).
General Records of the Department of State. Appointment Records Lists and
Record Cards. List of U.S. Consular Officers by post, 1789 – 1939.
Vol. 13 of 23, Record Group 59, NARS A-1 Entry 802.
Applications and Recommendations for Public Office, 1797 – 1901,
Administration of Madison, 1809 – 1817, Record Group 59, RM 438.
Appointment Records, Lists and Record Cards, Card Record of Appointments
made from 1776 to 1968. NARS A-1 Entry 798 (box 17).
Miscellaneous Permanent and Temporary Presidential Commissions, 1789 -
1952. Vol. 01 of 21 NARS A-1 Entry 774.
Journal of the Executive proceedings of the Senate of the United States of America,
1815-1829. Friday, December 12, 1817. (Removal of Wm. Kirkpatrick
as Consul at Málaga).
RG 59, Dept of State, Lists of U.S. Consular Officers by Post, A-1 Entry 802,
Vol. 13 of 23,
Journal of the Executive Proceedings of the Senate of the United States of America,
1815 – 1829, Friday December 12, 1817.
R.G. 59, Dept. of State, Despatches from U.S. Consuls in Málaga, Spain, 1793
– 1906 microfilm reel T217 (1) and T217 (2).

## Palacio de Liria, Archivo de la Casa de Alba, Madrid.

C.51-8. Letter to Count de Teba from William Kirkpatrick.

## Bedford County Council Record Office.

Correspondence between Thomas Robinson, 2nd Baron Grantham (1738-1786)
and John Kirkpatrick Escott. L 30/14/212, 10 October 1775.

## Ewart Library, Dumfries.

GGD74/3/9 – 17 documents. Letters of Miss Jane Kirkpatrick (see also GGD/55).
Court Books of the Commissariat of Dumfries, The Testament of William
Kirkpatrick of Conheath, 17 January 1788, and 14 November 1789,
copied by Janet Isabel Finney, 2002.

## Archivo Narsisco Diaz de Escovar, Museo de Arte Populares, Málaga.

Díaz de Escovar, *Cronista de la Provincia.*

## Georgetown University Library

1/28 Read, George, Date: 2/15/1843 Description: 1 brief AL (copy) dated 2/15/1843 from Washington Irving (1783-1859), U.S. Minister to Spain (1842-1846), to George Read, U.S. Consul at Málaga (Spain).

## Guildhall Library, City of London.

London Directories – *"Complete Guide"* 1760, 1765, Kent's *Directory* 1771, 1775, 1780, 1785, *London Directory* 1791 to 1796.

## Massachusetts Historical Society, 1154, Boylston Street, Boston, MA 02215.

Hooper-Sturgis Papers - 1798 –1857, 14 document boxes and 1 oversize box, call no. Ms. N-1435.

## Missouri Historical Collection Archives, St Louis, MO 63112-0040.

*Thomas Jefferson (1743-1826) Collection,* 1773-1826, Folder 15, 23 Sept. 1803 and folder 58, 4 Feb 1805.

## The Schlesinger Library, Radcliff College, Cambridge MA 02138.

*Cabot Family Papers, 91 NUCMC, 1712-1862*

## Library of Virginia, Richmond, VA,23219 –8000.

*Will of Joseph Gallego, 1818*, Richmond City Hustings Court Will Book 2.

## Staatsarchiv, Oldenburg, Germany

Correspondence with Mr. Axel Eilts, Archivist, on 20 Oct 2008. Ref. *Best. 22 Nr. 6.* Consul Thomas Kirkpatrick.

## Staatsarchiv, Hannover, Germany.

Correspondence with the Archivist, *Hof und Staats Hadnbuck fur das Konigreich Hannover*, 1829, and 1833.

## U.S. National Library of Medicine, Bethesda, MD 20894

MS B 025 Kerr, James. *Observations on natural history by Dr. James Kerr*, corrected and improved by Mr. Christopher Holland. 1790.

### Kirkpatrick Family References.

Kirkpatrick Mendaro, Enrique, Marquis de Placetas, Private papers and researches concerning the Kirkpatrick. Numerous references including Nota 8 bis.

Kirkpatrick, Major General Charles, *Records of the Closeburn Kirkpatricks,* The Grimsay Press, Glasgow, 2003.

Kirkpatrick, Major General Charles, Unpublished Manuscripts, Dean Lane White Parish, Wiltshire (by kind permission of his daughter Mrs Butler, 20 March 1996).

Kirkpatrick, Richard Godman, *Kirkpatricks of Closeburn, Memoir Respecting the Family of Kirkpatrick of Closeburn in Nithdale with notices of some collaterals*, London, privately printed, 1858.

Kirkpatrick, Alexander de Lapere, *Chronicles of the Kirkpatrick Family*, privately printed by Thomas Moring, de la More Press, London.

Kirkpatrick, Melvin Eugene**,** *A Kirkpatrick Genealogy, Being an Account of the Descendants of the Family*, David Hudson – 1995.


Anderson, William, *The Scottish Nation, Surnames, Families, Literature, Honours and Biographical History of the People of Scotland, Vol. II*, A. Fullerton & Co., Edinburgh and London, 1862.

Burke, Bernard, *A Visitation of the Seats of the Noblemen and Gentlemen of Great Britain*, Heraldry 1855. Herald's Office, Edinburgh, 16 May 1791.

Felthem, John, *A Tour Through the Island of Man 1797 – 1798*, from Manx Society Publications.

*Genealogical Table of the Family of Kirkpatrick of Closeburn in Nithdale*. Patent, Heralds Office, Edinburgh, 16 May, 1791.

Johnstone, C. L., *Historical Families of Dumfriesshire and the Border Wars*, 1878.

*Burke's Peerage and Baronetage*. 106th edition.

*Wigtown Pages Death Notices* from the *Wigtownshire Free Press* Transcribed by Diana Henry and Compiled by Randy Chapple.

## Near Contemporary References:

Alger, John Goldworth, *Napoleon's British Visitors And Captives: 1801 – 1813*. New York, 1904.

Anonymous, (a Diplomat) *Napoleon the Third and his Court*, London 1865.

*Boletín de la Sociedad Económica de Amigos del Pais de Málaga*, 31 Enero 1864.

Burke, Edmund, *The Annual Register of World Events*, 1808.

Carr, John, Sir, K.C., *Descriptive Travelling in the Southern and Eastern Parts of Spain and the Baleric Islands in the year 1809*. London, 1811.

De Cappell Brooke, Arthur, Sir, *Sketches in Spain and Morocco*, Vol. II, London 1831.

*Les Droits de l'Homme*, Paris, Sept. 1876.

*Edinburgh New Philosophical Journal, Exhibiting a view of the Progressive*, Eds. Robert Jameson, Sir William Jardine, Henry D. Rogers, 1842.

*The Edinburgh Annual Review, 1808 – 1826*, Editor, Walter Scott, 1824.

Johnson, T. B., *An Impartial History of Europe*, Vol. IV, London 1813.

Llanos y Torriglia, de, Félix, *María Manuela Kirkpatrick, Condesa del Montijo, La Gran Dama*, Primera Edition, Espase- Calpe, S.A., Madrid, 1932.

Llanos y Torriglia, de, Félix and Pierre Josserand, *Lettres Familierès de L'Imperératrice Eugénie*, 1935.

*The Memoirs of Dr. Thomas W. Evans, Recollections of the Second French Empire*, Ed. Edward A. Crane, T. Fisher Unwin, London, 1906.

Dodds, James, Rev., *Personal Reminiscences and Biographical Sketches*, Edinburgh, 1888, 2nd Edition.

Primoli. J-N, *L'Enfance d'Une Souveraine, Souvinirs Intimes*, Paris, 1923.

Mérimée, Prosper, *Lettres de Prosper Mérimée à Madame de Montijo*, Ed. Claude Schopp, Mercure de France, vol. 1, Paris, 1995.

*La Nouvelle Caprée, ou les Amours de Napoléon III, L'Apothéose Matrimonial de Bonaparte de César*, a pamphlet published in Stockholm, no date.

Novales, Alberto Gil *William Maclure, Socialism, Utopica en Espania*, Universidad Autónoma de Barcelona, 1979.

Saldoni, Baltasar, *Diccionario biográfico-bibliográfico de efemérides de músicos españoles*, Madrid, 1868.

Vésinier, Pierre, *Le Mariage d'une Espagnole*, Deuxième Edition, Londres, 1869.

*Vigésimo sexta Junta General de Accionistas del Banco Nacional de San Carlos, celebrada en la casa del mismo Banco en el día 20 de abril de 1808*. Madrid, 1815.

## Secondary Sources:

Abbott, John Stevens Cabot, The *History of Napoleon III, Emperor of the French*, B. B. Russell, Boston, 1868.

Barrionveno Serrano, Rosario, *Los expedientes de hidalguía del Archivo de Málaga*, in preparation for publication in late 2009. Málaga Municipal Archives.

Beatty, Charles R., *Ferdinand de Lesseps, A Biographical Study*, London, 1956.

Browning, Michael, Lovelace, *Lovelace's Charity, Affairs in Spain, 1803 Onwards*. http://www.lovelacetrust.org.uk/historyofthelovelacetrust.html

Bulloch, J. M., *The Curious Career of the Kirkpatricks and how they Begat Eugéne*, San Francisco Weekly Bulletin, 12 April 1898.

*Cambridge Historical Journal* 1937, v. 5-6, 1935-1940 citing PRO: *S.P.F.* Sp. 154 ( old PRO ref. no.) Mr Francis Aiskill writing to William Pitt in 1781.

Carlyle Collected Letters, Vol. 5, Jan. 1829 – Sept. 1831, Letter to Gustave D'Eichthal. The Carlyle Letters Online. http://carlyleletters.org. Accessed 4 March 2009.

Carr, Raymond, *New Cambridge Modern History*, vol. IX, CUP, 1965.

Cartlidge, Joyce, *Empress Eugénie: Her Secret Revealed*, Magnum Opus Press, London, 2008.

Carver, Michael, *Out of Step, Memoirs of a Field Marshall*, London, 1989.

Cobban, Alfred, *Aspects of the French Revolution*, Jonathan Cape, 1968.

Cruz, Jesus, *Gentlemen, bourgeois and revolutionaries, Political change and cultural persistence among Spanish dominant groups, 1750-1850.* Cambridge University Press, 1996.

Dalrymple, William, *White Mughals*, Harper Collins, 2002.

Demerson, de Paula, *La vida azarosa de D.Cipriano Palafox Portocarrero, padre de la emperatriz Eugenia de Montijo (1784 – 1839) Revista de Estudios Extremeños*, Badajoz, 1995, Tomo LI, No.1, Enero – Abril.

*Dictionary of American Biography*, Cabot, George.

Duff, David, *Eugénie & Napoleon III,* Collins, London, 1978.

Esdaile, Charles J., *Fighting Napoleon, Guerrilla, Bandits and Adventurers in Spain 1808 – 1814*, Yale University Press, 1988.

Esdaile, Charles J. *The Peninsular War, A New History,* Penguin Books, 2003.

García Montoro, Cristóbel, *Historia de Málaga*, Catedrático de Historia Contemporánea. Universidad de Málaga, Málaga.

García Montoro, Cristóbal, *'Inversiones agroindustriales de la burguesía mercantil a fines del siglo XVIII: La burguesía de negocios en la Andalucía de la Ilustración* . Cádiz, 1991, tomo II.

Glover, Michael, *Legacy of Glory, The Bonaparte Kingdom of Spain*, Leo Cooper, London, 1970.

Guedalla, Philip, *The Second Empire,* Hodder and Stoughton, London, (1922) 1946 edition.

Herr, Richard, *Flow and Ebb,* chapter 7 in *Spain a History,* editor, Raymond Carr, Oxford University Press, 2000.

Jeffrey, Brian, *Fernando Sor, Composer and Guitarist,* First Edition, Tecla Editions, 1977, and second edition 1994. www.tecla.com

Krauel Heredia, Blanca, *Viajeros británicos en Málaga (1769-1855),* University of Málaga, Málaga, 1986.

Kurtz, Harold, *The Empress Eugénie,* 1826-1920, Hamish Hamilton, London, 1964.

Legge, Edward, *The Empress Eugénie,* Grant Richards, 1916.

Leroy, Alfred, *The Empress Eugénie,* Translated by Anne Cope, Heron Books, Geneva.

Lesseps, de, Ferdinand, *Recollections of Forty Years,* Trs. C. B. Pitman, 1887, in 2 Vols.

Nepveux, Ethel S., *George Alfred Trenholm and the Company That Went to War 1861- 1865,* Charleston 1973. (Privately published)

Madroñero, Manuel Burgos, *Málaga, Siglos XVIII-XIX – Lose Extranjeros.,* Notas (5) from Málaga Archivo Municipal, Legajo 1979.

Malloy, Fitzgerald, *The Romance of Royalty,* New York, 1903.

Mévil, André, *Vie Espagnole de l'Impératrice Eugénie,* Editions Ventadour, Paris.

Torre Molina, María José de la, *La Música en Málaga Durante la Era Napoleónic (1808- 1814)* Universidad de Málaga, Colección Studia Malacitana, Málaga, 2003.

Muñoz Martín, Manuel, *Los promotores de l economía malagueña de siglo XIX,* Colegio de Eonomistas de Málaga, - Fundación Unicaja, Málaga 2008.

Parton, James and others, *Most Prominent Women of the Present Generation,* Hartford, CT., 1868.

Parmentier, Jan, Dr., *Het Gezicht van de Ostendese Handelaar, Studie van Ostende kooplieden, renders en ondernemers actief in de internationale handle en visserij tijdens de 18d eeuw.*

Payne, Stanley G. *A History of Spain and Portugal, Vol.2.* University of Wisconsin Press, 1976.

Pino, Enrique del, *Historia General de Málaga,* Colección Andalucía, Almuzara, 2008.

Platt, Christopher (1984), *Foreign Finance in Continental Europe and the United States, 1815-1870.* London, George Allen & Unwin.

Preston, Daniel, *A Comprehensive Catalogue of the Correspondence of James Monroe,* Vol. III Greenwood Publishing, 2000.

Ridley, Jasper, *Napoleon III and Eugénie,* Constable, London, 1979.

Ringrose, David R., *Spain, Europe, and the "Spanish Miracle", 1700 – 1900,* Cambridge University Press, 1996.

Rosario Barrionveno Serrano, *Los expedientes de hidalguía del Archivo de Málaga*, in preparation. Málaga Municipal Archives.

Rubio-Argüelles, Ángeles, *Apunte Históricos Málaganas*, 1954. Unpublished thesis.

Saint–Amand, Imbert, de, *Louis Napoleon and Mademoiselle de Montijo*, Hutchinson & Co. London, 1900,

Sencourt, Robert, *The Life of the Empress Eugénie*, Ernest Benn, London, 1931.

Seward, Desmond, Eugénie, *The Empress and Her Empire*, Sutton Publishing, Stroud, England. 2004.

Stoddart, Jane T., *The Life of the Empress Eugénie*, Hodder and Stoughton, London, 1906.

Soissons, Count de, *The True Story of the Empress Eugénie*, John Lane, The Bodley Head, New York, 1921.

Turnbull, Patrick, *Eugénie of the French*, Michael Joseph, London, 1974.

Villar García, María Begoña, *La emigración irlandesa en el siglo XVIII.*, Málaga: Universidad de Málaga, 2000.

Villar García, María Begoña, *Los Extranjeros en Málaga en el Siglo XVIII.* Cordoba 1982.

Whipple, Sydney B. *Scandalous Princess, The Exquisite Thérésia Cabarrús*, New York, 1932.

## Other References:

*The Writing of John Quincy Adams 1767 – 1848*, Edited by Ford, Worthington Chauncey, New York, 1913, Volume 6.

Ansted, Prof. D. T., *Scenery, Science and Art, being Extracts from the Note-Book of a Geologist and Mining Engineer*, London, 1854.

Blackall, Henry, Sir, *The Galweys of Munster, Part 2*, http://www.galwey.com/genedocs/galweys_of_munster2.htm

*Blackwood's Gentleman's Magazine*, 1781.

*Blackwood's Gentleman's Magazine*, 1822.

*Boletín de la Sociedad Económica de Amigos del País de Málaga*, Imprenta de Correo de Andalucía, Málaga, 1861.

Bosanquet & Fuller, Editors, *Report of Cases Argued and Determined in the Court of Common Pleas (etc.) Easter Term 1796 to Trinity Term 1799*, Butterworth, London, 1826.

Brayley, Edward Wedlake, F.S.A. *A Topographical History of Surrey*, Volume II Monuments of Chertsey, Godley Hundred.

Busby, James, Esq. *Journal of a Recent Visit to the Principal Vineyards of Spain and France - - with Observations Relative to the Introduction of the Vine into New South Wales*. Smith, Elder and Co. Cornhill, London, 1834.

*Calendar of Miscellaneous Letters Received by the Department of State from the Organization of Government to 1820*, U.S. G.P.O., 1897.

*The Cambridge Historical Journal*, 1937, v 5-6 1935-1940 citing P.R.O.:
    S.P.F., Sp 154

*Camden New Journal*, 6 July, 2008, concerning Spanish refugees.

*The Congressional Globe*, Published by the United States Congress, Ed. Francis
    Preston Blair, John Cook Rives, Franklin Rives, George A. Bailey.

*Estudios Regionales*, Nº. 49 (1997) Universidad de Alcalá.

Gaite, Carmen Martín, *Love Customs in Eighteenth-Century Spain*, Translated
    by Maria G. Tomsich, University of California Press, Berkeley 1991.

*The Gentleman's Magazine*, Vol. LVII, 1787, part I.

*Great-Grandma's Tales, The remembrances of Mary Westwater Campbell,(1772
    – 1865)*. www.myheritageimages.com transcribed by: Ellen Lawson,
    June 1993.

*Transactions of the Huguenot Society of South Carolina*, Issue 87, Huguenot
    Society of South Carolina

Kemp, Robert Philp, Ed. *The Family Friend*.

*The Papers of Henry Laurens,1782 – 1792*, Edited by David R. Chesnutt,
    Philip May Hamer, C. James Taylor, published by South Carolina
    Historical Society, Charleston, S.C.

Lea, Henry Charles *A History of the Inquisition of Spain Volume 1*. Appendix,
    Spanish Coinage.

*The Leisure Hour*, edited by William Haig Miller, James Macaulay, William
    Stevens, 1905.

*Lectic Law Library*, http://www.lectlaw.com/def2/m091.htm

*The London Polytechnic Magazine, and Journal of Science, Literature, and
    the Fine Arts*, ed. by T. Stone. Jan.-June, 1844, Published by John
    Mortimer, London, 1844.

Lydon, James G. *Fish and Flour for Gold, 1600 – 1800: Southern Europe in the
    Colonial Balance of Payments, Business History Review*, XXXIX, 1965.

Napier, Mark, *Memorial and Letters Illustrative of the Life and Times of John
    Graham of Claverhouse, Viscount Dundee*, (Marquis of Montrose),
    Edinburgh, 1859.

*Naval Documents Related to the United States Wars with the Barbary Powers*.
    Vol. 1, Washington 1939.

Norton, the Hon. Mrs., *A letter to the Queen on Lord Chancellor Cranworth's
    Marriage and Divorce Bill*. London, Longman Green 1855.

*Notes and Queries*, Oxford University Press 4th S VL, 3 September 1870.

*Notes and Queries*, Oxford University Press, January - June 1901.

*Notes and Queries*, Oxford University Press, Item notes: v. 167 Jul-Dec 1934.

Maclure, William, *The European Journals of Wm. Maclure*, with notes by
    John S. Doskey, American Philosophical Society, Philadelphia 1988,
    Memoirs Series, Vol. 171.

*The Spain That William Maclure Knew*, Indiana Magazine of History, June 1998.
    http://www.Málagahistoria.com

Malloy, Fitzgerald, *The Romance of Royalty*, New York, 1904.

Marryat, Frederick, *Code universale de signaux à l'usage des navires du commerce de toutes les monde*, – 1866.

Marx, Karl, *Revolutionary Spain*, New York Herald Tribune, August – November 1854 . A series of articles.

*The Mercantile Navy List and Annual Appendage to the Commercial Code of Signals for All Nations: 1856/57*. Edited by J. H. Brown.

*Miscellaneous Works of David Humphreys, Late Minister Plenipotentiary from the United States of America to the Court of Madrid,* New York, 1804.

Morilla Critz, José *La viticultura de Andalucía en 1831 vista por James Busby, padre de la viticultura Australiana*. Estudios Regionales No. 49, 1997.

Oliver and Boyd's *Edinburgh Almanac and National Repository*, 1835.

*Otago Witness, Ladies' Gossip column*, 29 August 1889, Otago, New Zealand. http://paperspast.natlib.govt.nz/cgibin/paperspast

Pearson, James, *The Chronicles of Clan Colquhoun*, Elachan Publications. 2007 and 2009.

Passenger Arrivals at the Port of Philadelphia 1800 – 1819. Baltimore Genealogical Publishing Co. 1986.

Raquet, Condy, editor, *The Financial Register of the United States*, Philadelphia, 1838.

*Reports from Her Majesty's Consuls on the Manufactures, Commerce,* &c. By Great Britain Foreign Office, 1868, 299 – 300, for Adra etc.

Rhind, William, *A History of the Vegetable Kingdom,* Blackie and Sons, Glasgow, 1857.

Ripley, George, *The American Cyclopedia*, 1858, D. Appleton, New York. www.rosaverde.com. Accessed 4 May 2010

*Scottish Notes and Queries*, 1898.

Sealey, Malcolm, *The Coolangatta Estate*, Published Privately by Lulu, Australia, 2006.

Story, William, *Essay upon the Agriculture of Victoria,* (Australia). The Victorian Government Prize Essays, 1860, Melbourne 1861.

SUR, English language newspaper, Spain, 2nd December to 8th December 2005.

Taché, Louis-H, *Les homes du jour galerie de portraits contemporains*, Montreal, Canada, 1894.

Thompson Cooper Ed., *The Register and Magazine of Biography*, 1869.

Walford, Edward, *Tales of our Great Families*, 1880.

www.wineonline.ie/library/australia.htm

# Notes

1.  Cartlidge, Joyce, *Empress Eugenie: Her Secret Revealed.*
2   Ringrose, David R. *Spain, Europe, and the "Spanish Miracle," 1700 – 1900.*
3   *Les Droits de l'Homme*, Paris, Sept. 1876.
4   De Cappell Brooke, Sir Arthur, *Sketches in Spain and Morocco.*
5   Mévil, André, *Vie Espagnole de L'Impératrice Eugénie.*
6   Taché, Louis-H, *Les homes du jour galerie de portraits contemporains.*
7   Mévil, André, *Ibid.*
8   *The Leisure Hour,* edited by William Haig, etc. page 328.
9   Ewart Library, Dumfries, GGD74/3/9 – 17 documents. (See also GGD/55).
10  Kirkpatrick General Charles. *Records of the Closeburn Kirkpatricks*, page 178, where he gives various sasine document references to these events.
11  The National Archives, of the UK: PRO, C213/460. Petition of the English Factory in Málaga
12  Blackall, Henry, Sir, *The Galweys of Munster,* Part 2, http://www.galwey.com/genedocs/galweys_of_munster2.htm
13  Lydon, James G., *Fish and Flour for Gold, 1600 – 1800: Southern Europe in the Colonial Balance of Payments.*
14  "The Masters Extraordinary perform the duty of taking affidavits touching any matter in or relating to the court of Chancery, [clerks to the Lord Chancellor] taking the acknowledgment of deeds to be enrolled in the said court, and taking such recognizances, as may by the tenor of the order for entering them, be taken before a master extraordinary." *Lectic Law Library,* http://www.lectlaw.com/def2/m091.htm
15  SMV/2/4/2/23/23, Society of Merchant Venturers, Bristol Record Office Archives.
16  The Gentleman's Magazine, Vol. LVII, 1787, part I, page 454.
17  *Vigésimo sexta Junta General de Accionistas del Banco Nacional de San Carlos, celebrada en la casa del mismo Banco en el día 20 de abril de 1808.*
18  See Appendix I for comparative values.
19  Archivo Histórico Provincial de Málaga, 3.945 f. 20.
20  Jesús Cruz, *Gentlemen Bourgeois and Revolutionaries, Political Change and Cultural Persistence Among the Spanish Dominant Groups 1750 –1850.*
21  Llanos y Torriglia, Felix de, *Lettres Familières de L'Impératrice Eugénie.*
22  Don Enrique Kirkpatrick Mendaro, Nota 8 bis.
23  The National Archives of the UK: PRO, PROB 11/1027 Will of Abraham Kirkpatrick
24  Archivo Municipal de Málaga, 1730 – 1732, 143/5
25  Notes and Queries, Oxford University Press, 1934, Item notes: v.167, Jul-Dec, page 352.
26  See Appendix Four for the Will of Robert Kirkpatrick.
27  Proceedings of the Court of Appeal, London, page 349 in the 29th year of the reign of George III.
28  The Cambridge Historical Journal 1937, v. 5-6, 1935-1940 citing PRO: *S.P.F.*, Sp 154

29 General Charles Kirkpatrick, *Ibid.*, page 187.

30 Kirkpatrick, Charles, *Ibid.*, page 95.

31 Bernard Burke, *A Visitation of the Seats of the Noblemen and Gentlemen of Great Britain*, page 145.

32 Alexander de Lapere Kirkpatrick, *Chronicles of the Kirkpatrick Family.*

33 *Otago Witness*, (New Zealand) Issue 1871, of 29 August 1889, page 33.

34 Rosario Barrionveno Serrano, *Los expedientes de hidalguía del Archivo de Málaga*, in preparation Málaga Municipal Archives.

35 Archivo el Ayuntamiento de Málaga, Signatura C-45 bis. (Málaga Municipal Archives).

36 Sencourt, Robert, *The Life of Empress Eugénie.*

37 Anderson, William, *The Scottish Nation, Surnames, Families, Literature, Honours and Biographical History of the People of Scotland, Vol. II*, page 617.

38 *Genealogical Table of the Family of Kirkpatrick of Closeburn in Nithdale.* Patent, Heralds Office.

39 See comments by Major General Charles Kirkpatrick in a commentary on a letter from the Countess Montijo to Madame J. Kirkpatrick at West Park near Bristol written in the 1850s at the time of Eugénie's marriage. This letter, and the commentary dated April 1952, is now in Dumfries Archives.

40 General Charles Kirkpatrick, *Ibid.*

41 Malloy, Fitzgerald, *The Romance of Royalty*, page 294/5.

42 Kirkpatrick Mendaro, Enrique.

43 Archivo Histórico Nacional, Madrid, Estados-Carlos 111, EXP.877 item 12, 1795.

44 *Boletín de la Sociedad Económica de Amigos del País de Málaga*, 31 March 1864 page 4.

45 *Notes and Queries*, January - June 1901.

46 Family history notes from Carlos Trías Vejarano, Marbella.

47 *Blackwood's Magazine*, 1822, page 500.

48 Private correspondence Enrique Kirkpatrick Mendaro to Carlos Trías Vejarano, 13 July 2003.

49 Beatty, Charles, *Ferdinand de Lesseps a biographical study*, pages 16- 19.

50 Beatty, *Ibid.*, page 18.

51 Beatty, *Ibid.*

52 *Miscellaneous Works of David Humphreys Late Minister Plenipotentiary from the United States of America to the Court of Madrid.*

53 *Hof und Staats Hadnbuck fur das Konigreich Hannover*, 1829, page 39, and 1833, page 50.

54 Papers of Mrs Butler, daughter of Major General C. Kirkpatrick, seen at Dean Lane, Whiteways, Somerset, England, 10 March 1996.

55 Carver, Michael, *Out of Step, Memoirs of Field Marshall Lord Carver*, page 2.

56 Nepveux, Ethel S., *George Alfred Trenholm and the Company That Went to War 1861- 1865.*

57 http://www.Málagahistoria.com/Málagahistoria/barrios/huelin.html

58 Anderson, William, *The Scottish Nation: Or The Surnames, Families, Literature, Honours, etc.* page 617.

59     Kirkpatrick, Melvin Eugene, *A Kirkpatrick Genealogy, Being and Account of the Descendants of the Family*, 1995 page 425. Also *Scottish Notes and Queries*, 1898, page 170.

60     Kirkpatrick, Richard Godman, *Memoir Respecting the Family of Kirkpatrick of Closeburn in Nithdale*, page 71. "the son and one daughter died young".

61     http://familtreemaker.geneaology.com/users/t/o/r/Jorge-Toro-San-Juan/ WEBSITE-0001/UHP-1085.html. No other validation has yet been found for this information.

62     Johnstone, C.L., *Historical Families of Dumfriesshire and the Border Wars*, 1878, Chapter V.

63     Demerson, Paula de, *La vida azarosa de D. Cipriano Palafox Portocarrero, padre de la emperatriz Eugenia de Montijo (1784 – 1839)*, page 19.

64     *Lettres de Prosper Mérimée á Madame de Montijo*, Volume I, page 26.

65     Abbott, John Stevens Cabot, *The History of Napoleon III, Emperor of the French*, page 512.

66     The National Archives of the UK: PRO, FO 185/90. Consular Papers.

67     William Kirkpatrick's Testamentary documents in the Archivo Histórico Nacional, Madrid. Leg 52, B.

68     Anonymous, *Napoleon the Third and his Court*, pages 243, 244.

69     Cruz, Jesus, *Gentlemen, Bourgeois, and Revolutionaries, Political Change and Cultural Persistence Among the Spanish Dominant Groups 1750 –1850*, page 114.

70     García Montoro, Cristóbal, '*Inversiones agroindustriales de la burguesía mercantil a fines del siglo XVIII: Tomás Quilty y la fabricación de azúcar en la costa malagueña*' (1779-1804), *La burguesía de negocios en la Andalucía de la Ilustración*, tome II, pages 151-162, and '*Inversiones industriales de los irlandeses en Málaga durante la etapa final del Antiguo Régimen*', and María Begoña Villar García, *La emigración irlandesa en el siglo XVIII*, pages 143-156.

71     Rubio-Argüelles, Ángeles, *Apunte Históricos Málaganas*, page 98.

72     Esdaile, Charles, J., *Fighting Napoleon, Guerrilla, Bandits and Adventurers in Spain 1808 – 1814*.

73     Anderson, William, *Ibid.*, page 617.

74     I am indebted to Gijs Speltincx of the Combined Anglican Parish of Ostende and Bruges for translating relevant passages from Dr. Jan Parmentier's book *Het Gezicht van de Oostendese Handelaar, Studie van OOstende kooplieden, renders en ondernemers actief in de internationale maritieme handle en visserij tijdens de 18d eeuw*. I have used many of his translated phrases for this chapter.

75     Buildings probably used by John Kirkpatrick in Ostende – The buildings were property of Liebaert & Jfr. Wwe Leep & d'Heer Leeps. Reference from Gijs Speltincx of the Anglican Parish of Ostende and Bruges.

76     Great-Grandma's Tales, *The remembrances of Mary Westwater Campbell (1772 – 1865)*.

77     Kirkpatrick General Charles, *Records of the Closeburn Kirkpatricks*, page 178, listing Kirkcudbright sasine numbers, 1426- 1429-2443-2879-3325 and 3324.

78     Cobban, Alfred, *Aspects of the French Revolution*, pages 233 - 234.

79     Evan Nepean, (1751 – 1822) see also *The Papers of Henry Laurens*, 1 September 1782 - 17 December 1792.

80    Kirkpatrick, Richard Godman, *Ibid.*
81    International Genealogical Index, (an uncertain source, but a useful guide). The remaining registers of the English Church are in the Guildhall Library and The National Archives of the UK: PRO, both in London. Other records are scattered in Archives in Belgium.
82    Parton, James and others, *Most Prominent Women of the Present Generation.*
83    Paterson, James, *The Kirkpatricks of the Isle of Wight,* The Chronicles of Clan Colquhoun, Issue No. 15, Autumn 2007.
84    *Wigtown Pages Death Notices* from the *Wigtownshire Free Press.* Transcribed by Diana Henry and Compiled by Randy Chapple, February 2006.
85    *Notes and Queries,* 4th Series, VL, 3 September 1870, page 187.
86    Correspondence with Mr. Axel Eilts Archivist, Staatsarchiv, Oldenburg, Germany, 20 Oct 2008. Ref. *Best. 22 Nr. 6.*
87    http://list.genealogy.net/mailman/archiv/hannover-l/2002-01/2002-01f.html
88    Kirkpatrick Mendaro, Enrique, unpublished manuscript, and Archivo Histórico Provincial de Málaga, Ref, (3.726/82).
89    Walford, Edward, *Tales of Our Great Families,* 1880, page 179.
90    Robert Kemp Philip, Ed. *The Family Friend,* page 171, also Thompson Cooper Ed., *The Register and Magazine of Biography,* page 333.
91    Anonymous, *Napoléon the III and his Court,* pages 243-4.
92    Consular Birth Registrations for Hamburg, International Genealogical Index.
93    Ayuntamiento de Málaga Archivo Año 18 Legajo núm. 176 numero 49 Censo.
94    Dalrymple, William, *White Mughals.*
95    Pearson, James, *The Chronicles of Clan Colquhoun.* See other volumes for further material on the Keston Kirkpatricks.
96    *Transactions of the Huguenot Society of South Carolina,* Issue 87.
97    The National Archives of the UK: PRO, C12/2133-1.
98.   *The Carlyle Collected Letters,* Vol. 5, Jan 1829 – Sept 1831, Thomas Carlyle to Gustave d'Eichthal, 17 May 1831; The Carlyle Letters Online, 2007, http://carlyleletters.org Accessed 4 March 2009.
99    Robert Kirkpatrick's Will dated 1781, TNA of the UK: PRO, PROB 11/1077 page 75.
100   US National Archives. NARA RG 59, Box 6, *Applications and Recommendations for Public Office, 1797 – 1901,* Administration of Madison, 1809-1817.
101   Correspondence between Thomas Robinson, 2nd Baron Grantham (1738-1786) and John Kirkpatrick Escott, L 30/14/212, Bedford County Council Record Office.
102   *Blackwood's Gentleman's Magazine,* 1781, page 195.
103   TNA of the UK: PRO, PROB 11/1077.
104   TNA of the UK, PRO, C 13/107/35 Kirkpatrick v. Kirkpatrick Escott.
105   Archivo Histórica Provincial de Málaga. Leg.2628, fol. 582 (the document reads Juan Kirkpatric Scott).
106   Brayley, Edward Wedlake, F.S.A. *A Topographical History of Surrey,* Volume II, Monuments of Chertsey, Godley Hundred, page 200.
107   Catastro de Ensenada, Volume 106. Folio 10.213 Málaga Municipal Archives.

108　US National Archives. RG 59, General Records of the Department of State, Applications and Recommendations for Public Office, 1797-1901, Madison 1809-1817 Box 6 (film M438).

109　TNA of the UK: PRO, FO 185/90, Málaga Consular Correspondence.

110　Madroñero, Manuel Burgos, *Málaga, Siglos XVIII-XIX – Lose Extranjeros,* Notas (5) Archivo el Ayuntamiento de Málaga, Legajo 1979.

111　British Parliamentary Papers, Reports of the Committees, Session 19 Feb.-10 Sept. 1835 Vol. VI page 127.

112　Oliver and Boyd's *Edinburgh Almanac and National Repository,* 1835, page 207, also *The Mercantile Navy List and Annual Appendage to the Commercial Code of Signals for All Nations: 1856/57,* page 170.

113　Frederick Marryat, *Code universelle de signaux à l'usage des navires du commerce de toutes les monde,* – 1866.

114　Ed. Edward A. Crane, *The Memoirs of Dr. Thomas W. Evans,* Page 621, Appendices.

115　Appointment Records of the Department of State, Applications and Recommendations for Public Office for the Administration of President Madison 1809 – 1817, dated 1814.

116　Archivo Histórico Nacional, Madrid, Expedientes de la Junta de Dependencia de Extranjeros, ESTADO, 625, Exp.21, 1801-03-12 and ESTADO, 637, Exp.8, 1807-03-07 and ESTADO, 625, Exp.19, 1801-01-15.

117　Lists of U.S. Consular Officers by Post, Dept of State, NARA, RG59, A-1 Entry 802, Vol. 13 of 23, U.S. National Archives.

118　*Journal of the Executive Proceedings of the Senate of the United States of America, 1815 – 1829,* Friday December 12, 1817. "I hereby nominate to the Senate for its concurrence, the persons whose names are stated on the annexed paper. – George G. Barrill of Massachusetts, to be Consul of the United States at Málaga, in Spain, in the place of William Kirkpatrick, removed".

119　Preston, Daniel, *A Comprehensive Catalogue of the Correspondence of James Monroe,* Vol. III, 2000, page 703, (citing an Autograph Letter signed, K' Hi: Perry Papers).

120　Norton, the Hon Mrs., *A letter to Queen Victoria on Lord Chancellor Cranworth's Marriage and Divorce Bill,* London, 1855.

121　*Naval Documents Related to the United States Wars with the Barbary Powers.* Vol. 1, Washington 1939, page 438.

122　Naval Documents, *Ibid.,* page 472.

123　Naval Documents, *Ibid.,* pages 476-477.

124　Naval Documents *Ibid.,* pages 540-541.

125　Naval Documents *Ibid.,* page 559.

126　Naval Documents *Ibid.,* pages 550-551.

127　Naval Documents *Ibid.,* page 602.

128　Naval Documents *Ibid.,* page 615.

129　Naval Documents *Ibid.,* page 540.

130　*The Congressional Globe,* United States Congress, page 2158.

131　US National Archives, College Park, Maryland, NARA, *Despatches from U.S. Consuls in Málaga, Spain, 1793 – 1906,* T217 (1).

132　Dodds, The Rev. James, *Personal Reminiscences and Biographical Sketches,* page 198.

133　TNA of the UK, PRO, FO 927/17 Málaga correspondence, 16 Feb 1821.

134 Málaga Municipal Archives, 99/194 – 195 Grivegnée, Enrique, comérciate. See also catalogue by Augustina Aquilar Simón, *Inventario de Documentos de la seccion de propios, rentas, censos, arbitrios positos, contribuciónes y repartos de Archivo Municipal de Málaga.* 84-9655-32-9.

135 Bedfordshire County Record Office - Correspondence between Thomas Robinson, 2nd Baron Grantham (1738-1786) and John Kirkpatrick Escott - ref. L 30/14/212, ref. file L 30/14/212, 10 October 1775.

136 *Thomas Jefferson Papers*, Bixby Collection, Missouri Historical Society, Saint Louis. MO.

137 Hailman, John, *Thomas Jefferson on Wine,* University Press of Mississippi, 2006, page 266.

138 Thomas Jefferson Collection, 1743-1826, Bixbey Collection, A0770 Folder 58, Missouri History Museum, St Louis, MO.

139 Hooper-Sturgis papers, Massachusetts Historical Society.

140 *Blackwood's Gentleman's Magazine*, 1781, page 195.

141 Ringrose, *Ibid.*, pages 209-210.

142 *Passenger Arrivals at the Port of Philadelphia 1800 – 1819.* Baltimore Genealogical Publishing Co. 1986.

143 U.S. National Library of Medicine, 8600 Rockville Pike, Bethesda, MD 20894 Bound Manuscripts MS B 025 Kerr, James. *Observations on natural history by Dr. James Kerr,* corrected and improved by Mr. Christopher Holland. 1790.

144 Busby, James, Esq. *Journal of a Recent Visit to the Principal Vineyards of Spain and France - - with Observations Relative to the Introduction of the Vine into New South Wales,* 1834.
See also: José Morilla Critz *La viticultura de Andalucía en 1831 vista por James Busby, padre de la viticultura Australiana,* Estudios Regionales Nº 49, (1997), pages 261-298, Universidad de Alcalá.

145 http://www.wineonline.ie/library/australia.htm.

146 Sealey, Malcolm, *The Coolangatta Estate,* 2006, page 21.

147 Demerson, Paula de, *La vida azarosa de D. Cipriano Palafox Portocarrero, padre de la emperatriz Eugenia de Montijo (1784 – 1839)*

148 *The Spain That William Maclure Knew,* Indiana Magazine of History, June 1998, Pages 100-101.

149 Wm Maclure, *The European Journals of Wm. Maclure,* Editor, with note by John S. Doskey, American Philosophical Society, Philadelphia 1988, Memoirs Series Vol. 171, page 155.

150 Novales, Alberto Gil, *William Maclure, Socialismo, Utópica en España,(1808 – 1840)* Universidad Autónoma de Barcelona, 1979, page 27 and note No. 47.

151 Carr, Sir John, KC, *Descriptive Travelling in the Southern and Eastern Parts of Spain and the Baleric Islands in the Year 1809,* London, 1811.

152 SUR in English, 2nd December to 8th December 2005. SUR is an English Language Newspaper in Andalusia.

153 *Edinburgh New Philosophical Journal, Exhibiting a view of the Progressive,* page 266. Editors, Robert Jameson, Sir William Jardine, Henry D Rogers, Science – 1842.

154 www.rosaverde.com. Accessed 16 March 2008.

155 Rhind, William, *A History of the Vegetable Kingdom*, 1857, pages 407-408.

156 Geo. Ripley, *The American Cyclopedia*, 1858, New York, page 400.

157     Wm. Story, *Essay upon the Agriculture of Victoria* (Australia), page 135. The
        Victorian Government Prize Essays 1860, Melbourne 1861.

158     Records at the Archivo Municipal de Málaga concerning his application for
        the status of Hidalgo show Calle St. Domino as his address.

159     Malloy, Fitzgerald, *The Romance of Royalty*, New York, 1904, page 293.

160     Translated from Díaz de Escovar, Cronista de la Provincia, Archivo Narsisco
        Diaz de Escovar, Museo de Arte Populares, Málaga, Courtesy of Dr. Trinidad
        Farcie Merron.

161     María José de la Torre Molina. *La Música en Málaga Durante la Era
        Napoleónica* (1808-1814) Servicio de Ediciones e Intercambio de la
        Universidad de Málaga, Pages 92 - 124.

162     Saldoni, Baltasar, *Diccionario biográfico-bibliográfico de efemérides de músicos
        españoles*, 1868, page 256.
        Translation by Brian Jeffrey– see reference below.

163     Jeffrey, Brian, Dr. *Fernando Sor, Composer and Guitarist*, First Edition, Telca
        Editions, page 128 and second edition 1994. www.tecla.com

164     Camden New Journal, 6 July, 2008, http://www.thecnj.co.uk/
        review/2008/042408/feature042408_01.html

165     Platt, Christopher *Foreign Finance in Continental Europe and the United States,
        1815-1870. Quantities, origins, functions and distribution*, 1984.

166     Bulloch, J.M., *The Curious Career of the Kirkpatricks and how they Begat
        Eugénie*, San Francisco Weekly Bulletin, 12 April, 1898.

167     Bosanquet & Fuller, Editors, *Report of Cases Argued and Determined in the Court
        of Common Pleas (etc.) Easter Term 1796 to Trinity Term 1799*, pages 350 – 353.

168     Ringrose, David, *Ibid.*, page 115.

169     Will of Joseph Gallego, 1818, Richmond City Hustings Court Will Book 2,
        pp. 273-294. The Library of Virginia, Richmond, VA.

170     Herr, Richard, *Flow and Ebb,* chapter 7 in *Spain a History*, editor, Raymond
        Carr, Oxford University Press, 2000, page 192. [by permission of Oxford
        University Press] I have drawn heavily on this very useful analysis of these
        complex events.

171     Browning, Michael, Lovelace, *Lovelace's Charity, Affairs in Spain, 1803 Onwards*.

172     Ringrose, David, *Ibid.*, page 113.

173     Herr Richard, *Ibid.*

174     Herr, Richard, *Ibid.*

175     Archivo Histórico Provincial de Málaga (3.949/730), and (3.873/13).

176     Muñoz Martín, Manuel, *Los promotores de l economía malagueña de siglo XIX*,
        page 187.

177     Alger, John Goldsworth, *Napoleon's British Visitors and Captives: 1801 – 1813*,
        pages 258, 250, and page 238 for Mme. Kirkpatrick.

178     Alger, *Ibid.*, page 257.

179     Esdaile, Charles J. *Ibid.*

180     Pino, Enrique del, *Historia General de Málaga*, chapter 13.

181     Carr, Raymond, *New Cambridge Modern History*, vol. IX.

182     Torres Molina, María, José, de la,. *La Música en Málaga Durante la Era
        Napoleónica (1808 – 1814)*.

183     Burke, Edmund, *The Annual Register of World Events*, 1808, page 185.

184    Johnson, T. B., *An Impartial History of Europe,* Vol. IV, 1813, page 310.

185    *The Edinburgh Annual Review* – Editor Walter Scott, 1824, page 299.

186    Esdaile, Charles J., *Ibid.,* page 197.

187    The National Archives of the UK: PRO, PC 1/3918, bundle of documents. Order in Council of 30 June 1810.

188    Rubio-Argüelles, Ángeles, *Ibid.,* page 188.

189    Glover, Michael, *Legacy of Glory, The Bonaparte Kingdom of Spain,* 1970, page 174.

190    Rubio-Argüelles, Ángeles, *Ibid.,* page 168.

191    Novales, Alberto Gil, *Ibid.,* page 111, note 47.

192    Krauel Heredia, Blanca, *Viajeros británicos en Málaga (1769-1855),* Universita de Málaga.

193    Kirkpatrick Mendaro, Enrique.

194    Brian Jeffrey, *Fernando Sor, Composer and Guitarist,* First Edition, Telca Editions, 1977, page 128 and second edition 1994.

195    Glover, Michael, *Ibid.,* page 162, *quoting Memoirs of Count Miot de Melito,* 1881.

196    Glover, Michael, *Ibid.,* page 162.

197    Glover, Michael, *Ibid.,* pages 150 – 170.

198    Esdaile, Charles E., *Ibid.,* from Blayney, Lord, *Narrative of a Forced Journey Through Spain,* 1.

199    Villar García, María Begoña, *Los Extranjeros en Málaga en el Siglo XVIII.* Cordoba 1982.

200    Muñoz Martín, Manuel, *Ibid.,* page 139.

201    The Will of Jospeh Gallegos of 1818, Richmond City Hustings Court Will Book 2, Library of Virginia.

202    Alger, John Goldsworth, *Ibid.,* pages 266- 270.

203    Rubio-Argüelles, Ángeles, *Ibid.,* page 287.

204    Kirkpatrick Mendaro, Enrique, *William Kirkpatrick Wilson, (1764 – 1837)* from family papers, pages 98- 99, extract from the bankruptcy papers of the Grivegnée family in the Archivo Histórica Provincial de Málaga.

205    Archivo Histórico de Málaga, Ref. (3.946/771) and (3.943/407) ex Manuel Muñoz Martín.

206    Kurtz, Harold, *The Empress Eugénie,* London, 1964, pages 8-10. Kurtz gives an analysis of Cipriano's situation when Napoleon's regime collapsed and the Bourbons were restored to government by the victorious Allies.

207    Seward, Desmond, *Eugénie, The Empress and Her Empire,* pages 2 -4.

208    Demerson, Paula de, *Ibid.,* page 191.

209    Archivo de la Casa de Alba, Madrid, C.51-8.

210    *A Comprehensive Catalogue of the Correspondence of James Monroe* - Oliver M. Perry to James Monroe. ALS. ICHi; Perry Papers, page 703.

211    *The Writing of John Quincy Adams 1767 – 1848,* Volume 6. pages 274 -5.

212    RG 59, General Records of the Department of State, *Applications and Recommendations for Public Office, 1797-1901,* Madison 1809 –1817, Box 6 (film M438) US National Archives.

213    *Calendar of Miscellaneous Letters Received by the Department of State from the Organization of Government to 1820.* U.S. G.P.O. 1897. U.S. National Archives.

214    Anonymous, *Napoleon the Third and His Court,* pages 243-244.

215    Manuel Muñoz Martín *Ibid.*

216 AHPM, 3,944/415, and Manuel Muñoz Martín, *Ibid.*, page 144.

217 AHPM 3,949 f.730, and Manuel Muñoz Martín, *Ibid.*, page 137.

218 AHPM 3,950 f.209.

219 Manuel Muñoz Martín, *Ibid.*, page 143 and from AHPM 3,631 f.312.

220 But whatever the arguments between Eugenio, Count de Montijo and his brother Cipriano, it is a curiosity that they both belonged to the first Masonic lodge to be set up in Madrid and that a Count of Montijo is reported to have married the widow of the Duke of Wharton, an Englishman, who instigated the setting up of this Lodge. Colonel Reitz who led the 1820 Revolution was also a member so it is hardly surprising that the Count de Teba hastened to his side.

221 *The Edinburgh Annual Register,* Editor: Walter Scott, 1808-1826 page 272.

222 García Montoro, Cristóbal, *Historia de Málaga*, Catedrático de Historia Contemporánea. Universidad de Málaga, page 31.

223 For an interesting take on these events see *Revolutionary Spain* by Karl Marx, New York Herald Tribune. August-November 1854 .

224 Payne Stanley G., *A History of Spain and Portugal*, Vol.2.

225 Archivo Histórico National, Madrid, Estado 3.158/8. from Gaite, Carmen Martín, *Love Customs in Eighteenth Century Spain*, California University Press, Berkeley, 1991.

226 Duff, David, *Eugénie & Napoleon, III*, pages 62- 36.

227 Duff, David, *Ibid*, page 59.

228 Sencourt, Robert, *The Life of the Empress Eugénie*, page 32.

229 *Reports from Her Majesty's Consuls on the Manufactures, Commerce, &c.*, by Great Britain Foreign Office, 1868, pages 299- 300, for Adra etc. (TNA of the UK).

230 *The London Polytechnic Magazine, and Journal of Science, Literature, and the Fine Arts*, edited by T. Stone. Jan.-June, 1844.

231 Ansted, Prof. D. T., *Scenery, Science and Art, being Extracts from the Note-Book of a Geologist and Mining Engineer,* page 158.

232 *Actividades Mercantiles de William Kirkpatrick y Wilson en Adra,* ex Enrique Kirkpatrick Mendaro from Archivo Histórico Provincial de Almería.

233 Research by Dr. Audrey Hayward, Bath Mineral Water Hospital, England.

234 Mévil, André, *Ibid.*, pages 19-21.

235 Deed of Aparcería, 29ᵗʰ August 1836, From National Archives, Madrid, Testamentary documents, Leg, 52 – b – 6.

236 This quote is credited to a letter Irving wrote to Mrs. Pierre M. Irving in 1853. The original with Georgetown University Library is dated 1843, see 1/28 Read, George, 2/15/1843. Description: 1 brief AL (copy) dated 2/15/1843 from Washington Irving (1783-1859), U.S. Minister to Spain (1842-1846), to George Read, U.S. Consul at Málaga (Spain), indicating that he never recommended Ignacio Figueroa as Vice-consul to Adra and mentioning a trip to Adra and William Kirkpatrick. Sent from Madrid to Málaga.

237 Stoddart, Jane, *The Life of Empress Eugénie*, 1906.

238 Archivo Histórico Provincial de Málaga (3.963/97)

239 Muñoz Martín, Manuel, *Ibid.*, page 188.

240 *The Financial Register of the United States*, edited by Condy Raguet, Philadelphia 1838 page 316.

241     These statements appear to have been conflated in the typewritten text of 1936 in the d'Alba Archives.

242     Archivo Histórico Nacional, Madrid, Lig. 52B No. 6 (a – h) Testamentaria de Guillermo Kirkpatrick Wilson.

243     Indiana Magazine of History *Ibid.*
        The National Archives of the UK: PRO, FO 927/17 Málaga Consular correspondence.

244     Lea, Henry Charles, *A History of the Inquisition of Spain, Volume 1,* Appendix, Spanish Coinage.

245     Stoddart, Jane T. *Ibid.,* page 9.

246     Napier, Mark, *Memorial and Letters Illustrative of the Life and Times of John Graham of Claverhouse, Viscount Dundee,* 1859, page xiii.

247     Correspondence with Cathy Gibb, Dumfries Archives Centre, 24 June 2008.

248     Taine, Hippolyte, *Les Origines de la France contemporaine: L'ancien régime,* (1875), 14th edition, Paris 1885, pages 221-222, from Alfred Cobban, *Aspects of the French Revolution.*

249     Esdaile, Charles, *Ibid.,* page 118.

250     Lea, Henry Charles, A History of the Inquisition of Spain, volume 1. Appendix, Spanish Coinage.

251     The National Archives of the UK, PRO, FO 927/17, Málaga Correspondence (Consular) 1816 - 1821.

252     Alger, John Goldsworth, *Ibid.,* pages 266- 270.

253     TNA of the UK, PRO, PROB11/1077 pp 75.

254     General records of the Department of State, Record Group 59, Applications and Recommendations for     Public Office, Admin. of Madison 1809 -1817 box 6 film no M438.

255     IGI records for South Carolina.

256     *Burke's Peerage and Baronetage,* 106th edition, page 1516.

257     This account is taken from General Charles Kirkpatrick's *Records of the Closeburn Kirkpatricks,* pages 177-178.

258     Felthem, John, *A Tour Through the Island of Man 1797 – 1798,* from Manx Society Publications.

# Index

Lightning Source UK Ltd.
Milton Keynes UK
21 February 2011

167920UK00001B/10/P